COMPARATIVE AND INTERNATIONAL EDUCATION SERIES

Volume 10

Girls and Young Women in Education

A European Perspective

COMPARATIVE AND INTERNATIONAL EDUCATION

Series Editor: PHILIP G. ALTBACH, State University of New York at Buffalo, New York

Editorial Advisory Board:

NOTICE TO READERS

Dear Reader

An invitation to Publish in and Recommend the Placing of a Standing Order to Volumes Published in this Valuable Series.

If your library is not already a standing continuation order customer to this series, may we recommend that you place a standing continuation order to receive immediately upon publication all new volumes. Should you find that these volumes no longer serve your needs, your order can be cancelled at any time without notice.

The Editors and the Publisher will be glad to receive suggestions or outlines of suitable titles, reviews or symposia for editorial consideration: if found acceptable, rapid publication is guaranteed.

ROBERT MAXWELL
Publisher at Pergamon Press

Girls and Young Women in Education

A European Perspective

Edited by

MAGGIE WILSON
Oxford Polytechnic, UK

PERGAMON PRESS

Member of Maxwell Macmillan Pergamon Publishing Corporation
OXFORD · NEW YORK · BEIJING · FRANKFURT
SÃO PAULO · SYDNEY · TOKYO · TORONTO

U.K.	Pergamon Press plc, Headington Hill Hall, Oxford OX3 0BW, England
U.S.A.	Pergamon Press, Inc., Maxwell House, Fairview Park, Elmsford, New York 10523, U.S.A.
PEOPLE'S REPUBLIC OF CHINA	Pergamon Press, Room 4037, Qianmen Hotel, Beijing, People's Republic of China
FEDERAL REPUBLIC OF GERMANY	Pergamon Press GmbH, Hammerweg 6, D-6242 Kronberg, Federal Republic of Germany
BRAZIL	Pergamon Editora Ltda, Rua Eça de Queiros, 346, CEP 04011, Paraiso, São Paulo, Brazil
AUSTRALIA	Pergamon Press Australia Pty Ltd., P.O. Box 544, Potts Point, N.S.W. 2011, Australia
JAPAN	Pergamon Press, 5th Floor, Matsuoka Central Building, 1-7-1 Nishishinjuku, Shinjuku-ku, Tokyo 160, Japan
CANADA	Pergamon Press Canada Ltd., Suite No. 271, 253 College Street, Toronto, Ontario, Canada M5T 1R5

First edition 1991

Library of Congress Cataloging in Publication Data
Girls and young women in education: a European perspective/edited by Maggie Wilson.—1st ed.
p.   cm.—(Comparative and international education series; v. 10)
Includes bibliographical references and index.
1. Women—Education—Europe—Cross-cultural studies.
2. Educational equalization—Europe—Cross-cultural studies.   3. Comparative education.   I. Wilson, Maggie.   II. Series.
LC2037.G57   1990   370.19'345—dc20   90–41074

British Library Cataloguing in Publication Data
Girls and young women in education: a European perspective. (Comparative and international education series, v. 10).
1. Europe. Female students. Education. Equality of opportunity.
I. Wilson, Maggie   II. Series
376.94

ISBN 0–08–037266–X Hardcover
ISBN 0–08–037267–8 Flexicover

Printed in Great Britain by B.P.C.C. Wheatons Ltd, Exeter

Introduction to the Series

The Comparative and International Education Series is dedicated to inquiry and analysis on educational issues in an interdisciplinary cross-national framework. As education affects larger populations and educational issues are increasingly complex and, at the same time, international in scope, this series presents research and analysis aimed at understanding contemporary educational issues. The series brings the best scholarship to topics which have direct relevance to educators, policy-makers and scholars, in a format that stresses the international links among educational issues. Comparative education not only focuses on the development of educational systems and policies around the world, but also stresses the relevance of an international understanding of the particular problems and dilemmas that face educational systems in individual countries.

Interdisciplinarity is a hallmark of comparative education and this series will feature studies based on a variety of disciplinary, methodological and ideological underpinnings. Our concern is for relevance and the best in scholarship.

The series will combine monographic studies that will help policy-makers and others obtain a needed depth for enlightened analysis with wider-ranging volumes that may be useful to educators and students in a variety of contexts. Books in the series will reflect on policy and practice in a range of educational settings from pre-primary to post-secondary. In addition, we are concerned with non-formal education and with the societal impact of educational policies and practices. In short, the scope of the Comparative and International Education Series is interdisciplinary and contemporary.

I wish to acknowledge the assistance of a distinguished editorial advisory board including:

Professor Suma Chitnis, Tata Institute of Social Sciences, Bombay, India.
Professor Kazayuki Kitamura, Research Institute for Higher Education, Hiroshima, Japan.
Professor Gail P. Kelly, State University of New York at Buffalo, USA.
Dean Thomas La Belle, University of Pittsburgh, USA.
Dr S. Gopinathan, Institute of Education, Singapore.
Professor Guy Neave, Institute of Education, University of London.

PHILIP G. ALTBACH

Acknowledgements

I wish to record my thanks for the encouragement given by colleagues at Oxford Polytechnic during the course of this project. I would also like to thank Patsy McIntosh for her detailed comments on the draft concluding chapters, Greta Ilott for her excellent typing and Bob Waugh for his invaluable support throughout.

Oxford 1989   MAGGIE WILSON

Contents

Contents

CHAPTER 1

Introduction

MAGGIE WILSON

WITHOUT equal access to educational experiences, skills and qualifications, girls and women have over the years been deprived in their personal development, in their choice of work, in their lives as citizens and family members and in their capacity to influence the local and national political decisions which affect their daily lives. The issue of women's rights re-emerged with renewed vigour in the 1950s and 1960s, expressed in the liberal concept of equality of opportunity. Throughout the 1970s, attempts were made to create the conditions which would remove formal barriers to sex equality and would give individuals equal access to education, training and jobs, on the assumption that equal treatment of men and women would result eventually in full social equality. The agenda of the post-war women's movement was far from parochial and the issue of equal educational participation attracted particular attention in both educational research and in national and international policy-making circles. The elimination of formal barriers to discrimination in this area is relatively amenable to state intervention and the notion of equality of educational opportunity was congruent with the upsurge of liberal-democratic concerns at that time.

Within Europe since the 1960s there has been a general and marked growth in female enrolment at all levels of education, which, together with a substantial increase in women's participation in the labour market, has brought about enormous changes in the social fabric and in the experiences of girls and women. The lifestyles of many young women today would have been scarcely conceivable by their grandmothers. Such changes are often portrayed as being irreversible and as having led to a full realization of equal opportunities in terms of qualifications and employment between men and women. However, despite the considerable progress made, stubborn and persistent divisions remain in both education and the labour market. This introductory chapter will outline international policy in the area of girls and educational opportunities, briefly review the main educational and employment issues for women in Europe and give a short overview of the book.

1

International Policy and Equality of Educational Opportunity

The right to receive an equal education has been a fundamental part of many human rights documents since the Second World War. This right has usually been expressed in terms of access to, rather than the content of, education, underpinned by the principle of non-discrimination. United Nations resolutions, such as the UN Declaration of Human Rights in 1948, the UN Declaration on the Rights of the Child in 1959 and the UNESCO Convention against Discrimination in Education in 1960, all upheld the principle of equality of opportunity in education. This was most clearly expressed in a 1967 resolution, subsequently incorporated into the 1979 UN Convention on the Elimination of all Forms of Discrimination against Women, to which all European countries were signatories. This stated that:

All appropriate measures shall be taken to ensure girls and women, married or unmarried, equal rights with men in education at all levels, and in particular

(a) equal conditions of access to and study in educational institutions of all types, including universities and vocational, technical and professional schools;
(b) the same choice of curricula, the same examinations, teaching staff with qualifications of the same standard, and school premises and equipment of the same quality, whether the institutions are co-educational or not;
(c) equal opportunities to benefit from scholarships and other study grants;
(d) equal opportunities for access to programmes of continuing education, including adult literacy programmes, and
(e) access to educational information to help in ensuring the health and well-being of families.
(United Nations Resolution 2263, 1967.)

Such resolutions are technically enforceable by a kind of peer review, in which signatories report to a committee elected by member states on progress made in the area concerned, but do not have the force of law (Rendel, 1988). Nevertheless, they are important in giving a high profile to agreed principles and in setting a kind of global moral tone to issues of international importance.

Fresh impetus was given to the issue of women's rights at this level in 1975 when the UN International Women's Year heralded the UN Decade for Women, which attempted to define ways in which women could fully participate in the economic, political and social life of their countries. The sub-themes adopted for the first five years of the Decade were those of equality, development and peace, followed by the themes of health, employment and education in 1980–1985. The Decade culminated in the Nairobi World Conference, which was attended by some 5,000 delegates from 157 countries and 1,400 journalists, with a further 12,000 participants at a parallel forum. The Conference recognized that, although the Decade had raised a general awareness of women's issues, many of its goals had not been met. This was partly because of the impact of world-wide economic recession and also because of a lack of political will in some countries such as the UK, where it has been dubbed the "invisible decade" (Ashworth and Bonnerjea, 1985) and because of a political backlash in some policy-making circles (Rogers, 1989).

The Conference issued a series of resolutions, or "Forward Looking Strategies to the year 2,000", which were later formally adopted by the United Nations and included the recognition of education as a key tool in the advancement of women, with specific recommendations in the areas of illiteracy, "second-chance education", training and the evaluation of textbooks and curricula (Women of Europe, 1986).

Although few international agencies kept statistics on enrolment until the 1980s, other international bodies, such as the International Labour Organisation (ILO) and the Organisation for Economic Cooperation and Development (OECD), have paid particular attention to the employment situation of women, which has necessarily involved an examination of vocational education and other educational measures. In 1980, for example, the OECD Ministers of Education agreed to give priority to developing "education to provide a full range of educational choices for young women and young men, both for further education and skill qualifications for employment" (OECD, 1985, p. 121).

Commitment to equal opportunities in employment was also a major component of European Community legislation. Article 119 of the Treaty of Rome, which established the European Community in 1957, enshrined the principles of equal pay for equal work and equality of opportunity in training. This was in turn strengthened by further Directives on equal pay in 1975 and on equality of treatment between men and women workers in 1976, which encompassed equality of opportunity in general vocational and technical education, initial and advanced training and retraining, as well as access to employment, promotion and working conditions. A 1978 Directive concerned equal treatment for men and women in matters of state social security. Directives are legally binding on member states, but member states are free to select the most suitable form for their implementation, which has sometimes resulted in evasive measures being taken to circumvent legislation (Buckley and Anderson, 1988). However, in this case, several member states already had legislation on equal pay and equal treatment for women and others followed swiftly.

The 1975 Directive had considerable implications for the upper levels of secondary education as well as for vocational education and was reinforced by the Standing Conference of European Ministers of Education of the twenty-two Council of Europe countries in 1979, which called for a coordinated policy to ensure that equality between the sexes became a reality. Specific recommendations included the preparation of all pupils to share in domestic and parental responsibilities, to earn an independent living and to participate in democratic decision-making and public life (Byrne, 1985). Commitment to this policy was renewed in 1985, with an additional resolution to pay particular attention to statistical monitoring to aid policy-making (*Council of Europe Bulletin*, 1985).

Sections of the European Parliament and European Commission have continued to maintain a high level of interest in equality of opportunity in employment and education. The Commission published a large-scale survey of sex inequality in secondary schools in 1978, which investigated inequality in educational leadership and patterns of achievement and equal opportunities in initial and in-service teacher education (Byrne, 1978). The Women's Information Bureau of the Commission produces the useful bulletin, Women of Europe, and the Commission established a permanent Advisory Committee on Equal Opportunities in 1981, which sanctioned two "positive action" programmes from 1982–1985 and 1986–1990. The latter included a wide range of educational measures to raise awareness of gender equality issues among educational personnel; to encourage girls to take up non-traditional courses of study and careers, especially in information technology; to develop non-sexist teaching materials and to develop training programmes for women of all ages, as well as a range of projects to combat inequality in employment (Women of Europe, 1985a). The European Parliament also has a permanent committee on women's rights.

The Nordic Council of Ministers of Culture and Recreation also made a formal commitment to an equal opportunities programme in employment, teacher-training, curricula and educational materials in 1972 and equality between the sexes has remained a consistent goal since that time (*Council of Europe Bulletin*, 1988).

The Pace of Change

Education

In response to international pressure, economic and demographic changes, to the demands of the women's movement and to other sources of political pressure, European governments have introduced measures which have resulted in rapid, and sometimes remarkable progress in the improvement of girls' educational opportunities since the early 1970s. These measures and their effects on the life chances of girls and young women will be explored in specific national contexts in the chapters which follow.

In terms of enrolment patterns, differences at the compulsory school level are now solely due to demographic variations in the birth-rate of boys and girls. Where access to upper secondary education is on a selective basis, girls equal or outnumber boys. It is also more common for boys to leave school without any qualifications than for girls to do so. In many countries girls now outnumber boys in the upper levels of academic secondary education which lead to entrance into higher education. Here young women have made substantial inroads into institutions which have been traditionally male-dominated and in some countries are now present in equal numbers (OECD, 1986). Table 1.1 below illustrates this substantial change during the period 1970–1986 in the twelve countries of the EEC:

TABLE 1.1
Full-time students in Higher Education Aged 19–24 as a Percentage of the Population in Selected European Countries, 1970–1986

	Belgium	Denmark	West Germany	Greece	Spain	France	Ireland	Italy	Luxembourg	Netherlands	Portugal	United Kingdom
Women												
1970–71	11	16	10	7	6	13	7	11	1	7	8	7
1975–76	15	25	16	11	12	18	8	16	1	11	9	9
1980–81	19	24	18	12	17	20	11	19	2	14	9	9
1981–82	20	24	19	13	18	22	11	18	2	15	9	9
1982–83	20	24	20	15	19	23	12	18	2	15	10	9
1983–84	21	25	20	17	20	22	12	18	2	16	11	9
1984–85	22	26	20	19	22	24	14	19	1	16	12	9
1985–86	25	26	21	..	24	25	14	19	..	17	..	9
Men												
1970–71	18	22	18	15	17	17	13	17	3	18	9	11
1975–76	20	27	25	18	21	20	13	25	2	23	10	13
1980–81	23	24	24	16	21	20	14	24	3	25	11	12
1981–82	23	24	25	17	21	23	14	23	3	24	10	13
1982–83	23	24	26	17	21	23	14	22	3	24	10	12
1983–84	23	24	27	17	21	21	14	21	2	24	10	12
1984–85	24	27	27	19	23	24	16	21	2	24	11	12
1985–86	28	26	27	..	24	24	16	20	..	24	..	12

Source: Eurostat (1987)

However, despite such progress, marked disparities remain in enrolment in vocational education and training and in patterns of subject choice in upper secondary and higher education. Some areas of vocational education remain virtually single-sex, while Engineering and Technology in further and higher education remain male bastions in Western European countries, despite progress in other areas such as Law, Administration and Medicine. Indeed it has been suggested that gender-based subject divisions have become stronger, as more women have been recruited into higher education in both socialist and non-socialist countries (Sutherland, 1988). Where higher education is organized in different institutions of varying prestige, more male students are generally to be found in the higher status establishments. Indeed, there is some evidence to suggest that areas of study become devalued in employment terms once large numbers of female students are enrolled, a "shifting of the goal posts", which has considerable implications for young women in the labour market (OECD, 1985). Within higher education, male postgraduate students still greatly outnumber female postgraduates, which in turn gives rise to a considerable under-representation of women in the academic workforce of universities and other institutions of higher education. At the lower levels of the education system teaching is becoming an increasingly feminized profession in many countries. As the OECD concluded in 1985, "the removal of formal barriers of access to girls and women (in education) is by no means tantamount to realizing actual equality of opportunity and results" (OECD, 1985, p. 121).

Although inequality of educational opportunity between the sexes in Europe may not be as acute as in the wider world context, differences between social groups within European societies may compound inequalities based on sex (cf., Kelly, 1989; Acker *et al.*, 1984). Much of the literature on gender and education tends to ignore the ways in which differences based on social class, regional origin, minority group status or race compound gender differences, with the result that only a partial picture of the position of girls in the education system emerges. Research into inequality of educational opportunity in terms of social class or race has likewise been impoverished by a lack of attention to gender differences.

There are notable exceptions to this tendency to ignore those pupils who are less educationally successful, for example in Byrne's statement of concern for those girls "whose alternative to staying at home for forty years is not the professions, nor even the skilled workbench, the high wage packet bringing financial independence, the industrial training which gives job security, responsibility and mobility, (but) is low pay, canteen cleaning . . . , the typewriter, the unskilled labour market, short-term employment" (Byrne, 1987, p. 24).

One reason for such a deficiency in the research may lie in the highly complex interrelationship between the factors involved. Contributors to this book reveal varying degrees of awareness of such issues, which are briefly addressed in the conclusion. It is, however, beyond the scope of this book to explore in any depth the educational fate of the estimated 4.5 million children of migrant workers in North-West Europe, the specific situation of migrant women in the economy (OECD, 1983, 1985) or the particular experiences of girls of Afro-Caribbean and Asian origin in Britain. Readers are referred to a small, but growing body of literature in this context (cf., Lynch, 1986; Braham *et al.*, 1982; Castles, 1984; Gundara *et al.*, 1988; Troyna, 1987).

Comparative statistical data on the participation of girls in the education system has little to say about the roots of sex differences in education, in the family or in the early years of education or about the different experiences of girls and young women in single-sex and co-educational establishments. The chapters on individual countries presented in this book give an indication of research into the qualitative dimension of gender differentiation in schools, which tends to be underpinned by assumptions derived from psychological social learning theories. This book does not explore psychological theories of gender difference and the reader is again referred elsewhere (cf., Sayers, 1984). However, in most cases contributors have analysed data in the context of changes in national labour markets. A brief overview of changes in the European context is given below.

Employment

The period 1975 to 1985 saw a massive influx of women into the labour force in the European Community and Scandinavian countries and an increasing tendency for women to stay longer in employment, taking a shorter break for rearing children. During this period 10.2 million jobs were created in service industries in the European Community, while in 1981–1982 alone 3.6 million jobs were lost in agriculture and 2.2 million jobs were lost in industry (Eurostat, 1988). At the same time there was a considerable growth in part-time employment between 1973 and 1981 (OECD, 1985). By 1988, 37.2 per cent of jobs in the countries of the European Community were held by women and in Sweden 46.2 per cent of the labour force was female. In the main, women have entered employment in the service sector, particularly in the public sector. By 1988, 45 per cent of service sector jobs and 70 per cent of part-time jobs in all sectors were held by women in the EC, albeit with fairly wide national variations (Eurostat, 1988). Table 1.2 below graphically illustrates the proportion of women in full-time and part-time employment in selected European countries in 1985, while Table 1.3 illustrates the change in labour force participation from 1950 to 1982.

Despite such advances, there is little parity between men and women in the labour market. Female wages in most countries are 20 to 40 per cent less than those of males, with variations according to industrial sector, occupation and country (OECD, 1985). Since official figures usually exclude employment in small enterprises and do not take into account the unpaid work which women perform, this is undoubtedly an underestimate. Part-time work, with its generally low wages pro rata, irregular hours and lack of training or promotion opportunities, is a strong factor here, along with differences in hours worked in manual jobs and in seniority and promotion in non-manual full-time work. Where the concept of equal worth of jobs has been incorporated into bargaining procedures, such as in Sweden, wage differentials between men and women have been greatly reduced.

In the early 1980s the economic recession, and consequent reduction in public sector expenditure, resulted in accelerated unemployment rates in Europe, albeit with wide regional and national variations. Women, especially those under the age of twenty-five, have been disproportionately affected in several countries. Overall, 13 per cent of economically active women in the EC were unemployed in 1986, as compared with 9.3 per cent of men, a figure which probably masks the real figure since social security measures in some countries discourage women from registering as unemployed (Eurostat, 1988). Women have been particularly affected by the recession because of a reduction

Maggie Wilson

TABLE 1.2
*Total Labour Force, by Sex and Employment Status in Selected European Countries,
1985*

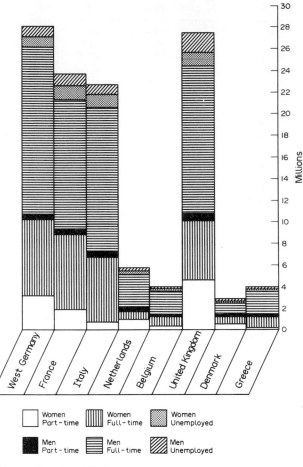

Source: Eurostat (1987)

in childcare services in some countries, a resurgence of traditional attitudes towards their employment and because of their concentration in precarious and vulnerable jobs (Women of Europe, 1985b). Although a new popular image of the modern career woman storming the citadels of the professions is often presented in the mass media, women are in reality still concentrated in a remarkably restricted range of jobs. Occupations where men and women are present in equal numbers are still a rarity, although this may be masked in enterprises and organizations where women occupy different levels of jobs within hierarchies of pay, status, rewards, conditions of work and degrees of

TABLE 1.3
*Female Share of the Labour Force of Selected
European Countries, 1950–1982*

	1950	1977	1982
Belgium	27.9	35.6	37.7[a]
France	35.9	37.6	38.6
Greece	32.1	27.7[b]	32.0[c]
Ireland	25.5	27.5	27.7
Italy	25.4	31.9	33.8
Netherlands	23.4	28.0	30.5
Spain	15.8	28.6	29.5
Sweden	26.3	43.7	46.2
United Kingdom	30.7	38.2	39.1
West Germany	35.1	37.6	38.2

[a] 1981.
[b] 1971.
[c] 1980.
Source: OECD (1985).

autonomy. The finer the level of analysis used to examine the situation of women in the labour market, the more occupational segregation becomes apparent and the slower the rate of change appears to be. Certain jobs, such as administration, have absorbed ever greater numbers of women, as they have entered the labour market. Women have had some success in entering new jobs in employment sectors with a history of female employment, such as teaching, but this does not appear to be the case where there is no such history (OECD, 1985).

Despite improvements in childcare facilities in many countries, facilities have fallen short of demand, particularly for extended day-care during school holidays, the full working day and in times of parental sickness, with some notable exceptions, such as Sweden (Women of Europe, 1988; Moss, 1988). While European women still bear the brunt of childcare and domestic responsibilities, reductions in social services in some countries have thrown the problem of elderly parents, and disabled children and spouses on to "carers" in the family, the majority of whom are women. Current trends across the industrialized world indicate that this will become a growingly significant issue as the age-structure of the population changes (Hunt, 1988).

Public Opinion

Contemporaneously with such changes, international opinion poll data has shown some liberalization of attitudes towards women in society. The European Commission has conducted surveys of public opinion in 1975, 1977,

1983 and 1987, the latter covering 11,650 respondents in twelve countries (Women of Europe, 1987). Although such surveys present a limited snapshot of public opinion, the findings are nevertheless instructive.

Respondents were asked whether they perceived the position of women in society as an important issue and whether they felt that legislation on a community or national level had been effective in improving women's employment conditions. In response to the first question, 25 per cent of respondents attached "considerable" importance to the issue of equality of employment and 54 per cent "average" importance, with a predictable sex difference in response, but little age difference. Only 27 per cent of respondents felt that legislation had been effective at the national level and 16 per cent at the EC level.

Attitudes towards the principle of women working in the occupations of bus driver, surgeon, obstetrician, barrister and Member of Parliament showed fairly strong support for women in these roles, from 62 to 67 per cent, albeit with quite wide variations by country. When men were asked whether they would prefer their wives to work or not, opinion was evenly divided, but the number of those in support of the idea had increased by 15 per cent from 1975 to 48 per cent in 1987 (although it should be noted that the 1975 samples was based on the then nine EC countries rather than the current twelve). In Germany, Luxembourg and Ireland the majority of men preferred their wives not to work, while respondents in Denmark, France and the United Kingdom gave the most positive responses to the principle of women at work. When responses to the two questions on the general principle of women working and personal choice in this area were correlated, only 24 per cent of men were strongly in favour of equality at work in the personal and public spheres. This finding reveals an interesting mismatch between expressed beliefs and actual practice, which is often mirrored in other contexts, for example in teachers' attitudes towards equal opportunities in general and in their own classrooms.

Respondents were also asked about role distribution within the family. Twenty-five per cent of respondents described their ideal family as one where the husband works and the wife runs the home, 29 per cent where the woman works and runs the home, and 41 per cent favoured equal role-sharing, results which showed a slight shift in opinion towards more equal tasks since the previous surveys. However, only 54 per cent of men and 53 per cent of women in households where the woman worked described their actual family arrangements as egalitarian. Among younger couples, women were less likely to bear the "dual role" of responsibilities at home and at work, but again there were wide variations between countries, with respondents in Greece, Spain, Portugal, France, Denmark and the United Kingdom expressing the highest degree of role-sharing and respondents in Luxembourg and West Germany the lowest. Table 1.4 presents the detailed responses to this question. Although very general, such data has profound implications for girls and women, which will be further explored in the concluding chapters.

TABLE 1.4

Desired Role Distribution in the Family in 1987 in European Community Countries, by Age, Sex and Country

	Equal roles	Woman does more housework	Woman in the home	None	No answer	Total
By sex and age						
All men	39%	29%	26%	3%	3%	100
Men aged 15–24	53	25	12	5	5	100
25–39	47	30	18	3	2	100
40–54	34	33	28	3	2	100
55 and over	26	28	41	3	2	100
All women	42	29	24	3	2	100
Women aged 15–24	61	25	12	1	1	100
25–39	49	27	19	3	2	100
40–54	37	32	27	2	2	100
55 and over	27	32	36	3	2	100
By personal circumstances						
Men with working wives	53	30	14	2	1	100
Men with non-working wives	25	30	40	3	2	100
Women with jobs (total)	55	31	10	3	1	100
– part-time jobs	60	26	8	4	2	100
– full-time jobs	45	39	13	1	2	100
Women with no job	36	29	31	2	2	100
By country						
EC.12 TOTAL	41	29	25	3	2	100
Belgium	34	30	25	8	3	100
Denmark	53	26	12	6	3	100
France	45	28	24	2	1	100
Greece	43	28	23	4	2	100
Ireland	34	20	39	5	2	100
Italy	42	31	25	1	1	100
Luxembourg	20	30	39	6	5	100
Netherlands	43	28	23	4	2	100
Portugal	43	24	25	6	2	100
Spain	47	19	28	4	2	100
United Kingdom	48	31	18	2	1	100
West Germany	27	34	32	3	5	100

Source: CEC (1987), *Women of Europe*.

An Overview of the Book

A great deal of comparative educational literature is both facilitated and constrained by the universality of the English language. A cursory glance at the contents lists of some of the international educational journals reveals a tendency to include a wide range of material, whose main source of common interest seems to lie in language rather than the social structure of the education systems concerned, or the social and political philosophies which underpin these. Studies which make unquestioning comparisons between the United States, where over 40 per cent of nineteen to twenty-one-year-olds are in some form of higher education, and the United Kingdom, where the figure is about 12 per cent, are a classic case in point. At the theoretical level, a common experience and pattern of education is sometimes assumed in analyses which extrapolate broad principles and tendencies from the American experience to the British.

Recent work on particular aspects of educational policy, such as vocational and multi- or inter-cultural education, has been more successful in integrating data from more comparable sources, even though the context of such educational initiatives varies quite widely within European countries (cf., Watson, 1985; Beattie, 1985; Lynch, 1986; Boos-Nünning, 1987). Comparative data is also available in some excellent reports and documentation produced by international organizations, such as the OECD and European Commission, but this tends to reach a fairly specialized reading audience. The intention of this book is to present an overview of the comparative situation of girls and education in Europe, which draws together contributors from a variety of European countries. For reasons of length, it has not been possible to include all European countries, and an attempt has therefore been made to include a fairly representative selection. As preparations for the next stage of European integration within the European Community in 1992 are intensified, a rather limited perception of the extent of Europe has often been presented in the mass media. Partly to redress this imbalance, a Scandinavian and an East European country have been included, despite obvious differences in the social and political structure of the latter country, Poland, with the other Western European countries. Indeed, the chapter serves to highlight persistently similar trends and yet substantial differences in a country where formal equality between the sexes has been enshrined in the Constitution since 1921.

Although broad similarities between educational systems and patterns of change, such as the democratization of compulsory education and the deferment of specialization, are to be observed in most of the countries covered, distinct differences also remain. Each chapter therefore gives a brief outline of the structure of the education system concerned to orient the reader, rather than to provide an in-depth understanding. Some structures and concepts, such as "non-university tertiary education" or religious-based state schools, will be unfamiliar to readers in some countries. Major differences also exist in the pace and timing of educational reforms, in the data – in the form of official statistics or research evidence – available to contributors and in the key issues which have dominated the educational headlines in each country. Each chapter presents core data on girls' access to and participation in the education system, but contributors have selected those issues which are most pertinent to their country's experience.

Chapter 2 presents an account of the failure of sweeping educational reforms and the introduction of co-education in French-speaking Belgium to mitigate strongly divergent patterns of curricular choice between boys and girls. Chapter 3 also examines curricular differentiation in England and Wales and focuses on women in teaching and academia as a case study of women in the labour market. The question of the match between qualifications and career opportunities in France is explored in Chapter 4, while Chapter 5 presents an analysis which queries whether researchers have underestimated the dynamic nature of the relationship between changes in education and the labour market in Greece. Chapter 7 presents data on sex differences in changing attitudes to science and technology in Poland, especially at the level of students and research workers in higher education. Chapters 8 on Spain and 10 on West Germany both examine the roots of such differences in attitudes and orientation in the classroom and in learning materials, while Chapter 6 contains the suggestion that girls are subject to dual pressures in the Irish context: to succeed in academic terms and to be "guardians of the moral order". Finally, the Swedish experience presented in Chapter 9 illustrates the extent and limits of changes brought about through a strong state policy. These themes are brought together in an overview chapter and some suggested policy implications are considered in the Conclusion.

References

Acker, S., Megarry, J., Nesbit, S. and Hoyle, E. (1984) (Eds.) *World yearbook of education: women and education*. London: Kogan Page.

Ashworth, G. and Bonnerjea, L. (1985) (Eds.) *The invisible decade: UK women and the UN Decade 1976–1985*. Aldershot: Gower.

Beattie, N. (1985) *Professional parents: parent participation in four Western European countries*. Lewes: Falmer Press.

Boos-Nünning (1987) *Towards inter-cultural education: a comparative study of children in Belgium, England, France and the Netherlands*. London: CILT.

Braham, P. *et al.* (1982) *Migration and settlement Unit 3: migrant labour in Europe*. Milton Keynes: Open University.

Byrne, E. (1979) *Equality of education and training for girls*. Brussels: Commission of the European Communities.

Byrne, E. (1985) Equality or equity: a European overview. In Arnot, M. (Ed.) *Equal opportunities policies: race and gender*. Oxford: Pergamon.

Byrne, E. (1987) Education for equality. In Weiner, G. and Arnot, M. (Eds.) *Gender and the politics of schooling*. London: Hutchinson/Open University.

Buckley, M. and Anderson, M. (1988) *Women, equality and Europe*. Basingstoke: Macmillan.

Castles, S. (1984) *Here for good: Western Europe's new ethnic minorities*. London: Pluto Press.

Council of Europe Bulletin (1985) 4. Strasbourg: Council of Europe.

Council of Europe Bulletin (1988) 3. Strasbourg: Council of Europe.

Eurostat (1987) Brussels: Commission of the European Communities.

Eurostat (1988) Brussels: Commission of the European Communities.

Gundara, J., Jones, C. and Kimberley, K. (1988) (Eds.) *Racism, diversity and education*. London: Hodder & Stoughton.

Hunt, A. (1988) The effects of caring for the elderly and infirm on women's employment. In Hunt, A. (Ed.) *Women and paid work: issues of equality*. Basingstoke: Macmillan.

Kelly, G. (1989) *International handbook of women's education*. Westport: Greenwood Press.

Lynch, J. (1986) Multicultural education in Western Europe. In J. Banks and J. Lynch (Eds.) *Multicultural education in Western societies*. Eastbourne: Holt Rinehart and Winston.

Moss, P. (1988) *Childcare and equality of opportunity*. Brussels: Commission of the European Communities.

OECD (1983) *Migrants' children and employment: the European perspective*. Paris: OECD.

OECD (1985) *The integration of women into the economy*. Paris: OECD.

OECD (1986) *Girls and women in education*. Paris: OECD.

Rendel, M. (1988) Women's rights to education. In Buckley, M. and Anderson, M. *Women, equality and Europe*. Basingstoke: Macmillan.

Rogers, B. (1989) *The domesticization of women*. London: Routledge.

Sayers, J. (1984) Psychology and gender divisions. In Acker, S. *et al.* (Eds.) *World yearbook of education: women and education*. London: Kogan Page.

Sutherland, M. (1988) Women in higher education: effects of crises and change. *Higher Education*, **17**(5).

Troyna, B. (1987) (Ed.) *Racial inequality in education*. London: Tavistock.

United Nations (1967) From resolution no. 2263 of The General Assembly of the UN *declaration on the elimination of discrimination against women*, 7 November 1967.

Watson, K. (1985) *Youth, education and employment: international perspectives*. Beckenham: Croom Helm.

Women of Europe (1985a) *Equal Opportunities*, Supplement 23. Brussels: Commission of the European Communities.

Women of Europe (1985b) *European women in paid employment*, Supplement 20. Brussels: Commission of the European Communities.

Women of Europe (1986) *The Nairobi World Conference*, Supplement 24. Brussels: Commission of the European Communities.

Women of Europe (1987) *Men and Women of Europe in 1987*, Supplement 26. Brussels: Commission of the European Communities.

Women of Europe (1988) *Women of Europe ten years on*, Supplement 27. Brussels: Commission of the European Communities.

CHAPTER 2

French-Speaking Belgium

NADINE PLATEAU

SINCE the beginning of the twentieth century, the issue of equality of opportunity in education has been of major concern to progressive politicians and educationalists. However, the question of sex discrimination has received little interest and has been raised only recently in the context of Belgium's obligation to conform to European agreements. Indeed, the reform of secondary education, carried out in the late 1970s, which endorsed the principle of equal opportunities for girls and boys by imposing co-education, can be said to have actually contributed to concealing girls' specific educational problems, as will be discussed later in this chapter. Since then co-education has been and still is considered, by the educational authorities, by the supporters of equal opportunities and by the public at large, to be the best way to eliminate inequality. It is precisely this commonly held belief that will be questioned here through examining some significant features of education in Belgium.[1] This chapter will firstly deal with the policies of the democratization of secondary education and the general establishment of co-education which were expected to improve girls' opportunities. It will then review the development of girls' schooling in secondary and higher education during the last fifteen years, a development marked by quantitative, though not qualitative, progress. It will finally indicate the reasons which account for this failure and review initiatives taken so far to redress the imbalance between the sexes in education.

The Structure of the Belgian Education System

Education in Belgium is characterized by the existence of two sectors: the public sector (réseau officiel) and the independent sector (réseau libre). Fifty-five per cent of schools belong to the public sector and are run by the state, provinces and communes. Forty-five per cent belong to the independent sector and are mostly run by the Catholic authorities. All schools, both public and independent, are free of charge from pre-primary until the end of secondary education, that is during the period of compulsory education, from the age of six until the age of eighteen. The independent sector, as well as the public

15

sector, is financed by the state. Subsidies are granted to the independent sector on condition that certain regulations are respected. These regulations are concerned with the structure of education, the compulsory elements of the curriculum, certificates and degrees and entry conditions. Certificates granted at the end of each year allow pupils to be admitted to the next year in any school, so that they can pass from the public sector to the independent sector and vice versa. The education system comprises:

Pre-primary education, which lasts about three years. Children can be admitted to pre-primary education as soon as they are two and a half years old.

Primary education, which lasts six years from the age of six and is organized according to a common core curriculum. At the end of the sixth year pupils who are awarded a certificate of basic education (certificat d'enseignment de base) enter secondary education. Those who have to repeat the school year are not allowed to stay longer than eight years in primary education, but must transfer to vocational or special secondary education, where they can be entered for the certificate of basic education.

Secondary education lasts six years, and is streamed or tracked, with the possibility of specialization between options within each track. A distinction is made between transition tracks (filières de transition) which include general academic and technical subjects and prepare pupils to go on into higher education, and qualification tracks (filières de qualification) which include more technical and vocational subjects and qualify pupils for a job. Transfer routes have been set up between the two types of tracks. In general and technical education, which includes thirty-two periods a week, the number of periods per week devoted to the common core curriculum decreases from twenty-eight in the first year to thirteen in the sixth year. At the end of the third year of general and technical education, pupils can be awarded the certificate of lower secondary education (certificat de l'enseignement secondaire inférieur) and at the end of the sixth year, the certificate of secondary education (certificat d'enseignement secondaire supérieure) and the diploma which gives access to higher education (diplôme d'aptitude à l'enseignement supérieur or DAES). Pupils in technical and vocational education can be awarded vocational certificates at the end of their fourth, fifth or sixth years in secondary education and can take the certificate of secondary education at the end of their seventh year. All certificates of secondary education and the DAES are awarded by the teachers' council in each school, and are issued under the authority of each educational institution, rather than by any national authority.

Higher education. The certificate of secondary education allows students to follow short courses in non-university tertiary education, lasting two to four years. The DAES qualifies pupils for admission into university and other tertiary courses, lasting from four to seven years.

The Democratization of Education

The Reform of Secondary Education

The issue of equality of opportunity for girls and boys has to be examined in the light of the historical process of the democratization of education which established in the public mind the democratic principle of equality of opportunity for all pupils.

Since the law of 19 May 1914 imposed compulsory education until the age of fourteen and made primary schooling free, primary education has had the status of a public service. The "Pacte Scolaire" (School Pact) of 1959 endorsed the principle of the extension and democratization of education in secondary education and education became non-fee-paying, though not compulsory, until the age of eighteen. This was made possible by a significant increase in the resources allocated to education at the end of the 1950s.

The "Pacte Scolaire" was signed by the three major political parties, the Christian Social Party, the Liberal Party and the Socialist Party. This was the first step in the unification of the secondary school system. It administered the organization not only of the public sector (schools mostly run by the state) but also of the independent sector (schools mostly run by the Catholic authorities). Both sectors became subsidized by the state on condition that certain regulations were respected. These regulations were concerned with the structure of education, degrees, conditions of admission, etc., but not the curriculum nor the teaching methods, each sector enjoying freedom in this respect. Despite this degree of autonomy, the content of the curriculum does not vary to any significant degree since there is a general agreement about what should be taught in Belgium throughout both sectors (Fourez, 1986).

The history of this reform and its application has been well documented (van Haecht, 1985). From the 1950s to the 1970s, the democratization of secondary education was carried out step by step, by successive reforms, mostly through the action of Socialist ministers who had been fighting to eliminate socio-cultural inequalities. This process culminated in the reform of secondary education called "Le Renové" ("renovated or reformed education") under the law of 19 July 1971. This was, on the one hand, a political reform aimed at democratizing society by encouraging young people from working class families to continue school and, on the other, it was an educational project designed to reduce socio-cultural handicaps and to encourage the development of all pupils' aptitudes. In order to fulfil these aims the structure of secondary education, with the exception of vocational education, became unified, all certificates gave access to university and transfer routes between general, technical and even vocational education were set up. Finally a core curriculum was established in the first two years, remedial courses were introduced and some subjects were taught in smaller groups. (These last three measures, designed to postpone option choice and to extend equality of opportunity, were dropped in 1986.)

The "Renové" was first introduced as an experiment in 1969 in state schools and became compulsory in those schools in 1978. Nowadays, the great majority of all schools have been reformed along these lines in French- and German-speaking Belgium; by 1987, 99 per cent of the state schools and 92 per cent of the independent schools had been reformed. Since these reforms, many of the formal barriers to equality of opportunity in school – which dated back to a time when education was strictly compartmentalized and selection was explicit – have been abolished so that education in Belgium, at least from a formal point of view, is a very democratic institution.

The Extension of Co-Education

The "Renové" reforms established co-education as an extension of the principle of equality to both boys and girls and as a logical consequence of an equal opportunities policy. But, whereas the democratic unification of all the forms of secondary education was the result of a long struggle and was a much debated subject, co-education has never been the subject of a public and political debate and was little discussed. It has rather come about in the course of time in response to changing social circumstances.

Co-education has a long tradition in Belgium. Co-educational schools already existed in the nineteenth century. In 1845, half the school population attended mixed primary schools. At that time, only financial concerns motivated the creation of those schools. As was the case in most countries, when there were insufficient pupils for two schools in the same area, boys and girls sat together in the same classes, although this did not exclude separate entrances, cloakrooms, playgrounds, sports, etc. (de Grandpré, 1973). From the beginning of the century until now co-education has made continuous progress, albeit at a different pace according to the sector concerned, starting earlier in the state schools than in Catholic schools.

By 1965, 67 per cent of the secondary state schools but only 0.2 per cent of the Catholic schools were already co-educational. This impressive difference has been explained by the impact of the Papal Encyclical "Divinis Illius Magistri" of 1929 on Catholic education at that time, in which Pope Pious XI stated that co-education was a method based on a belief in naturalism which denied original sin (Verbeke, 1984). For a long time, co-education was only permitted when practical circumstances necessitated it and the creation of each co-educational secondary school had to be submitted to papal authorization until 1971. This interdict contributed to maintaining resistance in Catholic circles to co-education and to delaying the irreversible trend towards it which was evident in state schools.

In spite of this different development it must be acknowledged that Catholic and secular views on sex differences, relations between the sexes, and sex roles show a great similarity and by the 1970s these ideas had changed under the pressure of cultural, social and economic factors from an understanding of the relations between the sexes as a complementary one to one based on equality between the sexes (Plateau, 1987).

The 1970s witnessed the rebirth of the women's movement, the growing participation of women in the labour market and the application on the 1975 EEC Directive on Equality of Treatment Between Men and Women Workers. In this context of women's demands and international recognition of women's rights, the debate on the meaning and purpose of co-education changed. This shift was evident at a national conference on co-education held in Brussels in 1979. The conference was set up by the Ministry of Employment, the Ministry of Education and the Commission on Women's Employment on the theme: "How to implement co-education and guarantee equality between men and women?" (Cahiers de la Commission du Travail des Femmes, 1980). The ideas which underpinned the conference were clearly inspired by the European Directive of 1975. In his opening address, the Minister for Employment, M. de Wulfs, expressed the purpose of the conference, which was to determine the obstacles to real co-education, a prerequisite for mixed employment, which is, in turn, necessary to implement equality between men and women in employment, occupational training and promotion. A direct relationship between education and employment is assumed here, as well as the idea that the structure of employment can be challenged by changing educational conditions.

At the conference, the main obstacle to equality was perceived to be the inadequacy of girls' training, to which their concentration in some sectors of the labour market was attributed. This inadequacy was said to be caused by a traditional conception of the role of women in society, which influences girls' aspirations. The participants expressed an optimistic faith in the effects of co-education in opening up to girls the whole range of study choices, challenging sex stereotyping and in changing girls' and boys' attitudes to life. Nowhere were the educational methods or content of co-education actually defined and it is quite significant that the conclusions of the conference included the proposal of a bill that would clearly define the purpose and the scope of co-education. This startling demand at the *end* of a conference on co-education only makes sense if we consider the way educational authorities had dealt with the issue up to that point. As mentioned above, the reform of traditional schools had automatically meant co-education. The ministerial circular of 9 August 1977, which had stipulated that all state schools had to introduce co-education, had not been accompanied by any guidelines concerning content or methods of education and had solely specified how practical problems of buildings (toilets!) had to be resolved. In addition, none of the circulars dealing with the purpose and the organization of the earlier "Renové", had alluded to the issue of gender. Indeed, the ministerial circular of 6 October 1966, had underlined the necessity to fight stereotypes, those "value judgements linked to parental occupation, social class, race, attainment at school . . .", without mentioning sex-role stereotyping. The neutral word of "pupil" used in these circulars enabled an obliteration of gender difference and consequently the real social inequalities between boys and girls. Whether this was as a consequence of progressive optimism and fear of discrimination, of unconscious sexism coupled with ignorance, or of both, these policies resulted in the disappearance of the category of girls as a group whose interests and specific problems needed to be analysed and addressed. Schools, though co-educational, remained male-defined, adapted to male interests and male needs, despite the progress which girls had made in gaining access to all forms of education.

So far the issue of co-education in the state sector of education has been considered. In the Catholic sector, co-education was introduced later between 1970 and 1975 and was expanded with the extension of the reforms in 1981. By 1987, 92 per cent of the secondary Catholic schools were co-educational. Unlike in the state sector there has been some reflection on co-education in Catholic circles. A recent publication on this subject by the Catholic educational authorities recommends co-education as an educational project true to the message of the Bible (Bureau Pédagogique, 1987). The publication opens with a quotation from Genesis 1.27: "So God created man in His image, male and female He created them", which is supposed to support the view that psychological differences exist between males and females, without affirming any hierarchy between the sexes. The purpose of education is thus "to educate boys and girls to meet each other on an equal but different footing". The text underlines that this difference should not be confused with minor differences which result from traditional socio-cultural patterns. In the Catholic view of co-education, the principle of equality does not exclude a recognition of sex differences, but does not treat boys and girls together in the neutral category of "pupil". It is too early to try to assess to what extent Catholic and non-Catholic views on equality will affect girls' destinies in school, but we can assume that the recognition of girls' specific identity constitutes a favourable ground for those who wish to raise awareness of girls' problems and to promote positive action.

By the late 1970s co-education had raised expectations among those committed to the issue of equality of opportunity for girls and boys. Ten years later, failure to achieve this was implicitly acknowledged in two documents: the first a large-scale survey on fifteen years of education in the Catholic sector conducted by the SNEC (Secrétariat National de L'Education Catholique) (Bureau Pédagogique, 1986), and the second a booklet on equal opportunities published by the Secretariat of Social Emancipation (Cabinet du Secrétariat d'Etat, 1987). Co-education had indeed not had the expected results in terms of diversification of girls' study patterns, as the next section will show.

The Development of Schooling for Girls

During the 1980s there was a 15 per cent decrease in the number of pupils in pre-school and primary education, due to the falling birth rate, and an increase in the secondary school population by 8 per cent until 1985 when the effects of the falling birth rate began to take effect at that level. In the "non-university" tertiary education sector there was a 59 per cent increase in enrolments during this period, mainly because of the increased take-up of education by young people of working class origin, while the number of students at university only very slightly increased by 0.8 per cent.[2] Girls, in particular, increased their participation in education during this period, as illustrated by Table 2.1 below.

TABLE 2.1

Changes in the Rate of Enrolment in Education of 15–25-Year-Olds, 1960–1981

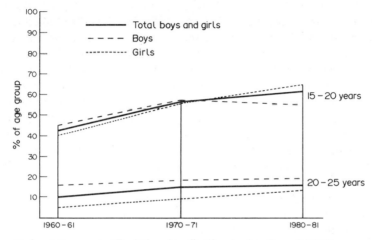

Source: *Etudes et Documents*, "Evolution des effectifs – Analyses", no. 8 (1985).

An analysis of pupil enrolment by age supports this assertion: girls have increasingly extended their studies to a later age, and in the academic year 1984–1985 they were only outnumbered by boys at the age of twenty-one. These figures indicate a quantitative progress in the development of girls' schooling. The extension of equal opportunities enabled pupils from less privileged social backgrounds in particular, and girls in general, to complete secondary education, even before legislation in 1985 extended compulsory education until the age of eighteen. However, there is some disparity between boys and girls in their uptake of the different forms of secondary education and higher education available.

Some trends at the level of secondary education are illustrated in Table 2.2 below. There has been an overall decrease in the percentage of pupils in general and technical education with a corresponding increase in uptake of vocational education, as a result of democratization. However, this trend is less marked among girls, whose uptake of general education has not decreased significantly in the ten years illustrated and whose representation in general

TABLE 2.2

Distribution of Male and Female Pupils in Secondary Education by Sector, 1974–1975 and 1984–1985

	1974–1975		1984–1985	
% in	*Boys*	*Girls*	*Boys*	*Girls*
General	61.15	60.97	56.59	59.67
Technical	25.37	17.33	19.15	15.82
Vocational	13.48	21.70	24.26	24.51
Total	100.00	100.00	100.00	100.00

Source: *Etudes et Documents*, "Evolution des effectifs – Analyses", no. 8 (1985).

education had surpassed that of boys by 1984–1985. This suggests that girls are tending to stay on longer in general education and indeed changes in the uptake of general education confirms this trend: in the academic year 1974–1975 there were 53 per cent of boys and 47 per cent of girls in upper secondary education but by 1984–1985 the proportion was reversed, with 46 per cent of boys and 54 per cent of girls studying at this level. By 1984–1985 both girls and boys were less represented in technical education than in 1974–1975, but the proportion of boys in vocational education had increased considerably, unlike that of girls. Within vocational education, girls still marginally outnumbered boys but the figures indicate an important increase in the number of boys: 2,242 boys and 8,729 girls completed this programme in 1974–1975. Ten years later, the figure for boys had risen to 9,022 and for girls to 10,482.

These trends can be explained by the different impact which the extension of secondary schooling had on the study choices of boys and girls. The significant overall increase of pupils in vocational education is due to increased uptake by pupils from the working classes, but, according to the 1986 SNEC survey on fifteen years of education mentioned above, 60 per cent of boys and only 51 per cent of girls from working class families attended vocational education, while 38 per cent of girls from working class families attended general education as compared with 28 per cent of working class boys. Several reasons have been put forward to account for this pattern. The first reason will be explored in a subsequent section: the system operates selection on the basis of school results so that failure in general education means that less academically successful pupils are steered towards technical education and eventually vocational education. As girls achieve better academic results than boys, they tend to "hold their own" in the academic track and not to be "channelled off" into technical education. Another reason which has been put forward is that technical and vocational education programmes are less adaptable to girls than to boys, in that they offer a wider range of "male" options. However, the question remains as to whether the increased number of girls in general education is actually favourable in terms of career qualifications. The CESS

(Certificat d'enseignement secondaire supérieure), which is awarded at the end of the sixth year of secondary school – at the age of about eighteen years – is a prerequisite to continuing higher studies but it has little value on the labour market as it does not provide pupils with a specific job qualification. Eleven per cent of girls who leave school with a CESS do not go on into higher education and this can leave them in a worse situation than the less academically successful boys who have at least some specific vocational or technical qualifications.

At the level of higher education, which includes "non-university" tertiary and university education, there is a different pattern in the distribution of male and female students as Table 2.3 shows.

TABLE 2.3

Distribution of Male and Female Students in Higher Education by Sector, 1974–1975 and 1984–1985

	1974–1975		1984–1985	
% on	*Males*	*Female*	*Males*	*Females*
University courses	64.59	47.45	58.66	45.39
Non-university short[a] courses	19.20	47.14	24.12	45.88
Non-university long[b] courses	16.21	5.41	17.22	8.73
Total	100.00	100.00	100.00	100.00

Notes: [a] Non-university short courses are one to two years of study.
[b] Non-university long courses are three years of study in tertiary education.
Source: *Etudes et Documents*, "Evolution des effectifs – Analyses", no. 8 (1985).

The decrease in the percentage of male students on university courses has been higher than that of girls and their increase in short-term study quite appreciable. Girls' choices have been more steady: they still enter short non-university courses in great numbers and are increasing their participation in the long non-university courses. Overall their numbers on "non-university" courses have constantly increased, from 41 per cent of total students in 1974–1975 to 47 per cent ten years later. At university level girls were 24.3 per cent of total students in 1964, a proportion which had risen to 40.7 per cent by 1984.

Girls and Educational Achievement at School and in Further and Higher Education

Patterns of Achievement

Achievement has a special significance in the education system in Belgium because of its impact on pupils' aspirations. However, the only available indicators are the figures concerning pupils' underperformance and the award of diplomas. Table 2.4 below illustrates gender differences in the number of pupils who have had to repeat the school over one or two years and who are thus not of the "normal" age for the level of education concerned.

The higher numbers of "repeaters" in technical and vocational education indicates the way in which failure in general education usually results in the transfer of pupils to technical and vocational education. At all levels and in all the forms of secondary education, female pupils experience less delay in their studies than males, except in the sixth year of vocational education, which may be related to their lack of motivation at this level, for these young women have been relegated after successive failures to typical "female" study options – hairdressing, waitressing, community service work – which are not associated with such good job prospects as the "male" study options of mechanics, carpentry, etc. The reasons commonly put forward to explain girls' relatively successful academic performance at school are their greater conformity to school rules and requirements and their better use of language. Unfortunately no research has been carried out on these topics in Belgium.

TABLE 2.4

Percentage of Pupils who have Repeated the School Year by Sex and by Level of Education, 1984–1985

	% girls	%boys
Last year of primary education	28	32
Third year of secondary education: general	32	40
technical	69	77
vocational	83	90
Sixth year of secondary education: general	32	44
technical	69	80
vocational	71	54
First year of higher "non-university" education	30	61

Source: Percentages derived from figures produced in *Etudes et Documents*, Enseignement primaire, no. 2, Enseignement secondaire, no. 3, Enseignement superieur, no. 5 (1985).

The second indicator of differential achievement is the number of pupils obtaining the school leaving certificate. In 1984 more girls than boys were awarded the CESS and they accounted for 56 per cent of the holders of this diploma. However, until 1987 university candidates also needed to pass an examination to obtain the DAES (a second diploma giving access to higher education) and here only 83 per cent of female compared with 88 per cent of male candidates gained this diploma.[3] Official statistics do not record whether girls failed or simply did not take the examination.

In higher education, young women also seem to outperform young men. In "non-university" tertiary education female students accounted for 57 per cent of successful diploma holders and at university they accounted for 48 per cent of graduates, but only 24 per cent of those successfully completing doctorates (Cabinet du Secrétariat d'Etat, 1989).

On the whole, the extension of educational opportunities appears to have been favourable to girls in quantitative terms. They have progressed at all levels of education, even outnumbering boys in some areas. However, this has not been accompanied by an equally favourable transition to the labour market, as the unemployment figures demonstrate. On the contrary, unemployment among young women is unexpectedly high in relation to the level of their qualifications. In 1989, for example, 22.7 per cent of female, as opposed to 10.1 per cent of male holders of the CESS were unemployed (Cabinet du Secrétariat d'Etat, 1989). The most widely suggested explanation for this discrepancy has been that the options chosen by girls do not offer good job opportunities.

Option Choice

Although girls have made progress in access to all levels of education, this has not been matched by corresponding progress in qualitative terms. On the contrary, despite the expectation that co-education would eliminate or at least reduce stereotypical choices of study options, there have hardly been any significant developments in this area. The classical polarization between male and female patterns of study has persisted at all levels and in all forms of education.

At secondary level, general education seems to be the form of education where girls have slightly progressed in the so-called "male" areas. No comprehensive survey of options taken by boys and girls has been published by the Ministry of Education. Available data concern the first grade of general education in 1984–1985 which includes 76 per cent of all the pupils in the first two years of education. The core curriculum of twenty-four periods a week consists at this level of French, Dutch, Mathematics, Sciences, History, Geography, Physical Education and Religious or Ethical Education. The remaining eight periods are allocated to options. Patterns of uptake are illustrated in Table 2.5 below.

In the second year girls chose Latin more often (30 per cent of girls to 21.5 per cent of boys). They chose scientific options less often (23 per cent of girls to 28 per cent of boys), they were greatly under-represented in Technical Education (8 per cent of girls to 28 per cent of boys) and over-represented in the Social Sciences (28 per cent of girls to 14 per cent of boys) and the Arts (3.5 per cent of girls to 2 per cent of boys).

The options system is developed over the next four years of schooling to a high degree of intricacy and in some schools pupils have to choose one out of more than twenty options or combinations of subjects. Although this has not been reviewed on a national scale, the SNEC survey, already mentioned, highlighted pupils' choices of basic options. A comparison between options

TABLE 2.5

Numbers of Pupils by Option in First Grade of
General Education, 1984–1985

	No. of girls	No. of boys
Latin	6741	5260
Science	5326	6896
Technical education	1890	6869
Arts	795	399
Social Sciences	6307	3535
Non-specified	1704	1501
Total	22763	24460

Source: *Etudes et Documents*, "Enseignement secondaire",
no. 3 (1985).

taken before the reform and the present pattern is difficult to make as the system has totally changed. However, the report points out significant trends and changes between 1969–1970 and 1984–1985. Firstly, the option of Latin had lost its leading position. Many pupils, more boys than girls, gave it up after two years, even without failing. The option of Science, which was non-existent in 1969–1970, was the most favoured option (57 per cent of pupils overall), but when permitted to specialize between the Sciences during the last two years at school 25 per cent of girls chose Biology to 18 per cent of boys, and 15 per cent of girls chose Physics to 30 per cent of boys in 1984–1985. Variation in choice in the number of hours of Mathematics studied is illustrated in Table 2.6 below.

The preference for Mathematics is striking: though more girls continued to

TABLE 2.6

Distribution of Pupils in Fifth Year Mathematics Options,
According to the Number of Mathematics Periods Taken

	1969–1970		1984–1985	
	% girls	% boys	% girls	% boys
3 hours	74.0	58.9	44.0	27.0
5 hours	17.8	7.1	43.6	46.3
7 hours	8.2	34.0	12.4	26.7
Total	100.00	100.00	100.00	100.00

Note: In the traditional system, i.e., before reform: 3 hours correspond to the sections Latin/Greek and Latin/Science; 5 hours to Science B and 7 hours to Latin/Mathematics and Science A.

Source: Percentages: derived from "L'Enseignement Secondaire Catholique après 15 ans de renovation, Bureau Pédagogique du Secrétariat National de L'Enseignement Catholique" (1986).

study Mathematics for three hours than boys in 1984–1985, there were more girls in the five hour option and the gap between girls and boys in seven hour option had narrowed. The "Renové" has given Mathematics a new legitimacy in the reformed system, and in this respect girls have benefited from the "Renové". In the traditional system the Science B programme with five Mathematics periods a week was predominant in all girls' schools, whereas the Science A programme with seven periods was predominant in all boys' schools, which explains the higher number of girls in the five hour option and of boys in the seven hour option in 1969–1970. The possibility of taking up either option in the "Renové" had created more balanced study patterns. The survey concluded that boys were still over-represented in Mathematics options, though the gap was closing, and that girls were still over-represented in the Arts and Social Sciences.

This polarization is repeated in technical and vocational education where many options are chosen by girls or boys only. In 1984–1985, for example, in the third stage of vocational education, seventy-nine options were available, but whereas boys were found in seventy-three options, girls were found in only fifty-four. Moreover, girls were concentrated in a very restricted number of options: 80 per cent opted for eleven courses in traditionally "female" areas, such as textiles, community service work, sales, art and domestic science.

At the level of non-university tertiary education changing study patterns reveal the persistence of stereotypical choices as illustrated by Table 2.7.

Young women accounted for 54 per cent of students in "non-university" tertiary education in 1984–1985 (*Etudes et Documents*, no. 8, 1985) and continued to outnumber young men in health-related and teacher training courses at this level, although there has been an overall decline in numbers due to the state of the labour market. In the technical education sector young women have made little significant progress.

At the level of university studies, this polarization of study patterns persists. A few examples are given in Table 2.8 below.

The over-representation of young women persisted in the Arts and in Psychology, where they accounted for 64 per cent of students. The case of Medicine is also interesting because here the gap between the number of male and female students narrowed due to the decrease in the number of male applicants. Finally, young women do not seem to have progressed greatly in Applied Sciences where they accounted for a mere 11 per cent of students (*Etudes et Documents*, no. 8, 1985).

In conclusion we can say that although the number of female students has increased in all faculties, there has been little overall change in their choice of subject and careers, which remain largely sex-stereotyped. At all levels of education, typically female and male study patterns can be noted. There has been no greater diversification of choice among boys than among girls and yet it is girls' choices which are generally criticized. This criticism is based on an implicit recognition of the different social value awarded to areas of study.

TABLE 2.7

Changes in the Student Population in "Non-university" Tertiary Education,
1974–1975 – 1984–1985

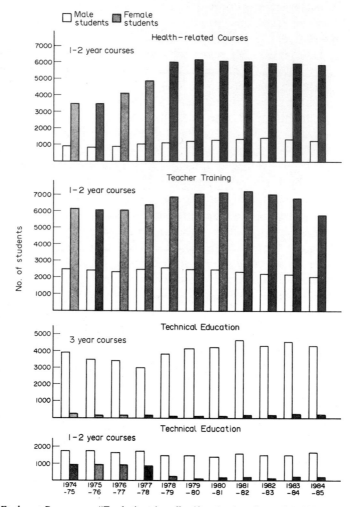

Source: *Etudes et Documents*, "Evolution des effectifs – Analyses", no. 8 (1985).

Higher social value, measured in terms of social status, prestige, responsibility and salary, is commonly attributed to male-dominated areas of study. Girls, as shown above, are over-represented in low-valued studies. There is a clear gender hierarchy in study patterns and this has been of predominant concern to those in official and non-official circles who are committed to the issue of equality. The overemphasis in the media on the poor uptake of girls of the Sciences and Technology is related to the conviction that these subjects lead to

TABLE 2.8

Changes in the Student Population at University, 1974–1975 – 1984–1985

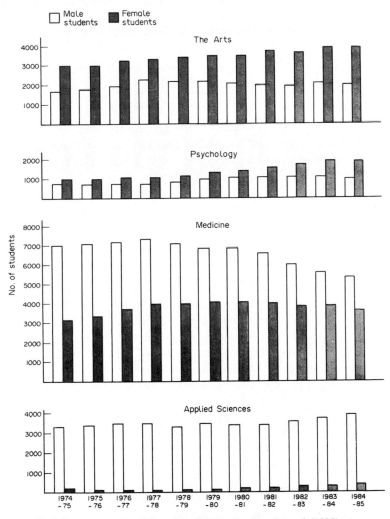

Source: *Etudes et Documents*, "Evolution des effectifs – Analyses", no. 8 (1985).

good employment prospects. In fact, even without raising the question of the validity of those judgements – after all why should teachers deserve less prestige than engineers? – it is questionable whether the so-called "under-achievement" of girls in study choices is sufficient to account for their weak position in the labour market. The very relationship between education and employment has been questioned in recent years by researchers, who have denounced the temptation in a period of crisis to blame the problems caused by a real lack of jobs on supposedly inadequate job training, and to look for educational solutions to the problems (Alaluf, 1986; Tanguy, 1986). According to recent research (Leroy and Godano, 1986) young people under twenty-five lost one-third of their employment opportunities between 1974 and 1984 because of the contraction of the demand for labour and an increase in the active population. Yet the question still remains as to why girls still make stereotypical choices despite current opportunities to act otherwise.

The Myth of Free Choice

It is the contention of this chapter that segregation based on class and sex, which used to be institutionalized in the education system through single sex schools or class-segregated forms of education, is still present today in ways which are not immediately apparent. This will be illustrated by the example of secondary education, a period where first choices have to be made which have the long-term effect of placing pupils in streams which practically, though not formally, lead to the exclusion of pupils from some options and occupations.

As mentioned at the beginning of the chapter, the reforms of the 1970 unified the previously separate programmes of secondary education and made all schools co-educational. A minimal core curriculum was established in an option system which becomes more complex as a pupil advances up the school, and which mainly determines the pupil's school and career destiny. The novelty of the reforms lay in the fact that the social and sexual division of knowledge embodied in the school system appeared to be not the result of any constraint but of free choice. The "Renové" was introduced within a framework of debate which stressed the advantage of option choices based on pupils' aspirations and aptitudes. The debate proved successful. It was widely heard and echoed by educational authorities, heads of schools and teachers so that most parents and pupils have become familiar with the idea of freedom of choice, an ideology which masks the real determinants of choice. Research conducted in reformed secondary schools in 1982 has disclosed the hidden mechanisms of segregation, differentiation and hierarchy which have tended to restore the rigid system of social recognition of the previous educational system (van Haecht *et al.*, 1982). This study was concerned only with reproduction of the social division of knowledge: gender was not used as a category of analysis or interpretation. However, the study is of use in dealing with the issue of gender and can be used to illustrate that a logic underpinning option choice can be discerned, in which the variables of social class and sex are interconnected.

Two main series of determinants of choice can be distinguished: firstly the institutional determinants which limit the real opportunities for choice within the school system and secondly the ideological and social determinants which influence strategies adopted by parents and pupils in the system. The study points out that the reformed education system, which had claimed that all options were of equal value, could not prevent options from becoming the means of selection. The implicit hierarchy of "orientations" (combinations of options), which appears by the second year, is by no means related to the difficulty of the subjects, but to the social image of these subjects, and is reinforced in the following years. "Orientations" are distributed in a pyramid with, at the top, "orientations" including the highest number of Mathematics periods (Sciences/Mathematics, Latin/Mathematics, Mathematics/Languages) and at the bottom "orientations" with the lowest number of Mathematics periods (Social Sciences, Arts). The hierarchy is thus founded on the Mathematics course so that a failure in Mathematics has irreparable effects on pupils' schooling. Within this mode of selection, girls are clearly disadvantaged, as they are over-represented in basic Mathematics and under-represented in intensive Mathematics. The question as to whether this is through failure or by choice has not been analysed, but it is possible to speculate that childhood games and toys have not provided girls with the same familiarity with the scientific and technological world as they have boys, and that parents put less pressure on girls to achieve well in these areas. Moreover, programmes of intensive Mathematics are so overloaded that very little time is spared to explain the possible use of this knowledge. The research mentions that one teacher in three says (s)he does not devote any time to this question and this might well discourage adolescent girls who are generally more anxious to see the social usefulness of what they learn and who are less inclined than boys to enjoy the intrinsic nature of Mathematics.

The Mathematics course has thus become the main instrument of selection, which is now not so much based on repeating an academic year after failure but on the "softer" form of selection through "re-orientation" (reallocation to option bands). The 1982 study emphasized that this policy has meant in fact a system of relegation to a less demanding set of options so that the school career of many pupils is the story of a step by step downgrading from high status "option bands" to devalued option bands. This sheds new light on what appeared to be a favourable feature of girls' schooling, namely their lower rate of repeating the academic year, as girls who are over-represented in less-valued "orientations" may well be victims of this progressive relegation. In summary, the structure of the school system now facilitates selection through streaming on the basis of mathematical aptitude and an effective narrowing of the range of academic opportunities with successive failure. In the same way failure in general education leads to relegation to technical education and failure here means relegation to vocational education.

Another determinant of opportunities for real choice lies in variations in school provision and policy. All schools do not provide the same choice of options. When co-education was imposed on schools, many ex-girls' schools could not, for example, organize an option in intensive Mathematics. Today, some schools do not offer the three forms of education (general, technical and vocational) and not all schools offer courses for the full six years of secondary education. Pupils are therefore not offered the same "menu" over the whole country. Provision is more limited in sparsely populated and in working class areas. And, above all, schools do not have uniform policies on admissions or allocation to option bands. These policies are not always determined by the best interest of the pupil, but are rather the result of practical considerations such as the necessity of retaining a certain number of pupils. According to the 1986 SNEC survey, a pupil is more likely to achieve academic success in a very small school than in a large school and more so in the province of Luxembourg than in Brussels.

Faced with these objective limitations on opportunities, pupils and their parents, especially those from a privileged social background, have developed strategies to cope with the situation. Once again there is a shift in the nature of discrimination: from a system with in-built discrimination to an unequal use of the system by parents. Parental strategies for choosing schools have not been documented but some observations have been made that suggest that the interconnection of class and sex should be analysed. In Brussels, for example, reformed schools in residential areas have lost a part of the school population to the few traditional schools regarded as more demanding and more disciplined. At the early stages of the reforms of Catholic schools, more girls were sent to "ex-boys" schools than the contrary because parents thought that a "male" education would give their daughters better life prospects. Schools which specialized in technical and industrial education remained highly segregated and very few girls went to ex-boys' schools with those "orientations".

Parents appear to develop strategies in the choice of "orientations" at the beginning of secondary schooling. In general education, for example, pupils have to choose between Latin, scientific or technical options. The 1982 research on reformed secondary schools mentioned above indicated that Latin was chosen more often by pupils from wealthy and educated families, and by more girls than boys, the scientific option more by middle-class pupils and the technical option more by working-class pupils. The study also recorded that some parents opted for their child to repeat the year rather than be reallocated to a different stream. Here again there might be evidence of different and less demanding parental attitudes towards sons and daughters, since girls repeated the year less often than boys. Unfortunately no attention has been directed towards this problem among educationalists and researchers and this absence of data leaves many unanswered questions. The research on reformed schools concluded that all these strategies imply a voluntarist attitude towards education which characterizes parents whose social origin and education have prepared them for an optimal use of school and who know what is at stake in education in terms of careers and future life. It may be supposed that the will to intervene in education will differ according to the sex of the child, but the issue of parents' lower expectations for girls has not been seriously dealt with in Belgium. There has certainly been a change in parents' expectations in that nowadays many parents expect their daughters to have a job in order to contribute to the standard of living of the family, but many still do not expect their daughters to have a career in the main. However, girls also have a role to play in their own school and career destiny, and their aspirations and strategies will be examined in the next section.

Women in the Labour Market

Girls' Occupational Aspirations

A piece of research on girls' study choices conducted in 1986 by Brunfaut highlights girls' attitudes and expectations towards education and life. The girls interviewed were attending technical, vocational and higher education; in other words, forms of education which give professional or occupational qualifications. When asked what they expected from life the majority of girls answered that they hoped both to succeed at work and to create a home and a family. Only a minority mentioned either a family or a job. Of those girls whose life project was to run a home, 15 per cent came from a working class and 4 per cent a middle class background. Although girls on the whole aspired to both a job and a satisfactory home life, they did not all agree on the practical means to achieve this. When asked: "Does a woman have to give up her career for marriage or is it possible to reconcile all the aspirations of the modern woman?" 10 per cent said that sacrifice was inevitable, 20 per cent thought of giving up their job for a time, and the rest thought that some sort of compromise could be reached. These responses support the view that the majority of girls, like boys, want to work, but that family and home are seen as more important than a job by a substantial minority of girls.

At this point the question as to whether the role of boys in the family has changed as much as that of girls and whether boys are more ready to share home and family tasks needs to be raised. Research conducted in France among young secondary school pupils in 1984 revealed a marked difference between the sexes in terms of future aspirations. Unlike girls, the majority of boys did not think of the future in terms of family and domestic work and it was significant that only a minority of girls and no boys at all contested the traditional division of labour in the family, as if they felt that this was not of concern to them (Camilleri and Tapia, 1984). This reflects the reality of the division of labour in wider society. In Belgium the rate of female employment is estimated at about 40 per cent of the overall working population. In 1970, it was 32 per cent. Women have increasingly continued to work after marriage: the employment rate of twenty-five to twenty-nine-year-old women rose from 68.1 per cent in 1975 to 77.7 per cent in 1980, and of thirty to thirty-four-year-old women from 51 per cent in 1975 to 69.4 per cent in 1980. Women have shown their willingness to enter the labour market but, despite the expectations of feminists who had thought that responsibilities in occupational and private life would be shared, the responsibility for household management and children is still mainly incumbent on women (Peemans-Poulet, 1984). According to French sociologists little significant progress has been made in this area and even in the very few families where partners agree that domestic work should be shared, men take up on an average 20 per cent of domestic duties. This in turn tends to affect girls' expectations of life and to have a profound influence over their study choices (Grignon, 1987).

A French sociologist, Mosconi, has argued that sex segregation in the labour market, which supports low salaries in "women's jobs", influences sex segregation in education and not inversely (Mosconi, 1983). She points out that girls' seemingly voluntary exclusion from certain study options and their choice of traditionally female occupations depends on the objective presence or absence of girls and women in given occupations and professions, which in turn influences the degree to which girls can imagine themselves in these roles. Thus, when girls overwhelmingly choose to become nurses or teachers and explain their choices through their desire to help others or through their desire for human contacts, they choose careers in which they can imagine themselves, careers which are available to them. In this respect their choices are realistic and do pay attention to the labour market, and rather than stemming from a "backward" frame of mind, the stereotypical choices of girls can be seen to be the result of the pressure of external factors such as the objective probability of getting a job and the constraints of future family life.

This internalization of sex roles, it can be argued, does not take place during childhood, but on the contrary through a constant process in which girls take real opportunities more and more into account, and in which they are less and less allowed to dream, even if all this happens unconsciously. Girls do not always underachieve in aspirations but social pressures can compel them to lower their expectations. A small-scale "action research" study conducted in three schools in Brussels in 1987 points out that the level of expectations of fifteen-year-old girls, especially immigrant girls, is significantly high, 73 per cent expressing the wish to go to university. Beyond this age, there is a levelling down of aspirations towards "non-university" tertiary education, especially short-term diploma courses (Thiebaut, 1987). This study also showed that positive intervention had resulted in raising girls' aspirations, especially those of eighteen-year-old girls who thought of studies they had never imagined before. This suggests that socialization in the shaping of typically female role behaviour is never perfectly fulfilled. Girls' identities, especially at adolescence, can be modified so that traditional female stereotyping can be challenged. What girls most need is the opportunity to think through their situation, and to understand the real constraints. The survey on girls' study choices mentioned above precisely revealed the difficulties girls have in understanding their own motives. Eighty-nine per cent of the girls answered they had chosen their options freely. However, when asked the more pragmatic question, "Have you received enough information about opportunities for study?", less than half answered that they had. Thus, they declared themselves free to choose but they did not really know what there was to choose. The myth of freedom of choice was so strong that the recognition of a limit to this freedom did not weaken their conviction and they had really internalized the constraints of their choices.

Reproduction of a Sexual Hierarchy in School

In this process of the internalization of sex roles, society, family, the mass media and school all play a role. However, this section will be limited to the part of the education system which in Belgium is not regarded, unlike the family and mass media, as reproducing sexism. On the contrary, co-education is said to be the very cornerstone of equality. But the commitment to equality of opportunity is contradicted by hidden messages and practices which reinforce sexual hierarchy. Patriarchal knowledge transmitted in schools and universities has never been challenged. Feminism has hardly reached academic circles. Courses in Women's Studies were only started in 1987 at the University of Antwerp and in 1988 in Brussels. Foreign feminist research is unknown except to the small feminist groups and rare feminist magazines. There has been so far no concern to tackle bias in the content of the curriculum and girls continue to swallow a culture and a knowledge which will always remind them of the inferior status of women. Only the tip of the iceberg has been touched, namely the sex-stereotyped imagery in school textbooks. Research on this subject has been well received by educational authorities but this did not, however, result in any plan to remove old textbooks from schools (Crabbé *et al.*, 1985).

This deprecating treatment of girls and women through the sexist content of school learning is reinforced by sexist practices. The hidden curriculum is a reality in Belgium, as in other countries. The only research in this field has been carried out in primary schools in Flanders on the interaction between teachers and pupils (Himpens *et al.*, 1985). From a quantitative point of view the authors noted that teachers used a greater variety of terms to address boys, that they made more positive and negative remarks to boys and that they provided them with more encouragement, questions and information. From a qualitative point of view, teachers used more superlatives in their remarks to boys, the girls receiving much weaker expressions of approval or disapproval. The research concluded that boys enjoyed preferential treatment by female as well as by male teachers in co-educational schools, and were given more time and more interest. Now how do girls feel about this? Are they aware of this differentiation? Can they understand it in terms of sexism or do they ascribe this preferential treatment to their own personalities? It seems highly plausible that girls do not perceive the roots of the situation but understand this treatment as natural to each sex, rather than the result of a social production of differences.

Besides the interaction between teachers and pupils in co-educational schools, social relations between the sexes should be taken into account in an analysis of the reinforcement of sexual hierarchy. The director of the centre of adolescent guidance at the UCL (Catholic University in Brussels) has declared in an interview that co-education feeds the war between the sexes: young people tend to adopt extreme positions, girls make fun of the boys who are more clumsy and less mature, and boys display an overt misogyny (Toussaint, 1988). It has also been argued that the presence of boys and girls exacerbates stereotypical attitudes and behaviour because these allow pupils to maintain their identities. Several observers have noted that boys and girls physically separate themselves in classes especially between the ages of twelve and sixteen, "mixing" being more frequent again at the end of secondary school when boys and girls are more self-confident, and in their leisure time where opportunities are provided for the development of sexual relationships. Adolescent sexuality in terms of power relations between the sexes has not been documented in Belgium. However, psychologists and psychiatrists with practical experience suggest that in love relationships, boys and girls often reproduce the traditional script of male and female behaviour. A psychologist from the Université des Femmes, has, for example, described how a girl is more often anxious to please and that she often gets involved in a sexual relationship because she fears her boyfriend might think she does not love him (Piron, 1989).

The physical "mixing" of the sexes was the great hope of the promoters of co-education. But is voluntary separation in classrooms a pupil strategy to avoid the conflict caused by the eruption of sexuality? Co-education has had to fight sexual taboos but it could only cast out sexuality by neutralizing gender differences. Analysis of teacher and pupil views has demonstrated that sexuality is seen by teachers as well as by pupils as dangerous, to teachers an obstacle to the transmission of knowledge and to pupils a source of conflict, so that both groups try to neutralize it (Mosconi, 1989). The non-sexual character of education is guaranteed by consensus on co-education with its implicit definition of equality as the absence of sex differences and by the expressed views of teachers who state they have a neutral attitude towards gender issues. Although contradicted in practice, these views have also often been internalized by girls. This is a deep contradiction in the system: on the one hand it pretends to extend equality to all, and on the other it leaves its patriarchal foundations unchanged. Girls may well believe themselves to be equal to boys, they experience – though without being able to define it – male dominance in everyday school life, in their personal interactions with teachers and peers. This accounts for their vulnerability, the symptoms of which we recognize in the so-called "feminine" characteristics such as self-doubt, lack of self-confidence, limited ambitions. This vulnerability makes life harder but it also gives girls an insight into gender relations and consequent potential for change. Recognizing this could be the starting point of worthwhile interventions with girls to allow them to think objectively about their situation and to empower them to change it.

Equal Opportunities Policies

The principle of educational equality for boys and girls was affirmed in the law of 4 August 1978 which endorsed the 1975 European Directive on Equal Treatment Between Men and Women Workers. Only equal access to professional and occupational training was covered by the law, and the last formal barriers to equal access to all forms of education were not removed until 1983. Official concern about inequality was not the result of a diffusion of feminist ideas, or of a growing awareness of the problem, but simply came about through Belgium's obligation to apply international agreements. This accounts for the very lukewarm way in which educational authorities have dealt with the issue. It has never received priority over other issues and dealing with the impact of gender on educational achievement and outcomes has never been viewed as an educational concern. Agreement in principle was accompanied by little commitment to action.

In 1979 an advisory committee, the Commission for Equal Opportunities for Girls and Boys in Education, was set up within the Ministry of Education to give advice, conduct research, and propose legal measures to implement equality of opportunity in preparation for professional life. The Commission can recommend methods of promoting education which aim to develop harmonious relationships between girls and boys in school, family, social and political life. Between 1979 and 1988 the Commission produced nine papers on equal opportunities, only one of which has had any worthwhile effect. The powerlessness of the Commission can be ascribed to the status it had been given, which reflects the political priorities of the educational authorities. Members work voluntarily, they have no secretariat and no funding has been granted.

The list of initiatives taken by the Ministry of Education to promote equal opportunities is short. The text of the 1985 European Resolution on Equality of Opportunity For Girls and Boys in Education was distributed to all teachers and inspectors of state sector education. A video about sex stereotyping was made available to all state schools and an official in charge of the issue of equal opportunities has conducted working groups of heads of PMS centres (centres of psychological, medical and social guidance) and organized training days to raise awareness among teaching staff. The only large-scale project at state level was not initiated by the Minister of Education but by the Secretary for Social Emancipation, Ms Miet Smet, a women deeply committed to women's issues. Since 1987 she has launched an annual campaign to make parents, pupils and teachers aware of the issue of girls' stereotyped choices.

These campaigns by the Secretary for Social Emancipation have had a great impact on the public and they are an encouragement to people committed to this issue. Despite the lack of commitment from the Ministry of Education, small-scale projects have been carried out both in the state and Catholic schools. These have focused on two issues: in-service teacher education in consciousness raising about stereotypes and sex bias in schools, and the diversification of girls' options choice at secondary level, both issues recommended by the European Resolution of June 1985 so that funding and support have been easier to find.

In the Catholic sector, the initiative came from a Catholic women's group "Vie Feminine" which organized seminars on equal opportunities for future primary teachers and seminars on co-education for future teachers of religious education. These were small scale and brief projects. In the state sector the initiative came from a feminist group, "Changeons les livres", which has made a video on sex stereotyping in school books and has supplied instructors at seminars for teaching staff organized in the state sector. It is worth emphasizing that in both cases initiatives came from feminist and women's groups and that the instructors were not academics but most often members of groups which have been committed to the issue for a long time. Moreover, an appreciable part of these projects or action research has been conducted in the context of the EEC programme, thus funded by the EEC.

At present an initiative in teacher training is being pursued in both the state and Catholic sector. Information has been given to teachers and parents in the Catholic schools by the authors of the Catholic publication on co-education mentioned earlier in the chapter. Experimental projects are being carried out to diversify girls' option choices, especially in the involvement of girls in new technology. The political implication of this priority is to adapt girls to a technocratic society without challenging its patriarchal foundations. However, it must be recognized that this can prove to be a tool in achieving a broader goal. These projects are well funded and have positive side effects for girls. The action research in Brussels schools mentioned above has not only provided girls with sound information about studies and job opportunities, it has also increased their self-confidence and helped them to see better what determinants act upon them and what they can achieve. In this way, these educational strategies, whatever their original purpose, can support girls in their aspirations to equality and emancipation and finally contribute to giving them greater power and freedom.

We cannot expect more from the state than we have had so far, for the present context is anything but favourable. The current economic crisis has provoked cuts in the education budget. Since 1 January, 1989, education has been devolved to the level of the linguistic communities and it is unlikely that the new policy will treat equal opportunities as a priority. At a recent meeting the Minister of Education for the French- and German-speaking community admitted little had been done and did not promise to do anything. Yet it is clear that small-scale projects are multiplying and in this respect the European

Resolution provided vital support to pressure groups and outlined the guidelines for the integration of the issue of sex equality into education.

References

Alaluf, M. (1986) *Le temps du labeur* (The age of labour). Université Libre de Bruxelles.

Brunfaut, E. (1986) Des femmes pour l'an 2000, une enquête sur les choix d'études des jeunes filles (Women in the year 2000: a survey of the study choices of young girls). *Bulletin de la Fondation André Renard*, **61**. Cahiers de la Commission du Travail des Femmes, FGTB LHV.

Bureau Pédagogique du Secrétariat National de l'Enseignement Catholique (1986) *L'enseignement secondaire catholique après 15 ans de rénovation* (Catholic secondary education after 15 years of reform). Brussels.

Bureau Pédagogique du Secrétariat National de l'Enseignement Catholique (1987) *La coéducation, un projet pédagogique* (Co-education: an educational project). Brussels.

Cabinet du Secrétariat d'Etat à l'Emancipation Sociale (1987) *Egalité des chances pour les garçons et les filles lors du choix de la profession* (Equal opportunities in occupational choice for boys and girls). Brussels.

Cabinet du Secrétariat d'Etat à l'Emancipation Sociale (1989) *Les femmes dans la société belge* (Women in Belgian society). Brussels.

Cahiers de la Commission du Travail des Femmes (1980) Comment realiser la coéducation dans l'enseignement, gagé de l'égalité entre les femmes et les hommes (How to bring about co-education, as a guarantee of equality between men and women). Brussels.

Camilleri, C. and Tapia, C. (1984) *Les Nouveaux Jeunes* (The New Generation). Paris: Privat.

Crabbé, B., Delfosse, M. L., Gardaio, L., Verlaekt, G. and Wilwerth, E. (1985) *Les femmes dans les livres scolaires* (Women in school books). Brussels: P. Mardaga.

de Grandpré, M. (1973) *La coéducation dans les écoles de 45 pays* (Co-education in the schools of 45 countries). Quebec: Pauline Sherbrook.

Etudes et Documents de la Direction Générale de L'organisation des Etudes (1985) *Enseignement Primaire* (Primary Education), No. 2. Service de Statistiques et Programmation, MEN, Brussels.

Etudes et Documents de la Direction Générale de L'organisation des Etudes (1985) *Enseignement Secondaire* (Secondary Education), No. 3. Service de Statistiques et Programmation, MEN, Brussels.

Etudes et Documents de la Direction Générale de L'organisation des Etudes (1985) *Enseignement Supérieur* (Higher Education), No. 5. Service de Statistiques et Programmation, MEN, Brussels.

Etudes et Documents de la Direction Générále de L'organisation des Etudes (1985) *Evolution des effectifs – Analyses*, No. 8. Service de Statistiques et Programmation, MEN, Brussels.

Fourez, G. (1986) L'école en perspective historique (The school in a historical perspective). *La Revue Nouvelle*, **9**.

Grignon, M. (1987) Des principes à la realité (Principles into reality). *Informations Sociales*, **5**.

Himpens, A., Verbeke, M. and De Gos, M. (1985) *Coeducatie, wat is dat?* (What is coeducation?). Ghent: Centrum voor de Studie van de Historische Pedagogiek.

Leroy, R. and Godano, A. (1986) *Bulletin de l'Ires*. Louvain: Université Catholique de Louvain.

Mosconi, N. (1983) Des rapports entre division sexuelle du travail et inégalités des chances entre les sexes à l'école (The relationship between the sexual division of labour and inequality of opportunity between the sexes at school). *Revue Française de Pédagogie*, 62.

Mosconi, N. (1989) *La mixité dans le secondaire, un faux-semblant?* (Co-education in secondary schools: a pretence?) Paris: Presses Universitaires de France.

Peemans-Poulet, M. (1984) Partage des responsabilités professionnelles, familiales et sociales (The sharing of family, social and occupational responsibilities). Brussels: Commission des Communautés Européennes.

Piron, P. (1989) Parler d'amour (To talk of love). *Chronique Féministe*, **33**, Brussels.

Plateau, N. (1987) La discrimination des jeunes filles dans l'enseignement (Discrimination against girls in education). *Un hommes sur deux est une femme*. Louvain-la-Neuve: Ciaco.

Tanguy, L. (Ed.) (1986) *L'introuvable relation formation/emploi* (The intractable relationship between training and education). Paris: Documentation Française.

Theibaut, C. (1987) *Une intervention destinée à une population de filles d'origine immigrée dans le cadre de l'égalité des chances* (An action-research project aimed at improving equality of opportunity among a group of girls of immigrant origin). Brussels: IRFEC.

Toussaint, Y. (1988) Les Hommes (Men). *Le Soir.*

Van Haecht, A., Genard, J. L. and Karnas, A. (1982) *Problématique actuelle dans l'enseignement secondaire et aspirations professionnelles dans le champ scolaire* (Current problems in secondary education and occupational aspirations at school). Programmation de la Politique Scientifique, C.I.P.S., Programme national de recherches en sociales: Brussels.

Van Haecht, A., Genard, J. L. and Karnas, A. (1985) *L'enseignement renové: de l'origine à l'éclipse* (Educational reforms: from their inception to their eclipse). Université Libre de Bruxelles.

Verbeke, M. (1984) *Jongens en meisjes samen in de klas* (Boys and girls together in class). Ghent: Centrum voor de Studie van de historische Pedagogiek.

Notes

1. Between 1959 and 1989, education which fell within the sphere of one ministry (Ministré de l'Education Nationale) was submitted to a gradual process of "communautarisation" (decentralization): two ministers were appointed in 1968, one for the French- and German-speaking communities and one for the Flemish community, and since 1 January, 1989, all the important educational administrative functions have been transferred to the communities. This chapter will focus on the French- and German-speaking communities where the reforms were implemented on a much larger scale than in Flanders.
2. All the tables produced in this section come from *Etudes et Documents de la Direction Genérale de L'organisation des Etudes* (1985), published by the Service de Statistiques and Programmation of the Ministry of National Education, Brussels.
3. Percentages derived from figures produced in "Diplômes-Certificats-Brevets delivrés en 1984" (Diplomas and certificates awarded in 1984. In *Etudes et Documents*, 6.

CHAPTER 3

England and Wales

MAGGIE WILSON

THE 1944 Education Act gave some recognition to the notion of equality of educational opportunity and paved the way for a massive increase in resources allocated to the education system over the next two decades. During the 1960s it became, however, apparent that girls were not getting their fair share of the "educational cake". Early concerns centred on patterns of underachievement in examination results, on equal access to educational institutions and on the removal of formal barriers to educational opportunities. Years of lobbying in other areas of public life resulted in the 1970 Equal Pay Act and the 1975 Sex Discrimination Act, which was concerned with the areas of employment, the provision of goods, facilities and services, the disposal and management of services, education and training. It provided some measure of legal redress to discrimination and established the Equal Opportunities Commission as an arbitration facilitator, "watchdog" and research organization. In 1976 the United Kingdom adopted the 1975 EEC Directive on the Equality of Treatment Between Men and Women Workers, which endorsed the principle of equal treatment in the areas of vocational training and in education.

Since then the United Kingdom has been signatory to other international agreements in this area and several reports produced by the Department of Education and Science (DES) have include statements about the desirability of equal opportunities in education, particularly in terms of subject choice. However, no coherent national plan of action has been evolved (Byrne, 1985). This is partly the product of what has been traditionally a highly decentralized system of education in England and Wales, in which many major educational decisions are left to the discretion of the 104 Local Education Authorities (LEAs) and to the judgements of school staff and governors.[1] Many would also argue that there has been an absence of will to tackle this area of underachievement (Arnot, 1987).

More recently some educationalists have criticized what has been termed a "deficit" approach to research in this area, which has tended to adopt the norms of the most "able" and successful pupils as the criterion for achievement in the education system. Maximizing opportunities in higher education, it has been argued, may only lead to improved opportunities for the most able of a

41

disadvantaged group and tells us little about the experience of the great majority of girls in the education system (Acker, 1984). An overemphasis on differences in patterns of study may lend support to the view that girls are inappropriately socialized by their families and the education system and that disparities in job opportunities may be attributed to this. Research in the 1980s was thus directed towards the experiences of girls in school and towards ways in which to make schools more "girl-friendly" (Mahoney, 1985; Browne and France, 1985).

This chapter will briefly outline the structure of the education system of England and Wales, review evidence of the achievement and under-achievement of girls in this system and explore some of the areas of school life which may bring about such patterns. It will then turn to patterns of employment in the labour market, where the greatest disparities between the sexes may arguably be found, and give a brief account of equal opportunities policies in education.

The Education System of England and Wales

Education in England and Wales is compulsory and free of charge between the ages of five and sixteen. The great majority of children attend state schools, but attendance at private schools is increasing: 6.4 per cent of children attended private schools in 1987. These are mostly single-sex and a minority are based on religion. The state sector also contains "voluntary" schools, usually Church of England or Catholic, at primary and secondary level. In 1987, 23 per cent of children in England attended such schools (*Social Trends*, 1989).

Nursery Education. This is provided at the discretion of the Local Education Authorities. In 1987 only 47.6 per cent of three to four-year-olds were in state-sponsored nursery education, the majority on a part time basis (DES *Statistics of Education*, 1988). A variety of arrangements exist for other children, including private nurseries, play groups and child-minders, some state-sponsored day nurseries and a small, but increasing, number of company crèches.

Primary Education, State sector primary schools are co-educational. Most pupils transfer to secondary education at the age of eleven, but in some local education authorities middle schools exist for nine to thirteen-year-olds with transfer to upper secondary school.

Secondary Education. Selective education, which divided children into grammar, technical and secondary school attendance at the age of eleven, still exists in some areas. Eighty-five per cent of English and 98 per cent of Welsh state secondary schools are, however, comprehensive in their intake. Because many of the schools under the old tripartite system were single-sex, a few comprehensive schools are not co-educational. The majority of secondary schools offer education from eleven to eighteen years of age, although some schools do not offer education beyond the age of sixteen.

Until the 1988 Education Reform Act the only compulsory subject by law was Religious Education. In practice, all pupils took Mathematics, English and a cluster of core subjects, but they were also able to choose between a wide variety of options at the age of fourteen. The 1988 Act has now established a compulsory national curriculum for all pupils in state schools, comprising a core curriculum of Mathematics, English (and Welsh in Welsh language schools), Science, Technology and Design, Physical Education, Art, Music, a Modern Language at secondary school level, History and Geography plus Religious Education, with a consequent reduction in the opportunity to take optional subjects. This is being introduced in schools over a phased period.

From the early 1970s pupils were able to take CSEs (Certification of Secondary Education or the more difficult O-levels (Ordinary levels), usually at the age of fifteen or sixteen, the majority taking five or more subjects. Since 1986 a unified examination, the GCSE (General Certificate of Secondary Education) has been introduced.

In 1986–1987, 19 per cent of pupils in the United Kingdom took A-levels (Advanced levels) or Scottish Highers at the age of seventeen or eighteen in one to four subjects. Two or three good A-level passes are required for entrance into higher education in England and Wales, depending on the course and institution. They are highly specialized examinations, chosen according to the student's wishes.

The 1988 Act has also introduced testing according to national criteria at the ages of seven, eleven, fourteen and sixteen in addition to these public examinations, the first tests are to be administered to seven-year-olds in 1991.

Further and Higher Education. In 1987, 32 per cent of all sixteen to eighteen-year-olds in the United Kingdom were in non-advanced further education on a full-time or part-time basis, mostly at Colleges of Further Education, which offer courses in such vocational areas as Engineering, Construction and Business Studies, as well as academic GCSEs and A-levels (*Social Trends*, 1989).

In 1986–1987, 14 per cent of nineteen to twenty-year-olds in the United Kingdom attended courses in higher education in universities, polytechnics or other colleges such as colleges of higher education or art colleges on a full-time or part-time basis. The present government wishes to raise this figure to 20 per cent by the year 1990, to bring it more in line with other Western European countries. A system of income-related grants has been available to support students in higher education. This will be replaced by a part-grant, part-loan scheme from 1990.

The Open University was founded in 1970 to offer "second-chance" education by correspondence. In addition, the number of mature students (aged over twenty-one) has risen dramatically, particularly in the polytechnic sector, since 1980.

Girls and Educational Achievement at School and in Further and Higher Education

In general, girls show a slight advantage in the early years at school compared with boys, particularly in the areas of reading ability, spelling, grammar and verbal skills. A large-scale survey, Primary Education in England and Wales, conducted by the government's inspectorate in 1978 found a higher average reading score for girls between the ages of eight and eleven, although boys had tended to catch up by the age of eleven. There has been some evidence to suggest that boys under the age of eleven have superior numerical skills and a better sense of spatial awareness and this supposition has been used to explain later divergent patterns of study and employment (Kaminski, 1982). However, other research has presented a more complex picture. Girls have been found to have better computational skills at the age of ten (Ward, 1979), but eleven-year-old boys have been found to score higher in tests of assessment of length, capacity, rate and ratio (APU, 1980). It has also been suggested that such differences may be limited to high achievers rather than be typical of the average boy or girl, or may be a product of differences in the rate of maturation and may have been exaggerated (Steedman, 1983).

At secondary level boys and girls exhibit a strong divergence of interest and study patterns. The performance of girls in the application of concepts to Physics and, to a certain extent, Chemistry declines, while the performance of boys improves. However, when such patterns are explored in greater depth, the picture becomes more complex. The Assessment of Performance Unit of the DES tested a range of scientific skills between the ages of eleven and fifteen in 1986 (Johnson and Murphy, 1986). It was found that girls tended to have better observational skills, to have a slight edge in the use of graphs and charts at the age of eleven and in planning investigations at the age of eleven to thirteen. Boys exhibited superior computational skills at the age of fifteen, had a slight edge in interpreting and presenting information and in handling some scientific instruments. These differences are reflected in patterns of curricular choice, which are outlined in the next section. In terms of overall performance in public examinations at school level, girls outperform boys as a group to a high level, as illustrated by Table 3.1 below.

Fewer girls than boys leave school without any qualifications at all. Girls have shown a slight advantage in the number of pupils leaving school with five or more O-levels (now GCSEs) at the top grades and with one A-level. More boys than girls continue to attain two or three A-levels at school, although the gap between these results has narrowed considerably since the 1970s. Slightly more girls than boys stay on at school after the age of compulsory education at sixteen (DES Statistics of Education, 1988).

The number of young women entering higher education has also increased in recent years. In 1953 just over 1 per cent of girls reached university and just under 2 per cent entered teacher training in Colleges of Education (DES

TABLE 3.1

School Leavers-Highers Qualification by Sex, 1976–1977 and 1986–1987[a]

| | % Boys | | % Girls | |
	1975–1976	1986–1987	1975–1976	1986–1987
Percentage with:				
2 or more "A" levels	14.3	15.0	12.1	14.7
1 "A" level	3.5	3.6	4.0	4.2
5 or more "O" levels/grades:				
A–C grades	7.2	9.5	9.4	11.8
1–4 "O" levels/grades:				
A–C grades	23.9	24.7	27.0	29.2
1 or more "O" levels/grades:				
D or E grades, or CSE grades 2–5	29.9	34.5	28.4	31.0
No GCE/SCE or CSE grades	21.2	12.7	19.1	9.1
Total	100.0	100.0	100.0	100.0

Source: DES *Statistics of Education* (1988).

[a] These figures relate to school-leavers only and exclude qualifications gained in Colleges of Further Education.

Statistics of Education, 1953). The overall number of students in higher education has increased over the last twenty years, although still remains relatively low in comparison with other European countries. In 1987–1988, women accounted for 45 per cent of full-time students in higher education at degree level and 39 per cent of part-time students. Overall women have increased their share of higher education over the last twenty-five years despite a reduction in the number of places available for teacher training, an area with a high uptake of female students. Between 1980 and 1987 the number of women students in higher education increased by 20 per cent and the number of male students by 4 per cent, an increase particularly marked in public sector higher education and on part-time courses. At postgraduate level, representing just 4 per cent of the age group of eighteen to twenty-four-year-olds, 37 per cent of university postgraduate students are women (DES Statistics of Education, 1988, 1989). Differences between the sexes thus remain at this level, although are not as marked as those between social classes. In 1986–1987 28 per cent of children from managerial and professional families went to university compared with 2 per cent from families in manual occupations. Overall about 45 per cent of students in higher education are from a professional and managerial background, although they only constitute about a quarter of the population (*Social Trends*, 1989).

Despite the amount of research attention paid to the access of women to higher education, a far greater proportion of school-leavers enter further education. About half of all sixteen to eighteen-year-olds are to be found here and young women are more likely to take up such provision than young men. Colleges of further education offer a variety of educational courses below degree level, including GCSE and A-level work and courses leading to a range of technical qualifications. Female students are heavily concentrated in the less prestigious, non-advanced sector. In 1984 two-thirds of students on such courses were young women, pursuing courses in home economics, catering, secretarial and office skills, health and welfare. Four times as many young men as young women pursued courses which led to more prestigious technical and vocational qualifications (Blunden, 1984). Ninety-nine per cent of those on engineering courses at this level are male. One researcher has estimated that in 1980 two-thirds of courses in further education are foreclosed to female students because of prior subject specialization (Harding, 1980). Although nearly half of sixteen to eighteen-year-olds on part-time day-release schemes are female, many more male students over the age of eighteen obtained day-release from their employers to enhance their qualifications.

From the mid 1970s on the government has sponsored special youth training programmes to combat rising levels of youth unemployment. These are funded by the Department of Employment, but many of these courses take place in colleges of further education. Nearly half of the trainees on current Youth Training Scheme programmes are girls. In 1986 two-thirds of female trainees were concentrated in the areas of clerical work, personal services, sales, health and community service work, reflecting similar patterns in further education (Wilce, 1986).

Curricular Choice

Although, as has been shown, girls tend to "outperform" boys at primary school and to match boys' examination achievements at secondary school, differences in the choice of subjects which girls and boys pursue remain marked and persistent. As outlined earlier, the education system of England and Wales has traditionally allowed for early specialization and schools have enjoyed considerable latitude in offering a wide variety of subjects in comparison with their European equivalents. The introduction of the national core curriculum will dramatically alter this situation for pupils up to the age of sixteen, although it remains to be seen how choices within the broad subject divisions and within optional areas will pan out.

Despite an acknowledgement of sex differences in curricular choice by government reports such as the 1943 Norwood or 1963 Newsom Reports, the issue did not become one of central government concern until the 1970s with the publication of a national survey, Curricular Differences for Boys and Girls, by the Department of Education and Science in 1975. This showed a considerable polarization in subjects taken by boys and girls at examination level and also in courses designed for early school leavers, such as design or construction courses, child-care or home economics. Since then, most research and interest has focused on the issue of the relatively poor uptake of science and technology subjects by girls at all levels, and on the career consequences of such choices. The Department of Education and Science has continued to publish statistics on subject choice in public examinations and at degree level, while a major study of secondary school option choices published in 1984 casts light on pupil choice at the critical stage prior to public examinations (Pratt *et al.*, 1984). Surveying over one hundred secondary schools, this revealed some startling differences. While one in five boys took Engineering at the age of thirteen plus, only one in five hundred girls did so. One in three boys took Technical Drawing at this stage to one in fifty girls. Three times as many boys took Physics as girls and twice as many Chemistry, Commerce and additional Mathematics options. Twice as many girls took Biology and Modern Languages and four times as many girls took Human Biology as boys. Only one in one thousand boys took Needlework as an option. There were no major differences in Humanities subjects. The survey reported little change in option choice since the 1975 DES survey and Sex Discrimination Act.

This pattern is supported by trends in public examination results. At O-level and CSE level in 1985–1986 under 10 per cent of girls and over 20 per cent of boys obtained a pass in Physics and over 11 per cent of girls to over 15 per cent of boys obtained a pass in Chemistry, as illustrated by Table 3.2 below. These disparities are continued at A-level, where over three times as many boys obtained a pass in Physics as girls and over three times as many boys obtained passes in Craft, Design and Technology. A-level results for 1985–1986 are given in Table 3.3 below. These results represent an increase in the number of girls taking Science and Technology at examination level, but from a low number overall. Even in the new technological area of Computer Studies, girls only attained 27 per cent of O-level and 16 per cent of A-level passes in 1985–1986 (DES *Statistics of Education*, 1988).

Modern Languages and the Creative Arts tend to be the preserve of female candidates and this pattern is continued into higher education, as illustrated by Table 3.4, where women predominate in Education, Modern Languages and the Arts. Even within subject groupings, differences in uptake emerge. In the Social Sciences, for example, more male students take Politics and Economics, rather than Sociology or Social Administration, and in the Sciences, Biology rather than Physics. Broad subject groupings also mask status hierarchies within subject areas, such as Medicine and health-related courses. At postgraduate level only a third of students overall are female and the proportion of women students falls even within "feminine" areas, such as Education, where 50 per cent of postgraduates are women.

During the 1980s a considerable amount of research has been conducted into what has been called the "massive avoidance of the sciences" by girls (Kelly, 1981; Kahle, 1985; Harding, 1983). Reasons put forward by the Assessment of Performance Unit and the other studies cited include early socialization patterns, experience and play activities, subject images, teacher attitudes mediated in interaction in the classroom and the organizational

TABLE 3.2

Distribution of School-Leavers with Higher Grade Passes at "O" level or CSE in Selected Subjects, 1975–1976 and 1985–1986

	1975–1976			1985–1986			Percentage change 1975–1976 to 1985–1986		
	% Boys	% Girls	Total % all leavers	% Boys	% Girls	Total % all leavers	% Boys	% Girls	Total
Any subject	48.0	52.0	49.9	51.5	57.6	54.5	+7	+11	+9
English	31.0	40.9	35.8	34.7	45.4	40.0	+12	+11	+12
Mathematics	27.0	20.2	23.7	33.3	27.8	30.6	+23	+38	+29
Physics	16.5	4.5	10.7	21.9	9.4	15.7	+33	+109	+47
Chemistry	12.4	5.8	9.2	15.8	11.4	13.7	+27	+97	+49
Biological sciences	11.5	17.5	14.4	12.6	18.6	15.6	+10	+6	+8
Craft, design, technology and other science	18.3	3.6	11.2	17.6	3.8	10.9	−4	+6	−3
French	11.2	16.9	13.9	11.0	18.1	14.5	−2	+7	+4
History	13.4	14.6	14.0	13.5	15.4	14.4	+1	+5	+3
Geography	17.8	13.7	15.8	18.5	14.1	16.4	+4	+3	+4
Creative arts	10.5	14.9	12.6	10.1	17.3	13.6	−4	+16	+8
Commercial and domestic studies	1.4	15.5	8.3	3.4	16.9	10.0	+143	+9	+20
General studies	2.5	2.0	2.3	2.6	2.7	2.6	+4	+35	+13

Source: DES *Statistics of Education* (1988).

TABLE 3.3

Distribution of School-Leavers with "A" Level Passes in Selected Subjects. (Percentage of the 17 year old age group) 1975–1976 and 1985–1986

	1975–1976			1985–1986			Percentage change 1975–1976 to 1985–1986		
	% Boys	% Girls	Total % all 17 year olds	% Boys	% Girls	Total % all 17 year olds	% Boys	% Girls	Total
Any subject	16.7	14.3	15.5	16.4	15.7	16.1	−2	+10	+4
English	3.4	6.6	5.0	2.6	5.9	4.2	−24	−11	−16
Mathematics	6.0	2.0	4.1	7.4	3.6	5.5	+23	+80	+34
Physics	5.5	1.2	3.4	5.9	1.7	3.8	+7	+42	+12
Chemistry	4.1	1.8	3.0	4.6	2.7	3.7	+12	+50	+23
Biological sciences	2.6	2.8	2.7	2.4	3.4	2.9	−8	+21	+7
Craft, design, technology and other science	1.2	0.2	0.7	1.1	0.3	0.7	−8	+50	—
French	1.3	3.0	2.1	1.0	2.6	1.8	−23	−13	−14
History	3.3	3.4	3.4	2.6	3.0	2.8	−21	−12	−18
Geography	3.7	2.5	3.1	3.1	2.3	2.7	−16	−8	−13
Creative arts	1.2	2.1	1.7	1.3	2.7	2.0	+8	+29	+18
Commercial and domestic studies	0.1	0.8	0.5	0.5	1.0	0.7	+400	+25	+40
General studies	3.2	2.1	2.6	4.2	3.3	3.7	+31	+57	+42

Source: DES *Statistics of Education* (1988).

TABLE 3.4

Distribution of Students in Higher Education by Sex and by Subject Group, 1986–1987

First Degree Subject	Thousands		Females as % students
	Females	Males	
Languages and Literature	28.1	13.3	68
Administrative, Business and Social Studies	55.5	61.7	47
Medicine, Dentistry and Health	18.8	16.5	53
Arts other than Languages	15.2	13.0	54
Science and Mathematics	34.7	60.9	36
Engineering and Technology	8.2	61.5	12
Veterinary Science, Agriculture and related	2.3	2.9	44
Creative Arts and Design	20.2	14.2	58
Education	27.5	7.9	78
Architecture and other vocational subjects e.g. Librarianship and Information Science	7.4	9.3	44
All subjects	217.9	261.2	45.5

Source: Department of Education and Science, Further and Higher Education Statistics (1988).

features of the school. These will be explored in some detail in subsequent sections. It is worthy of note, however, that the same level of attention has not been directed towards the under-representation of boys in such areas as English and Modern Languages, in which girls tend to perform well, and which have traditionally provided society with its politicians, writers, creative artists and communicators of all kind. Shortages of personnel in scientific and technological areas of employment have also caused a shift in governmental support towards such areas of study at the expense of Arts and the Humanities, a trend which will disproportionately disadvantage young women.

Option Choice and Timetabling of Subjects

One reason to which the polarization of girls and boys into different avenues of knowledge has been attributed is the organization of the school timetable. The 1975 DES survey, Curricular Differences for Boys and Girls, found that in 98 per cent of secondary schools studied boys and girls were separated for some subjects, especially craftwork. Subject choices were often pre-empted by earlier specialization, particularly in the sciences, languages, commerce and crafts. Option choices were often arranged in timetabled blocks which precluded non-traditional choices. A later report on secondary education published in 1979 by the government's inspectorate, the HMIs, estimated that only 11 per cent of secondary schools offered a wholly "common curriculum" and that two thirds operated some form of sex discrimination in the range of crafts offered to pupils (HMI, 1979). Over half of male and female pupils took only one science at the age of fourteen to sixteen and 9 per cent of boys and 17 per cent of girls took no science at all at this age.

The large-scale 1984 survey of option choices cited earlier revealed some improvement in the situation but a continuation of discriminatory practice (Pratt *et al.*, 1984). Eleven per cent of schools surveyed still allocated pupils to craft subjects on the basis of sex alone and over a third took the sex of pupils into account when balancing class groups nominally based on ability. However, only half as many schools pre-empted subject choice as compared with in 1975 and 90 per cent of schools claimed to offer a rotational crafts timetable, which offers pupils the experience of a variety of craft subjects. This had resulted in some improvement in non-stereotyped crafts options, although in practice such schemes were often fairly nominal, restricted to the first two years of secondary school and with weak teacher support. About a quarter of the schools surveyed inferred that some vocational subjects were only open to one sex.

Although the relatively low uptake of the sciences by pupils is often attributed to pupil preference alone, many schools effectively enabled pupils to avoid the sciences. In 86 per cent of the schools surveyed, Biology could be taken as the compulsory science and 22 per cent of the schools allowed pupils to take no scientific or technological subjects after the age of fourteen. In only 2 per cent of the schools was one of the physical sciences compulsory.

The study also confirmed a higher uptake of the sciences by girls in single-sex schools, despite the poorer facilities commented on by the 1979 HMI survey. Over twice as many girls in single-sex schools took Physics as an examination option as in mixed schools, 41 per cent of girls in single-sex schools took Chemistry compared with 26 per cent in mixed schools. Boys were also more likely to take French or German, History and Geography in single-sex schools rather than in mixed schools.

Single-Sex Schools

The issue of subject choice in single-sex schools raises a number of other issues in connection with the co-education debate. The provision of single-sex schools was exempted from the terms of the 1975 Sex Discrimination Act. As outlined earlier, the great majority of state secondary schools in England and Wales are co-educational, with the exception of many selective grammar schools. The majority of private schools are also single-sex, although there has been an increasing tendency for boys' schools to admit girls into sixth forms (*Social Trends*, 1989). Single-sex schools are thus in the main concentrated in the most prestigious and well-endowed areas of school provision, a point which has not always been adequately recognized by researchers, concerned with the "superior" performance of pupils in such schools.

Co-education in the public sector was, in general, a by-product of the comprehensivization programme of the 1960s. It was assumed that all pupils would benefit from better facilities and would also experience a more "normal" school environment in mixed schools (Dale, 1975). The 1975 DES report on curricular choice acted as a catalyst for re-evaluating the issue of pupil performance in single-sex and mixed schools, both in terms of subject choice and overall levels of attainment. During the 1980s, some researchers began to reassess the role of single-sex schools and to put forward arguments against mixed schools as detrimental not only to girls' performance in examinations but also to their self-esteem (Sarah and Spender, 1980). Indeed, one study concluded that mixed-sex schools "constitute a disaster area for girls" (Mahoney, 1985).

A closer investigation of examination results in single-sex schools reveals a more complex picture. In a large-scale study commissioned by the Equal Opportunities Commission in 1983, differences in the performance of pupils in single-sex schools compared with those in mixed schools were greatly reduced or disappeared when allowances were made for the social background of pupils or selective basis of such schools (Steedman, 1983). In single-sex girls' schools, pupil performance in the Sciences was generally superior to girls' performance in mixed schools and girls in the top ability range tended to excel over a broader range of subjects. However, the study concluded that the results presented no clear-cut case for or against single-sex schools on the basis of academic achievement. Although analysis of results in Mathematics has also shown that girls do better in single-sex schools, it has been suggested that no valid comparisons can be made without taking into account curricula taught, quality of teaching staff and the catchment area of schools (Smith, 1984).

A small minority of mixed schools have offered special classes for girls in Mathematics, the sciences or technical subjects. These are usually restricted to the pre-public examination level and have tended to show consistently better results for girls. Boys' performance tends to remain unaffected and both boys and girls are reported to enjoy the classes more (APU, 1980). Arguments against the provision of single-sex groupings centre on discipline problems in boys-only classes and the possibility that such classes may provide second-class compensatory education. No attempts have been made to set up single-sex classes in subjects in which boys are under-represented, such as Languages. However, arguments for single-sex groups are also put forward on broader grounds in relation to the perceived marginalization of girls in mixed classrooms, where, it is suggested, girls constitute a negative reference group for boys to enhance their own sense of success and achievement (Mahoney, 1985).

Organizational Features of the School and Classroom

In addition to the formal school curriculum, researchers have pointed to a number of aspects of the "hidden curriculum" of schools which differentiate between boys and girls. Some of these concern interaction between teachers and pupils within the classroom; others concern the organizational features of the school. Indeed, one writer has argued that schools are more conservative than wider society in their treatment of boys and girls (Delamont, 1983). Schools tend to segregate the sexes more rigidly in playgrounds or classroom areas, and to enforce exaggeratedly different clothes, behaviour and activities. The majority of schools in England and Wales have a school uniform or code of dress for pupils and this usually precludes trousers or jeans for girls. Most schools have separate sports facilities and classes for boys and girls; most keep separate registers and record cards. It has been estimated that pupils can be classified according to their sex up to twenty times a day (Buswell, 1981). Schools often operate different codes of discipline and punishment, although corporal punishment is now illegal in state schools.

Within the classroom, teachers often exploit rivalry between the sexes to motivate or to manage pupils. Several studies confirm the view that teachers pay more attention to boys because of their potential disruptiveness (Clarricoates, 1978; Spender, 1980). Teachers reprimand boys more often but also give more praise to boys and more attention. Girls are often addressed collectively and boys by their first names. Boys tend to dominate classroom talk and there is some evidence to suggest that teachers deliberately gear the content of lessons towards boys' interests in order to retain attention and control (Clarricoates, 1978). At infant school level boys are often seen as untidier, noisier, rougher, more immature and more lacking in concentration than girls (Hartley, 1978). Although primary school teachers tend to favour the diligence and neatness of girls in the early years, secondary school teachers have been found to express a preference for male pupils as being more challenging and stimulating to teach. In a small-scale study of A-level Humanities classes by Stanworth, both male and female teachers perceived the boys as more able and rated their prospects more highly than the girls in their classes. The girls remained largely passive and "invisible" in class and teachers consistently downgraded their achievements (Stanworth, 1983). Having learned to gain teacher approval through quiet diligence in class, girls find that this strategy can often backfire when different demands are made of pupils at the upper levels of schooling when more active and assertive verbal contributions are often expected.

Boys learn to monopolize physical space in the playground and in the classroom, often dominating the teacher's main line of vision in formally arranged classrooms (Spender, 1980). From an early age pupils show a marked preference to work in single-sex work groups (Tann, 1981). Inside and outside the classroom boys often use ridicule in verbal and non-verbal behaviour to denigrate girls who are assertive or "bright" in class. Such tactics can also be employed against boys who are seen to be too "brainy" or to be "swots", but can take on sexual innuendos when levelled at girls. One teacher collected seventy-two such "put-down" names employed in her school (Mahoney, 1985). Boys have been reported to routinely employ petty physical harassment and bullying to solicit favours from girls and from weaker boys, such as borrowing pencils and rulers and being supplied with food. More serious incidents of sexual harassment in mixed schools are also coming to light and these contribute to arguments put forward for a return to single-sex groups or schools, where a sense of confidence and solidarity can be bolstered. The apparent passivity of many girls in class, it is maintained, is often a defensive reaction against such behaviour and a form of voluntary withdrawal from abuse. Mixed classrooms, it is argued, provide an arena in which unequal sexual identities are learned, practised and endorsed.

The Development of Girls' Self-Image

The seeds of such divisions at the age of puberty have already long been sown, according to a wealth of research in this area, well documented in the 1986 OECD report on girls and education (Safilios-Rothschild, 1986). By the age of three, a child's sexual identity has already become a crucial filter through which experiences and stimuli are perceived. Through differential treatment, language employed, play activities, and toys, children develop strong notions of sex-appropriate behaviour, which become accentuated in their primary school years. Safilios-Rothschild summarizes the role of parents in this process as follows: "This projection into future sex role tracks permeates . . . every geture, thought and expectation of the parent for the child and creates the climate for the teaching of sex roles" (Safilios-Rothschild, 1986, p. 30).

At nursery or infant school, pressures to conform to prescribed patterns of behaviour are often greater on young boys than on girls. Underachievement in boys at this age is often attributed to lack of effort rather than of ability and boys are encouraged to be more independent and self-reliant in their play activities. Girls tend to receive less criticism and more direct supervision and to be rewarded for conformity and acquiescence. Girls who break loose from such patterns are often seen as doubly deviant, as "trouble-makers" and as "unfeminine" (Browne and France, 1985).

Although girls often exhibit positive attitudes to Science and Mathematics at primary school level, boys' leisure activities lend themselves to a greater familiarization with scientific activity, especially activity related to Physical Science. Girls tend to be encouraged to work with animals or plants, while boys tinker with mechanical equipment, constructional toys and measuring instruments. The polarization of hobbies is illustrated by Table 3.5 below.

Reading habits also vary. Girls tend to read more than boys and as a group tend to be more interested in narrative material, especially romantic fiction. Much of this literature presents girls as passive and immobile, usually engaged in indoor activities and seldom in a leadership role (Cowie, 1984). Book publishers have paid greater attention to such criticisms in recent years but comics, the staple diet of many children, remain highly sex-stereotyped (Whyte, 1985). Many more boys than girls read science fiction or science information materials, which further reflect and probably reinforce their

TABLE 3.5

Differences in the Percentages of 11-Year-Old Boys and Girls Reporting to have "Quite Often" Engaged in Particular Activities at Home or Otherwise Out of School (1984 APU national survey data)

Activity	% Boys	% Girls
Make models from a kit (Airfix)	42	6
Play pool, billiards or snooker	59	30
Play with electric train sets	45	16
Create models using Lego, etc.	50	23
Take things apart to see inside	38	18
Go fishing or pond dipping	30	13
Watch birds	30	27
Sow seeds or grow plants	30	34
Look after small animals/pets	52	57
Collect/look at wild flowers	8	27
Weigh ingredients for cooking	29	60
Knit or sew	5	46

Source: S. Johnson and P. Murphy, *Girls and Physics*, APU/DES (1986).

general interest in science and things scientific (Johnson and Murphy, 1986).

Several researchers have explored the issue of images of girls and women in school literature and publications. Females are all too often portrayed as helpmeets to boys and men in children's reading schemes, bystanders to the narrative drama of stories (Penman, 1986). School textbooks have been found to follow this trend, exhibiting a recurrent and serious under-representation of women in text and in visual imagery, not only in the Sciences but also in such "neutral" areas as Geography and the Social Sciences (Whyld, 1983). Careers literature has also been said to reflect similar divisions between the sexes and to put forward the image of science and industry as solely masculine areas of activity (EOC, 1980). Whether such imagery has an immediate and direct effect on the aspirations and self-concepts of girls is a debatable point. However, it seems highly plausible that such images, in conjunction with those presented by wider social experience, present girls in school with such a limited and narrow range of futures that stereotyped notions of appropriate spheres of work and activity remain unchallenged.

The Position of Women in Teaching

Women teachers themselves provide "role models" for pupils in school. Teaching has been a traditional area of occupational advancement for women since the nineteenth century, which has been seen to offer the opportunity for combining employment with childcare. However, as Deem has argued, if teaching does provide an occupation for women, with relatively good rates of pay, career prospects and status, "it does so only in comparison with other

jobs for women, which also reflect the existing division of labour in society"
(Deem, 1978, p. 115).

Women constitute about 60 per cent of the total school teaching force of
England and Wales. They are concentrated at the lower end of the educational
hierarchy where in 1987, 79 per cent of primary school teachers, 98 per cent of
the nursery and infant teachers and 47 per cent of secondary school teachers in
the public sector were women. Yet women are disproportionately under-
represented at the headteacher grade and in other senior positions, such as
Heads of Departments in secondary schools, as illustrated in Table 3.6. Forty-
seven per cent of primary headteachers and 17 per cent of secondary
Headteachers were women in 1987. Seventy-five per cent of teachers on the
lowest pay scale are women and the great majority of part time teachers are
women.

TABLE 3.6

Distribution of Full-Time Teachers in England and Wales by Salary Scale, 1986

| | Primary and Nursery | | Secondary | |
Grade	% Women	% Men	% Women	% Men
Head Teachers	7.5	32.1	0.8	3.3
Deputy Head, 2nd Mistresses/ Masters, Senior Teachers	8.5	20.1	3.4	6.4
Scale 4	0.1	0.3	7.5	21.4
Scale 3	7.5	12.4	20.4	27.8
Scale 2	41.0	26.2	30.4	23.7
Scale 1	35.0	8.9	37.5	17.4
Total	100.0	100.0	100.0	100.0

Source: Derived from DES *Statistics of Education* (1987).

With the amalgamation and closure of many single-sex secondary schools,
it is estimated that the proportion of women secondary school headteachers
fell by 25 per cent between 1963 and 1983 (Wilce, 1983). The number of part
time posts has also declined since the 1970s, with considerable implications for
those women teachers who hope to use part-time work as a route for re-entry
into the teaching profession after a career break for child rearing (Trown and
Needham, 1980). The average rate of pay for full time female teachers in 1983
was 88 per cent of the average male rate (DES, 1983).

In secondary schools women tend to be concentrated in certain subject
areas and to hold promotional positions concerned with pastoral care rather
than academic matters. At head of department level, women tend to be in
charge of English, Home Economics or Modern Languages departments.
Overall there are four times as many male as female Physics teachers and twice
as many male as female teachers of Mathematics, Geography and History.

One reason commonly put forward to explain the lack of women in senior positions in teaching is that women simply do not apply for the available promotional posts. This issue has been investigated by the National Union of Teachers in 1980 and by two further studies in 1983 and 1985. The NUT's survey sampled the views and experiences of over three thousand teachers. The survey found that nearly a third of women teachers were sole breadwinners, single, divorced or widowed (NUT, 1980). In contrast to the findings of earlier research, the survey revealed a high "promotion orientation" among women (Hilsum and Start, 1974). Eighty-one per cent felt that they were consciously pursuing a career and 76 per cent of married teachers defined their job as equally important to that of their husband. About half had sought promotion in the previous five-year period, either within their own school, externally or both. This figure was evenly spread between married and non-married women. Internal applicants were twice as successful in securing positions as external applicants, especially in primary schools. Sixty-nine per cent of women felt that they had been discriminated against, particularly in applications for external posts. Over 40 per cent had been asked questions about their personal and family life and discrimination against married women appeared to be particularly strong in the case of external applications.

A later smaller-scale study of applications for thirty-six secondary headships in fifteen Local Education Authorities in 1985 found a smaller proportion of women applying for headships (Davidson, 1985). Here, women constituted 11 per cent of applicants and of subsequent appointments. However, the study concluded that appointment panels often brought non-job-related criteria based on minor inferences into their judgements. The predominant image of the "ideal" headteacher was of a tough leader figure, to which most women and some quieter men failed to match up. The prevailing image of the woman teacher was further explored in a study of one Local Education Authority in 1985. Women were seen as less well qualified than men, lacking ambition, taking more time off work for personal or family illness and as handicapped by taking a break in service to rear children. Such "unfriendly myths" did not, however, stand up to scrutiny. Years of experience and absentee rates were similar between the sexes. Women's career aspirations appeared to be as strong as men's and an equal number had taken further qualifications in their own time in the previous three years. Only 3 per cent of the sample were on maternity leave in 1982–1983 (compared with 6 per cent in the 1980 NUT survey). However, well over twice as many male teachers had obtained secondment to upgrade their status and qualifications and generally obtained promotion faster. The study concluded that it is essential for schools and LEAs to organize training programmes for those involved in selection and promotion at school and local authority level, in order to monitor staffing patterns and to defuse such damaging assumptions about women teachers.

The issue is seen as not only important for women teachers themselves, but also because of the "role model" women teachers provide for boys and girls in school. If, it is argued, teaching is seen as a feminine "semi-profession", in which women teachers are concentrated in stereotypically female areas and in humbler positions, pupils may subconsciously receive a deficit image of women in the job market where, in general "women serve and men manage" (Acker, 1983). This may in turn delimit girls' occupational aspirations and skew the expectations of boys of their future working lives. In addition, the lack of men in the education of young children may serve to reinforce the image of teaching as an extension of the traditional maternal role.

Although, as has been emphasized earlier, the majority of pupils do not go on into higher education, the situation is perpetuated and intensified in this sector as well. Here women make up about 14 per cent of lecturers in universities and polytechnics, concentrated particularly in the areas of Education, Medicine, English, Biology and Modern Languages. In some arts departments where there is an overwhelmingly female uptake of subjects, there are no women lecturers at all. As in school teaching, the number of women represented declines the further up the educational ladder one proceeds, as illustrated in Table 3.7 below. Indeed, the proportion of female professors in England and Wales has remained more or less constant at 2 to 3 per cent of university professors over the last twenty-five years, and the proportion of women lecturers rose by only 4 per cent between 1930 and 1985 (Sutherland, 1985). The 1980s has seen a rise in the number of part-time and untenured posts in higher education, which are largely occupied by women. This position is partly a result of the smaller pool of female postgraduates from which to draw, but it is also argued that lack of confidence in producing research, a lack of academic sponsorship and low "visibility" on academic committees contribute to this situation, in addition to an image of the female lecturer similar to that of the woman teacher. The net result is again a role model of women in higher education which can discourage young women from entering non-traditional areas of higher education and can reinforce lower career aspirations in female students.

Women in the Labour Market

The unequal position of women in teaching and the academic world mirrors the position of women in the labour market as a whole. Women comprise over 40 per cent of the United Kingdom labour force and about two-thirds of women, whether married or single, are in employment. However, in common with other European countries, the majority of women are concentrated in areas of work which are characterized by low levels of pay, low skills, low status and poor job security. They are to be found in particular in the service industries, in light factory work and in the public sector, as Table 3.8 illustrates.

It has been estimated that over two-thirds of jobs are specific to one sex and that under 20 per cent of jobs are fully integrated in the sense that roughly equal numbers of men and women are present within them (Martin and

TABLE 3.7

University Academic Staff: Ratio of Men to Women

Grade	1966–1967			1986–1987		
	No. of women	No. of men	% women	No. of women	No. of men	% women
Professors	40	2,790	1	120	4,350	3
Readers and Senior Lecturers	340	4,500	7	710	8,540	8
Lecturers	} 2,580[a]	} 17,770[a]	} 13	5,320	22,900	19
Others				1,900	3,190	37
Total	2,950	25,060	11	8,060	38,980	17

Source: University Grants Committee (1988)

[a] Separate figures for lecturers and research staff not available for 1966–1967.

TABLE 3.8

Women as a Percentage of the Occupational Labour Force: Selected Occupations

	Full-time	Part-time
General management	6.0	5.0
Professional and related supporting management and administration	19.0	2.0
Clerical and related	56.0	18.0
Professional and related in science, engineering, technology	8.0	1.0
Selling	26.0	32.0
Literary, artistic and sports	23.0	8.0
Catering, cleaning and personal services	21.0	54.0
Professional and related in education, welfare and health	45.0	24.0

Source: Department of Employment, *New Earnings Survey* (1987).

Roberts, 1984). Part-time work accounts for over 40 per cent of all women's work and there has been a considerable increase in the number of women "homeworkers", who assemble products at home at low piece rates (Dex, 1985). The average female manual employee earns about 66 per cent of the average male rate. When overtime earnings are taken into account, this figure reduces to 55 per cent, but the earnings gap is greater within non-manual work (*New Earnings Survey*, 1987).

In the non-manual sector, the bulk of female employees are in clerical and secretarial work. This is often represented as a stepping stone to "higher things", but in practice such promotion rarely occurs. In this area there are arguably greater divisions between the levels which men and women occupy within organizations than between the types of jobs which men and women perform. The predominant popular image of the non-manual sector is one of increasing career opportunities for pioneering young women, especially for female graduates. The proportion of women employed in professional and managerial work has indeed risen from 16 per cent in the 1960s to 28 per cent in 1985. However, this is in line with a general expansion of such jobs in the last twenty-five years and the proportion of men in professional and managerial work has risen at a still faster rate. Young women have succeeded in entering non-traditional spheres of work, such as medicine, journalism and banking, in far greater numbers than before, yet the majority of female graduates tend to enter employment in education and in certain branches of public administration, usually those connected with welfare rather than fiscal matters. The proportion of women in "top jobs" remains low, as illustrated by Table 3.9. Only 2 per cent of engineers and 6 per cent of Members of Parliament are women.

Even where educational qualifications are held constant, statistical analysis reveals disparities in earnings and job levels. Overall, the average female non-manual wage is about 60 per cent of the average male rate. In 1985 the average

TABLE 3.9

Female Membership of Selected Professional Bodies, 1987

	Total membership	No. of women members	Women as % of membership
Institute of Personnel Management	30,842	14,145	46
British Medical Association	71,519	18,305	25
Institute of Bankers	112,016	20,380	18
Chartered Insurance Institute	65,819	10,250	15
The Law Society	41,309	6,262	15
Association of Certified Accountants	29,617	2,955	10
Institute of Chartered Accountants	84,738	6,479	8
Institute of Marketing	21,433	1,703	8
British Institute of Architects	21,685	1,127	5
Institution of Chemical Engineers	17,974	947	5
Royal Institute of Chartered Surveyors	77,576	3,434	4
British Institute of Management	74,052	2,548	3
Institution of Mechanical Engineers	76,504	771	1
Institution of Engineers and Technicians	7,500	8	0.1

Source: HMSO: *Women and Men in Britain, A Statistical Profile* (1987).

rate of pay for female degree-holders was still about 75 per cent of the male rate and nearly six times as many male degree-holders were in professional work as female degree-holders (*General Household Survey*, 1985).

Studies of employers' attitudes towards women employees at all levels reveal continuing patterns of discriminatory practice in appointments to and promotion within jobs. Access of women employees to occupational training schemes is a relatively under-researched area, but the pattern which emerges suggests that employers have been more reluctant to invest in training female employees than male employees (Byrne, 1978). As in the educational sector, employers' perceptions of women employees tend to overplay absentee rates and length of time taken for maternity leave and to underestimate women's commitment to their work. Of those women who return to work after taking maternity leave, over a third return to a job on a lower grade than before. There are few opportunities for a staggered return to work, except at fairly senior levels in such areas as the new technological industries or banking. In the United Kingdom particularly low levels of state-subsidized child care support are available (Moss, 1988). In addition, although there have been some changes in the traditional "division of labour" within the home, women still undertake the major share of domestic work, whether or not they are in paid employment.

Government sponsored industrial training has tended to be dominated by a conception of skills derived from the craft skills of male manual workers. Women were largely excluded from postwar training initiatives until fairly recently and male apprentices on private and public schemes far outnumbered female apprentices (Wickham, 1982). More recent government programmes have included a formal commitment to positive action for adult women in training but according to some observers, this remains very much at the level of rhetoric. In 1980, for example, although nearly half the participants in the government's Training Opportunities Scheme were women, only 1.5 per cent of those on higher level skills courses were women (Wickham, 1985).

Attitude surveys among school leavers report a high level of commitment towards positive action for girls in education. Girls express strong support for the idea of encouraging pupils of both sexes to enter non-traditional areas of work, although boys tend to be generally less committed to this issue (Pratt *et al.*, 1984). Most young school leavers, however, aspire to entering fairly traditional areas of the labour market, particularly in the less skilled areas of work. Working class girls, in particular, tend to accept jobs in the local labour market through family connections, whatever the prospects involved (Roberts, 1986). Boys tend to nominate preferred jobs on the basis of status and opportunities for on-the-job training or promotion, while girls tend to opt for jobs on the basis of content and interpersonal relationships. Aspirations for white-collar work, such as journalism, computing or medicine, reflect the least marked preferences by sex. What such aspirations reflect is probably a realistic assessment of occupational futures, based on daily experience and observation of available opportunities. Whatever the strength of commitment to equality of opportunity in the school, disparities in the labour market and at home may well prove to be the more enduring and decisive factor in the destinations of young school leavers, especially in periods of economic recession.

Equal Opportunities Policies

In a survey of teachers' attitudes published by the *Times Educational Supplement* in 1987, 68 per cent of teachers polled expressed the view that every school should have an anti-sexist school policy (*Times Educational Supplement*, 1987). An earlier survey reported over 90 per cent of teachers in favour of reducing sex discrimination in schools in general, but a smaller figure in support of positive action in their own curriculum area (Pratt *et al.*, 1984). Variations in attitude exist between the sexes and between teachers of different subjects rather than according to age, seniority or type of school (Adams, 1985). Action research projects have reported that teachers are often not willing to admit that there is a problem in their own school and that men and women teachers diverge over the issue of the priority of curricular over extra-curricular matters (Millman and Weiner, 1985).

A minority of schools and LEAs have formal equal opportunities policies and still fewer have designated posts in equal opportunities. Such formal initiatives may amount to little more than paper statements or to a means of pigeon-holeing such concerns, but may lend legitimacy and support to those teachers who are anxious to bring about change. In 1984 it was estimated that about three-quarters of schools conformed to the letter of the 1975 Sex Discrimination Act, that some 15 per cent exhibited features of "bad practice" in the area of equal opportunities, but that only 10 per cent conformed to a third of the policy guidelines of good practice drawn up by the Equal Opportunities Commission in 1982 (EOC, 1982a; Pratt *et al.*, 1984). In 1982 the Commission itself assessed that few schools included statements about positive action or equal opportunities in their brochures for parents or careers material for pupils and that a minority of courses in initial and in-service teacher training featured input on equal opportunities policies (EOC, 1982b). This situation is, however, changing in a number of areas. Guidelines put forward by the DES in 1989 about the content of courses for intending primary teachers, for example, included the recommendation that issues of gender and equal opportunities should be included, although this has not been a major part of the systematic review process of initial teacher education courses by the Council for Accreditation of Teacher Education carried out since 1984. Since the 1975 HMI survey into curricular differentiation, there have been no major government investigations into the area of gender and equality of opportunity and no major funding from central government for work in this area, despite some recommendations by the HMIs (Arnot, 1987). Equality of educational opportunity is also not a high profile aim of the new national curriculum.

The picture which emerges, then, is one of a mixture of contradictory pressures and change. There has been an increased awareness of the disparity in educational achievement between the sexes. There have also been significant efforts at all levels of the education system directed towards redressing this imbalance, which have resulted in real advances in the quality of educational experience of some girls. However, a combination of deep-seated cultural attitudes and a background of economic recession have limited the effectiveness of attempted changes. Whether girls will continue to make progress or whether some of the gains of the last two decades will be reversed remains an open-ended question.

References

Acker, S. (1983) Women and teaching: a semi-detached sociology of a semi-profession. In L. Barton and S. Walker (Eds.) *Class, gender and education*. Lewes: Falmer.

Acker, S. (1984) Women in higher education: what is the problem? In S. Acker and D. Warren-Piper (Eds.) *Is higher education fair to women?* Slough: SRHE and NFER.

Adams, C. (1985) Teachers' attitudes to issues of sex equality. In J. Whyte *et al.*, *Beyond the Wendy house*. New York: Longman.

Arnot, M. (1987) Political lip-service or radical reform? In M. Arnot and G. Weiner *Gender and the politics of schooling*. London: Hutchinson/Open University Press.

Assessment of Performance Unit (1980) *Maths development: a secondary survey report*. London: HMSO.

Blunden, G. (1984) Vocational education for women's work in England and Wales. In S. Acker (Ed.) *World yearbook 1984: women and education*. New York: Kogan Page.

Browne, N. and France, P. (1985) Only cissies wear dresses. In G. Weiner (Ed.) *Just a bunch of girls*. Milton Keynes: Open University Press.

Buswell, C. (1981) Sexism in school routines and classroom practice. *Durham and Newcastle Research Review*, **9** (46).

Byrne, E. (1978) *Women and education*. London: Tavistock.

Byrne, E. (1985) Equality or equity? A European overview? In M. Arnot (Ed.) *Race and Gender: equal opportunities policies in education*. Oxford: Pergamon.

Cowie, H. (1984) *The development of children's imaginative writing*. Beckenham: Croom Helm.

Clarricoates, K. (1978) Dinosaurs in the classroom: a re-examination of some aspects of the hidden curriculum in primary schools. *Women's Studies International Quarterly*, **1** (4).

Dale, R. (1975) Education and sex roles. *Educational Review*, **22** (3).

Davidson, H. (1985) Unfriendly myths about women teachers. In J. Whyte *et al.*, *Girl-friendly schooling*. London: Methuen.

Delamont, S. (1983) The conservative school? Sex roles at home, at work and at school. In L. Barton and S. Walker (Eds.) *Gender, class and education*. Lewes: Falmer.

Deem, R. (1978) *Women and schooling*. London: Routledge & Kegan Paul.

Department of Education and Science (1953) *Statistics of Education*. London: HMSO.

Department of Education and Science (1975) *Curricular differences for boys and girls*. London: HMSO.

Department of Education and Science (1983) *Statistics of teachers in service in England and Wales*. London: HMSO.

Department of Education and Science (1987) *Statistical Bulletin*. London: HMSO.

Department of Education and Science (1987) *Statistics of Education*. London: HMSO.

Department of Education and Science (1988) *Statistics of Education*. London: HMSO.

Department of Eduction and Science (1989) *Statistics of Education*. London: HMSO.

Department of Education and Science (1988) *Further and Higher Education Statistics*. London: HMSO.

Department of Employment (1987) *New Earnings Survey*. London: HMSO.

Dex, S. (1985) *The sexual division of work*. Brighton: Harvester.

Equal Opportunities Commission (1980) *Guide to equal treatment of the sexes in careers materials*. Manchester: EOC.

Equal Opportunities Commission (1982a) *Do you provide equal opportunities?* Manchester: EOC.

Equal Opportunities Commission (1982b) *An investigation of the implications of courses on sex discrimination in teacher education*. Manchester: EOC.

General Household Survey (1985) London: HMSO.

Harding, J. (1980) Sex differences in performance in science examinations. In R. Deem (Ed.) *Schooling for women's work*. London: Routledge & Kogan Page.

Harding, J. (1983) *Switched off: the science education of girls*. Harlow: Longmans Resources Unit for the Schools Council.

Hartley, D. (1978) Teachers' definitions of boys and girls: some comparisons, *Research in Education*, **20**.

Her Majesty's Inspectorate (1978) *Primary education in England and Wales*. London: HMSO.

Her Majesty's Inspectorate (1979) *Aspects of secondary education in England and Wales*. London: HMSO.

Hilsum, S. and Start, K. B. (1974) *Promotion and careers in teaching*. Slough: NFER.

Johnson, S. and Murphy, P. (1986) *Girls and physics*. London: Assessment of Performance Unit Occasional paper, London: HMSO.

Kahle, J. B. (Ed.) (1985) *Women in Science*. Lewes: Falmer Press.

Kaminski, D. M. (1982) Girls in maths and science: an annotated bibliography of work. *Studies in Science Education*, **9**.

Kelly, A. (1981) *The missing half*. Manchester: Manchester University Press.

Mahoney, P. (1985) *Schools for the boys*. London: Hutchinson.

Martin, J. and Roberts, C. (1984) *Women and employment: a lifetime perspective*. London: DOE/OPCS, HMSO.

Millman, V. and Weiner, G. (1985) *Sex differentiation in schooling: is there really a problem?* York: Longman Resources Unit.

Moss, P. (1988) *Childcare and equality of opportunity*. Brussels: Commission of the European Communities.

National Union of Teachers/Equal Opportunities Commission (1980) *Promotion and the woman teacher*. London: National Union of Teachers.

Penman, D. (1986) Confronting gender bias in children's books. *English in Education*, **20** (1).

Pratt, J., Bloomfield, J. and Searle, C. (1984) *Option choice: a question of equal opportunity*. Slough: NFER-Nelson.

Roberts, C. (1986) After sixteen: what choice? In R. G. Burgess (Ed.) *Exploring society*. London: Longman.

Safilios-Rothschild, C. (1986) Sex differences in early socialisation and upbringing and their consequences for educational choices and outcomes. In OECD *Girls' and women's education*, Paris: OECD.

Sarah, E. and Spender, D. (Eds.) (1980) *Learning to lose*. London: Women's Press.

Smith, S. (1984) Single-sex settings. In R. Deem (Ed.) *Co-education reconsidered*. Milton Keynes: Open University Press.

Social Trends (1989) London: HMSO.

Spender, D. (1980) *Man-made language*. London: Routledge & Kogan Page.

Stansworth, M. (1983) *Gender and schooling: a study of sexual divisions in the classroom*. London: Hutchinson.

Steedman, J. (1983) *Examination results in mixed and single-sex schools*. London: EOC.

Sutherland, M. (1985) The situation of women who teach in universities: contrasts and common ground. *Comparative Education*, **21** (1).

Tann, S. (1981) Grouping and group work. In B. Simon and J. Willcocks (Eds.) *Research and practice in the primary classroom*. London: Routledge & Kogan Page.

Times Educational Supplement (1987, June 12).

Trown, A. and Needham, G. (1980) *Reduction in part-time teaching: implications for schools and for women teachers*. London: EOC/AMMA.

University Grants Committee (1988) *University statistics 1988–9 Vol 1 student and staff*. Cheltenham: University Statistics Record.

Ward, M. (1979) Mathematics and the ten year old. London: Schools Council Working Paper, No. 61, London: Evans/Methuen.

Whyld, J. (Ed.) (1983) *Sexism in the secondary school curriculum*. London: Harper and Row.

Whyte, J. (1985) *Beyond the Wendy house*. New York: Longman.

Wickham, A. (1982) The state and training programmes for women. In E. Whitelegg (Ed.) *The changing experience of women*. Oxford: Martin Robertson.

Wickham, A. (1985) Gender divisions, training and the state. In R. Dale *Education, training and employment*. Oxford: Pergamon.

Wilce, N. (1983, July 29) Continual fall in the number of women who become heads. *Times Educational Supplement*.

Wilce, N. (1986, May 16) New scope hope for girls. *Times Educational Supplement*.

Notes

1. Separate and more centralized systems exist in Scotland and Northern Ireland. It has been beyond the scope of this chapter to cover these as well, but further comparative study of these countries would be rewarding.

CHAPTER 4

France

FRÉDÉRIC CHARLES

SINCE the late 1960s, schooling for girls in France has been characterized by, on the one hand, profound and important changes, and on the other, by permanent structural features which still seem to outweigh the increasing opportunities for girls and women to fully participate in working life.

This chapter will firstly analyse the position which girls occupy within the different strands of the education system. It will then try to show the connection between these and the traditional situation of women within the structure of the labour market. Finally, the chapter will examine developments which have occurred during this period to the benefit of women, which can be seen to be linked to their increasing use of the education system and which have had the effect of increasing to some extent their opportunities in the labour market.

The French Education System

The French education system consists of three stages of education:

The first stage of pre-school education from three to six years and primary education from six to eleven years.

The second stage of secondary education is in "collèges" (lower secondary schools) from the age of eleven to fifteen, the so-called "first cycle". Students can then transfer to "lycées d'enseignement professionel" (technical upper secondary schools) at the age of thirteen or fourteen, or can continue into the "second cycle" of secondary education at lycées (upper secondary schools) from the age of about fifteen to eighteen. Pupils at the lower-status technical upper secondary schools may leave at sixteen or go on to take the technological Baccalauréat. The highest examination taken at the lycées is also the Baccalauréat, which is subdivided into broad bands of subjects around a common core of Philosophy, French, History, Geography, Mathematics, Physical Education and a Modern Language. Students can specialize in the weighting given to subjects in the Bac. options. Thus in Bac. A, Philosophy is predominant; in B Economics and Social Sciences, in C

Mathematics, Physics and Chemistry, in D Mathematics, Physics, Chemistry and Biology. Bac. E is similar to C but with Technology in addition. These days Bac. C is considered to be the most prestigious option.

The third stage of post-secondary or higher education is offered by the lycées (in the higher technical sections or preparatory classes for the "grandes écoles"), and by specialized colleges and universities. The "Concours" is also taken at the lycées after one or two years of extra study. Here it is important to note the increasing pre-eminence of the "grandes écoles", the most prestigious institutions of higher education in France, to which entry is gained through an open competition. The nearest equivalent to the "grandes écoles" in England would be the universities of Oxford and Cambridge or in the United States, the Ivy League universities, and their social role in the reproduction of an élite is largely similar.

Higher education is again subdivided into three cycles of studies:

— The first cycle leads to the DEUG (Diplôme d'Etudes Universitaires Générales) (General Diploma of University Studies), two years after the Baccalauréat.
— The second cycle leads to a degree, three years after the Baccalauréat or to a Masters degree, four years after the Baccalauréat.
— The third cycle leads to the DEA (Diplôme d'Etudes Approfondies) (Diploma of Advanced Studies) five years after the Baccalauréat, or to the DESS (Diplôme d'Etudes Specialisées Supérieures) (Diploma of Higher Specialized Studies). Those who are awarded the DEA can then prepare for a doctorate taken roughly three years afterwards.

The system is also divided between a state and private sector, with a total of 19.6 per cent of pupils attending the latter in 1987. In the private sector 52.6 per cent of pupils were in mainly Catholic schools, 42.8 per cent in secondary schools and only 4.6 per cent in institutions of higher education (*Repères et Références*, 1988).

Girls and Educational Achievement

Girls' Attainment at Primary and Secondary School

From primary school onwards, girls tend to attain better results at school than boys. National surveys of pupil attainment show that they occupy a favourable position at school, both in terms of results in tests and in overall educational development. A recent survey of primary education, for example, found that for every hundred boys who successfully completed the first year of primary education, a hundred and ten girls successfully completed this stage (Duthoit, 1988).

Once at secondary school, girls continue to hold their own in those streams which lead to the prestigious **Baccalauréat** (the academic examination for entry into higher education) and their uptake of vocational education, which tends to have a lower status in France, is significantly less than that of boys, as Table 4.1 below illustrates:

TABLE 4.1

Percentage of Girls in the Different Levels of Education in the Public and Private Sector, 1984–1985

	% Girls	% Boys	Total
General Education			
First stage (11–15 years)			
Sixth grade	48.5	51.5	100.0
Fifth grade	49.9	50.1	100.0
Fourth grade	53.5	46.5	100.0
Third grade	54.5	45.5	100.0
Second stage (15–18 years)			
Second grade	55.7	44.3	100.0
First grade	55.5	44.5	100.0
Final grade	56.3	43.7	100.0
Vocational Education			
CPPN – (Classe préprofessionnelle de niveau)	41.0	59.0	100.0
CPA – (Classes préparatoires à l'apprentissage)	31.8	68.2	100.0
CAP – 3 year course (Certificat d'aptitude préprofessionnelle)	41.3	58.7	100.0
– 2 year course	48.6	51.4	100.0
BEP – (Brevet des études pro; fessionnelles)	55.9	44.1	100.0

Source: Author's own calculations from the *L'Annuaire Statistique de la France*, INSEE (1985) vol. 90, p. 290.

It is interesting to note from this data that girls become increasingly in the majority throughout the first and second stages of education and comprise a substantial majority by the last year of secondary school, at 56.3 per cent of the total number of candidates for the Baccalauréat.[1] In addition, girls also obtain better results at this level. In 1987–1988 girls comprised 56.7 per cent of candidates, while 57.2 per cent of those accepted to sit the examination had a success rate of 71.3 per cent. In comparison the boys' success rate was 69.2 per cent (*Note d'Information*, 1988). So, in summary, throughout their school careers, girls are less likely than boys to be eliminated from the competitive school system at any point.

Possible Explanations of Girls' Greater Success

There has been little research in France into the reasons for the better patterns of achievement of girls at school. Indeed, there has been a paucity of research in the social sciences in France into the question of sex discrimination in schools. From 1974–1982 there were scarcely thirteen references in the Centre de Documentation des Sciences de L'Homme in this area, and less than thirty in the Index of L'Institut Nationale de la Recherche Pédagogique in 1989 – a third of which concerned education in other countries. One reason for this may be that teacher training has never been fully integrated into the universities as it has been in England and the United States, so creating a lack of research experience and interest in this area.

One study by Sirota in 1988, however, concluded that there were virtually no differences between the amount and kinds of verbal contributions and attention-seeking behaviour which boys and girls made in primary school classes, contrary to research findings in the United States and Britain (Sirota, 1988). Sirota did, however, find that boys engaged in some kind of active and passive forms of behaviour, which are qualitatively different from those of girls. They chatter in class more often, especially about non-task matters, they fidget and are distracted more often. On the other hand, they leave their seats less often than girls and go up to the teacher's desk half as many times as girls. Although the author concluded that there "are no major differences in feminine and masculine behaviour in daily school life", it does appear that the behaviour of girls is closest to the image of the "good pupil". The tendency of girls to fidget and chatter less often gives an impression of greater stability and better concentration than boys and this "esprit de sérieux" leads to a more favourable image of girls. All this seems to indicate, along with a consensus in recent research findings by psychologists and social-psychologists, that far from being an indicator of greater docility on the part of girls, these differences in behaviour are on the contrary the outcome of a greater measure of self-reliance and a higher level of adaptability than that of boys (cf., Hurtig, 1982; Zazzo, 1982). These characteristics are far from being innate and can doubtless be ascribed to gender differences in socialization in the family. This was highlighted by a survey of 1,300 families conducted in 1978 by the Féderation Nationale des Ecoles, de Parents et d'Educateurs, which illustrated how early in their lives girls take on board their "apprenticeship" in the family (cf., Sirota, 1988). Girls were shown to be more involved in domestic tasks than boys and to play a far greater role in the running of the household. On the other hand, parents took a greater interest in their daughters' studies at primary school level than their sons' and, as a consequence, girls invested more effort in their time at school and valued it more. This evidence seems to show that the early socialization processes of the family and school complement each other to the benefit of girls in terms of their educational achievement (Sirota, 1988). However, despite all this, there remain substantial inequalities between boys and girls in later patterns of study and in their participation in different forms of education, as the following section will show.

Option Choices and Patterns of Study in Secondary and Higher Education

At the level of the Baccalauréat, girls and boys are unevenly distributed within the different study options, as illustrated by Table 4.2 below. From these figures it is clear that the participation of girls in the Baccalauréat options diminishes the more "scientific" these programmes are. So, for example, in 1988 girls comprised 82.8 per cent of candidates for the Baccalauréat in Literature and Philosophy and only 3.3 per cent of candidates for the Mathematics and Technology option. In the less "applied" option of Mathematics and Science, girls were in the minority, comprising 34.3 per cent of candidates but were in the majority in the Technology and Economics option, which largely comprises the Social Sciences, at 60.7 per cent of candidates. Here one can see a very similar general pattern to other European countries, with girls opting in large numbers for the Arts and Social Sciences rather than the Sciences. The fact that girls are relatively better represented in the Sciences than in some other countries may be partly due to the structure of the French education system which delays specialization until entry into the second stage of secondary education and also because at the level of preparation for the Baccalauréat, subject boundaries are less marked than in many other European countries.

Table 4.3 shows that sex differences are even more marked where differential patterns of study in the technological Baccalauréat lead on to different patterns of uptake of short courses in the Technological Institutes of the universities. It should be remembered that the technological Baccalauréat is taken by those pupils "cooled out" of mainstream studies in secondary education between the ages of fourteen and sixteen and is considered to be a lower status qualification. However, what Table 4.3 clearly shows is that while female students represented 54.3 per cent of the total number of candidates for the technological Baccalauréat in 1987, they were heavily under-represented in these sections which directly lead to employment in industry and technology, where they comprised a mere 9.9 per cent of candidates. In contrast, they are greatly over-represented in the sections which lead to employment in service industries, which generally afford a lower level of remuneration than the manufacturing sector, as will be illustrated in Table 4.4.

This gender difference in study patterns is similarly to be observed in the short courses which lead to the vocational CAP and BEP diplomas, as illustrated by Table 4.4. Here one can again very clearly see the way in which young women are concentrated in those vocational training courses which lead to service sector employment. In 1986–1987 young women represented 15.1 per cent of the candidates for the CAP and BEP in the extractive and manufacturing sectors and 81.2 per cent of candidates in the service sector area.

Even if one cannot totally agree with the comment in the 1979 OECD

TABLE 4.2

Sex Differences in Baccalauréat Options, 1959–1988

	Series A: Literature and Philosophy		Series B: "Technology" and Social Sciences		Series C: Mathematics and Sciences		Series D: Experimental Sciences		Series E: Mathematics and Technology		TOTAL
	% Boys	% Girls	% Boys	% Girls	% Boys	% Girls	% Boys	% Girls	% Boys	% Girls	% Girls
1959	35.0	65.0	62.0	38.0	78.5	21.5	46.0	54.0	100.0	0.0	48.5
1964	33.5	66.5	40.5	59.5	74.6	25.4	47.0	53.0	99.6	0.4	50.4
1969	31.6	68.4	49.7	50.3	73.5	26.5	49.4	50.6	98.7	1.3	53.2
1974	24.5	75.5	40.0	60.0	64.4	35.6	45.9	54.1	97.5	2.5	56.7
1988	17.8	82.2	39.3	60.7	65.7	34.3	47.5	52.4	94.7	3.3	57.2

Source: Author's own calculations based on statistics from *Résultats des Examens du Baccalauréat* (1959, 1964, 1969, 1974); Repères et Réferénces Statistiques sur les Enseignements et la Formation (1988), Ministry of Education (1988).

TABLE 4.3

Changes in the Distribution of Candidates for the Technological Baccalauréat Option and by Gender 1974–1987

| | Bac.F1–7 | | Bac.F8 | | Bac.F9 | | Bac.F10 | | Bac.F11–12 | | Bac.G | | Bac.H | | TOTAL | |
| | Industrial training, e.g. Electronics Building | | Paramedical Studies | | Building and Construction | | Micro ELectronics | | Visual Arts Music and Design | | Commercial and Administrative Studies | | Information Technology | | | |
	% Males	% Females	% Males	% Females	% Males	% Females	% Males	% Females	% Males	% Females	% Males	% Females	% Males	% Females	% Males	% Females
1974	88.3	11.7	0.4	99.6	N/A	N/A	N/A	N/A	41.8	58.2	24.5	75.5	61.4	38.6	44.6	55.4
1987	90.1	9.9	1.7	98.3	93.3	6.7	88.7	11.8	37.0	63.0	31.0	69.0	67.5	32.5	45.7	54.3

Source: Author's own calculations based on statistics from *Résultats des Examens du Baccalauréat* (1974, 1987) Ministry of Education.

TABLE 4.4

Distribution of Female Candidates for the CAP and BEP Diplomas by Occupational Group, 1986–1987

Occupational group	% Female candidates	Total number of candidates
Agricultural Studies and Forestry	20.9	416
Fishing and Maritime Studies	00.0	58
Civil Engineering, Cartography	11.2	617
Building and Construction	2.7	4,232
Roofing, Plumbing and Heating	0.5	4,535
Industrial Painting and Decorating	8.5	2,346
Metallurgy, Boilermaking	0.7	13,009
General and Precision Mechanics	1.8	48,368
Electrical Engineering	1.6	28,723
Electronics	3.9	5,600
Ceramics and Glasswork	54.5	425
Photography and Graphics	42.8	1,270
Papermaking	47.5	164
Chemistry, Physics, Bio-Chemistry	39.7	569
Baking	7.8	574
Butchery	4.0	126
Other Food Specialisms	18.0	7,001
Textiles and Clothing	97.7	16,919
Leatherwork	65.7	388
Woodwork	3.2	10,968
Engine driving		1,709
Architectural Draughtsmanship	22.6	1,899
Industrial Design	11.1	2,921
Total for Extractive and Manufacturing sectors	15.1	153,567
Administrative Skills	79.9	43,282
Shorthand and typing, office skills	98.2	29,305
Finance and Accounting	65.5	38,719
Commerce and Distribution	72.1	16,095
Paramedical health care, social services	95.8	13,837
Nursing	91.2	6,180
Hotel Management	84.3	15,829
Total for the Service Sector	81.2	163,247
Overall Total	49.2	316,824

Source: Author's own calculations from *Repères et Références Statistiques sur les enseignements et la formation*, Ministry of Education (1988) p. 153.

report, "Women and Equality of Opportunity", that in France Science and Mathematics "remain in practice the private hunting-ground of men", it is nonetheless true that the division of the sexes in secondary study options has profound repercussions at the level of higher education (OECD, 1979).

As can be seen from the figures shown in Table 4.5, young women are overwhelmingly in the majority at this level in the Arts and Pharmacology and also in Law, where they represented 68.8, 63.1 and 54.8 per cent of candidates

TABLE 4.5

Percentage of Female Students on University Courses and in Preparatory Classes for the Grandes Écoles by Subject Area and Level, 1987

Universities	Law	Economics	The Arts	Science	Medicine	Technical University Studies	Pharmacology	Total
1st Stage	59.5	49.5	73.3	35.9	55.9	37.6	—	56.1
2nd Stage	53.6	46.4	70.6	33.1	45.1	—	65.0	54.0
"Concours"	—	56.1	69.9	52.6	—	—	—	63.7
3rd Stage	44.2	33.0	50.3	28.1	38.2	—	53.6	39.0
Total	54.8	46.5	68.8	33.5	45.3	37.6	63.1	52.7

Source: *Repères et références Statistiques sur les enseignements et les formations*, Ministry of Education (1988) p. 209.
[a] The Sciences include 1 and 2 year courses, 19 per cent of students on the two-year courses are female and 50 per cent of students on one-year courses, which largely lead to veterinary schools and higher business diplomas.

respectively. In contrast, they are in a slight minority in Medicine at 45.3 per cent, Economics at 46.5 per cent, and particularly in the Sciences at 33.5 per cent and Engineering and Technology at 37.5 per cent. In addition, although female students are in an overall minority in the preparatory classes which lead to the highly prestigious "grandes écoles", representing only 33.5 per cent of entrants, as opposed to 52.7 per cent of university students, their distribution among study options reveals similar disparities.

Women in the Labour Market

Patterns of Employment

Contrary to popular belief, although the representation of women in the workforce has increased since the turn of the century, this has not been a profound change. In 1901 women represented 37.7 per cent of the workforce and in 1981 41 per cent (*Données Sociales*, 1987). If one looks carefully at the sexual division of labour in French society, it is apparent that women's work is concentrated in two main areas: service sector employment and unskilled work. In 1984, for example, women comprised 51.7 per cent of service sector employees as opposed to 25.5 per cent of the industrial workforce and 17.9 per cent of the agricultural workforce (*Données Sociales*, 1987). To put this another way, out of all women in employment in 1984, 0.7 per cent were in the agricultural sector, 21.1 per cent in industry and 78.2 per cent in the service sector (*Données Sociales*, 1987). In addition, if one looks in more detail at the kind of work which women undertake, it is clear that although they are to be found in all kinds of work, they are largely concentrated in clerical, routine white-collar work and at the level of intermediate supervisory work, and are most often to be found in particular service sectors. As Table 4.6 shows, women's employment is mainly limited to a number of "feminine" occupations, such as secretarial, cleaning or retail work, where women represent a large proportion of the workforce. This is equally the case in the areas of health and the social services, where women constitute 80 per cent of nurses and social workers, and in teaching, where they represent 75.2 per cent of primary teachers. These figures lend support to the contention that, despite important changes, the pattern of women's employment in the labour market nevertheless exhibits some permanent features, which will be examined in greater detail below. Again, as Table 4.6 shows, women occupy only roughly a quarter of the positions in the most highly paid and socially prestigious occupations. Within each occupational grouping, women are concentrated in the least well paid jobs with the least promotion prospects at each level of employment. So, for example, within the industrial labour force, women are largely concentrated in unskilled work, rather than at the more lucrative levels of foreman or skilled worker, while at the other end of the social hierarchy in and in management, women are largely confined to teaching rather than employment in engineering or senior management.[2]

Analyses of such data reveals the existence of strong parallels and a relatively strong relationship between the structural position of girls in the education system and their structural position in the labour market on leaving school or college. Although nowadays sex discrimination in admission and selection procedures to educational institutions is illegal, there are few studies which attempt to explain this relationship. One exception in this area was a study carried out by Mosconi in 1983, in which the author maintains that it is the unequal gender division in the labour market which largely determines the different options which girls take up at school. However, in addition, the author states that this is not a foregone conclusion. Society does not mechanistically determine what goes on in schools and the education system does have a measure of relative autonomy from the economy, which serves to conceal indirect sex discrimination just as effectively as it legitimizes the reproduction of the social class hierarchy through seemingly meritocratic selection (cf., Bourdieu and Passeron, 1970; Bourdieu, 1989). Girls appear to make choices according to their "tastes" and "aptitudes", which are incorporated into a hierarchy of subject disciplines and status, and which can be explained away in such negative psychological terms as "lack of motivation" or the different orientation of girls and boys towards different subjects. This process, in turn, results in the internalization of external constraints linked to the process of sex-role socialization for both boys and girls and results in, among other things, the labelling and identification of subjects as "masculine" and "feminine" (Safilios-Rothschild, 1986). Prejudices and beliefs, it can be argued, thus take on the air of personal conviction, which masks the social origins of such beliefs, a kind of alchemy, which transforms what is a direct product of the social division of labour into vocational choice or the resigned acceptance that "this is not a job for a boy/girl" (Mosconi, 1983). So the link between the education system and the division of labour in the workforce does not have to operate in an explicit way or with any degree of constraint. Selection into different options or streams is carried out with the agreement of pupils and their families, for the most part, who eliminate themselves from certain courses of action and direct themselves towards others. If so few girls are to be found on industrial training courses today, it is because their whole upbringing since their early childhood has led them to disengage from things mechanical or technological. This has the effect of making girls unable to imagine themselves as pupils in these areas and so ensures "voluntary exclusion" as a kind of self-fulfilling prophecy.

The Relationship Between Qualifications and Salary or Wage Level

In France there is a strong connection between the awarding of diplomas and the jobs to which they give access on the labour market. Diplomas are valued

TABLE 4.6

Main Characteristics of the Socio-Professional Groups in 1982 (as % of Women Employed, by Academic Qualifications, Average Salary and Salary Differential between Men and Women)

	Occupational sector as % of labour force	Women as % of occupational groups	% of diploma-holders			Index of average salary in 1982 (Norm=100)	Salary differential between men and women as %
			At degree or diploma level and above	At Baccalauréat level and above	At CAP level and above		
Liberal Professions		27	80			—	—
Civil Service		45	56			183	24.7
University and Secondary Teachers, Scientists			89			172	1.1
Information and the Arts		40	34			143	24.8
Private Sector Management and Administration		20	36			216	22.6
Engineers and Senior Technicians		6	56			219	22.5
Total: Administration and Higher Professions	8.6	25	58			200	26.9
Primary Teachers and para-educational Workers		63		87		113	7.5
Health Services and Social Work		74		79		106	7.1
Clergy, Religious Orders		44		52		—	—
Public Sector Administration Intermediate Level		47		46		124	19.0
Private Sector Administration Intermediate Level		39		35		123	15.3
Technicians		9		48		124	13.6
Foremen, Supervisors		6		19		126	21.2
Total: Intermediate Occupations	17.7	40		53		118	14.4

Craftsmen	24	45	—	—
Small Traders	47	32	—	—
Business Employing 10+ people	17	53	—	—
Total: Craftsmen, Small Traders and Businessmen	8.5	40	—	—
Public Sector Clerical Workers	75	38	45	−7.0
Police and Armed Services	5	41	41	2.4
Private Sector Clerical Workers	76	56	40	−8.1
Commercial Sector Employees	77	31	51	−23.2
Other White Collar Service Workers	83	20	50	−13.3
Total: Routine White-Collar Workers	25.6	42	45	−15.0
Skilled Industrial Workers	10	42	89	22.8
Skilled Manual Workers	8	45	82	15.6
Drivers	2	23	85	—
Transport, Construction and Maintenance Workers	7	28	85	16.3
Unskilled Industrial Workers	37	17	71	14.7
Unskilled Manual Workers	28	18	68	12.8
Agricultural Workers	14	14	63	15.6
Total: Manual Workers	32.7	29	79	20.7
Farmers	6.9	19	—	—
OVERALL TOTAL: Nos. IN LABOUR	100.0			
OVERALL TOTAL: % WOMEN IN LABOUR	39.23			

Source: *Données Sociales*. INSEE (1987) pp. 41, 43, 43, 47, 53, 60, 67.

for both their objective "purchasing power" and for their symbolic value. Very often sex differences in wage or salary levels are justified by the fact that the categories of seemingly identical jobs in fact conceal greatly dissimilar situations. Comparisons between male and female areas of work are often not valid because one is not comparing like with like. Nevertheless, if one looks at the question in terms of returns on qualifications, a comparison becomes more valid, since men and women often hold identical qualifications on leaving the education system. If one looks in detail at the income levels of men and women, disparities in income between types of jobs held and social position become even greater when qualifications held are taken into account.

As column seven of Table 4.6 shows, whatever their educational level, men's incomes generally exceed those of women and particularly where the highest qualifications are held. Male holders of the Higher Diploma can expect to command a salary higher than that of women with a similar qualification, for example, men in senior management and the professions can command a salary on average 26.9 per cent higher than women. The only areas of work where women can expect to earn a higher salary are in those occupations where they represent a great majority of employees, such as in secretarial work, so that there is a greater probability of promotion.

Differences in income may be in part linked to the fact that a higher proportion of women work part-time and take career breaks for child rearing – for example, in 1986 23.1 per cent of women and 3.4 per cent of men were in part-time employment and 83 per cent of all part-time work was taken up by women (cf., Belloc, 1987) – but these two factors are not sufficient to explain the differentials in themselves since disparities in income of some 15–20 per cent are discernible from the outset of working life at the lowest level of qualifications (Canceill, 1984). Indeed, there almost appears to be two job markets in the private sector in terms of income, one reserved for women and one for men. In the public sector, a similar pattern, although much reduced, can be discerned, where an income differential of about 20 per cent exists, whatever the level of qualifications (*Données Sociales*, 1987). Whether in the private or public sector, this data suggests that a hard core of discrimination against women continues to influence salary and promotion prospects.

The public sector, nevertheless, continues to attract a large number of women because of its equal opportunities policies in terms of entry and promotion. The teaching profession in particular recruits women in large numbers as it allows them to combine the role of mother with a career, as many sociological studies have shown, and as women teachers often provide a role model for girls whose mothers have not worked outside the home (Cacouault-Bitaud, 1985; Charles, 1988). Yet here, as elsewhere, women are generally concentrated in the lowest paid positions within the teaching hierarchy, as Table 4.7 shows.

Here one can clearly see how the "feminization" of the teaching profession is in inverse proportion to the most prestigious positions in this area. Massively

TABLE 4.7

Women in the Teaching Profession, 1984–1985 and 1985–1986

	% Women on Teaching Staff 1984–1985	% of Women Headteachers 1985–1986
Primary Education		
Pre-School Education	97.2	100.0
Primary Education	67.1	44.8
Special Education	63.0	a
Total % in Primary and Pre-School Education	75.2	a
Secondary Education		
Collège (Lower Secondary School)	62.0	a
Lycée (Upper Secondary School)	49.6	a
Lycée d'Enseignement Professionel (Upper Technical Schools)	42.0	a
Total % in Secondary Education	55.1	23.0
Higher Education		
Associate Lecturers	33.6	
Lecturers	30.4	
Professors	9.0	
Total % in Higher Education	25.4	

a No figures available.

Source: *Donées Sociales*, INSEE 1987; Eurydice, *Répartition par sexe des effectifs d'inspecteurs et des directeurs d'établissement* (1987).

concentrated in primary education, where they represent 75 per cent of the teaching force, women comprise only 44.8 per cent of headteachers at this level. In secondary education, women comprise 55 per cent of teachers and are again disproportionately under-represented at the level of headteacher or principal where they hold 23 per cent of headships. In higher education women are both in an overall minority at 25 per cent of lecturers and hold only 9 per cent of professorships. More detailed analysis reveals that women are more often to be found in the less prestigious lower secondary schools than in lycées and that they are massively concentrated in the Arts, a direct result of patterns of study in higher education. So, in 1987, for example, 67.7 per cent of teachers of English and 63 per cent of teachers of Classical and Modern Literature were women in contrast to 46.4 per cent of Mathematics teachers and 39 per cent of History and Geography teachers (Canceill, 1984). Again, if one looks at the level of the Inspectorate, women comprised only 23 per cent of this body in 1986. Within the Inspectorate, women were particularly under-represented in the most prestigious areas and at the national level, at 8 per cent of inspectors of academies and 12 per cent of general inspectors (Eurydice, 1987).

Education: Instrument of Reproduction or Emancipation?

Several studies have shown that in France the connection between the possession of higher qualifications and entry into careers is becoming ever tighter on the one hand, but on the other that diplomas or degrees from different types of higher educational establishments have a very different purchasing power (cf., Bourdieu and Passeron, 1964; Bourdieu and Passeron, 1970; Bourdieu, 1989; Baudelot *et al.*, 1981; Baudelot and Establet, 1971; Charlot, 1987). The number of students in higher education has increased enormously since the late 1960s as opportunities in the education system have been seized by all social classes, as a means of securing or improving their social position. However, this growth has resulted in a devaluation of university and college degrees in contrast to the relatively stable value of degrees from the "grandes écoles", where recruitment has expanded to a lesser extent during this period (cf., Passeron, 1982). Between 1960–1982 the number of students at university quadrupled from 214,600 to 889,500 while the number of students in the preparatory classes of the grandes écoles only doubled, from 21,000 to 40,800 students (*Données Sociales*, 1984, p. 479).

If one looks at the composition of the growth rate in universities and IUTs (Institutes of Technology) between 1955 and 1987, illustrated in Table 4.8 below, it is clear that girls have taken the lion's share of this growth rate, increasing their representation from 37.9 to 52.7 per cent during this period.

TABLE 4.8

Distribution of Students in Universities and IUTS by Sex, 1955–1987

	Total number of students	% Males	% Females
1955–1956	140,633	62.1	37.9
1969–1970	459,997	55.6	44.4
1977–1978	702,252	49.4	50.6
1981–1982	828,590	48.7	51.3
1986–1987	957,770	47.3	52.7

Source: (1955–1977 Statistics): C. Baudelot *et al. Les Etudiants, L'Emploi et la Crise*, Petite Collection Maspero: Paris; (1981 Statistics): *Données Sociales*, INSEE, p. 480; (1986 Statistics): *Repères et Références Statistiques sur les enseignement et la formation*, Ministry of Education, 1988, pp. 199 and 209.

In contrast, Table 4.9 below shows how under-represented female students were in 1985 in the "grandes écoles", the pinnacle of the French higher education system. Even where girls succeeded in gaining access to the engineering "grandes écoles", they are more highly concentrated in the less prestigious of these colleges.[3]

Even if women are relatively under-represented in these élite institutions, it is nevertheless true that a minority of women have still begun to penetrate a better remunerated sector of employment, hitherto the province of men, by

TABLE 4.9
Distribution of Students in the Grandes Écoles by Sex, 1984–1985

	% Males	% Females
Law and Administrative Schools	59.1	40.9
Business and Management Schools	59.8	40.2
"Ecoles Normales Superiéures" for advanced Educational Studies	65.4	34.6
Veterinary Schools	66.9	33.1
Architectural Schools	67.9	32.1
Engineering Schools	78.7	21.3

Source: *Données Sociales*, INSEE (1987).

virtue of their increased use of higher education and consequent improvement in their qualifications since the late 1960s. These changes have been most profound in the middle classes, where women have been able to take up posts in higher level white-collar work, such as in teaching or administration, and this has contributed to a modification of the social image of women in the middle classes, to the more positive image of "the modern, active, dynamic, independent, self-reliant and responsible woman" (Lenoir, 1985). Table 4.10 below highlights this substantial rate of increase of women in administration, management, teaching and the liberal professions over a twenty-three year period, from 1962–1985. During this period, the proportion of women in the civil service, for example, rose from 10.8 per cent to 24.6 per cent and the number in private sector management and administration from 12.8 to 23.4 per cent. However, it should be noted that while women have made substantial advances in management, this has been largely in the areas of training and personnel work rather than in accountancy or general management. In the intermediate occupations, such as nursing and primary education, the proportion of women has remained largely the same although overall numbers more than trebled in the first case and doubled in the second. The slowest rate of growth has occurred in manual industrial and agricultural work where numbers have only grown by a factor of 1.6 in the first case and have been halved in the second, and the proportion of women has actually declined in some areas. These figures also further illustrate the dramatic growth in white-collar work in general and the relative decline in blue-collar work, characteristic of many European economies. Expansion in overall numbers has largely been facilitated by the recruitment of well-trained and intellectually able women at several levels of the economy.

Thus one can conclude that the position of women in the education system and in the labour market has changed significantly during the last thirty years. The increased use made by girls and women of higher education, albeit mainly in certain subject areas and institutions, has without doubt contributed to expanding the range of jobs open to women and has helped women to be protected against economic crisis and unemployment. The higher the

TABLE 4.10

Distribution of Women in the Labour Force and Changes in Overall Employment Patterns, 1962–1985

	Women as % occupational groups		Total No. of employees in occupational groups		Sector as % of labour force	
	1962	1985	1962	1985	1962	1985
Liberal Professions	18.3	24.6	133,000	238,000		
Civil Service	10.8	24.4	157,000	244,000		
University and Secondary Teachers, Scientists	38.8	47.7	98,000	413,000		
Information and the Arts	39.0	30.0	59,000	623,000		
Private Sector Management and Administration	12.3	23.4	281,000	398,000		
Engineers and Senior Technicians	3.1	6.3	159,000	398,000		
Total: Administration and Higher Professions	16.3	25.9	892,000	2,095,000	4.7	9.8
Primary Teachers and Para-educational workers	64.9	63.2	383,000	757,000		
Health Services and Social Work	71.1	71.0	190,000	670,000		
Clergy, Religious Orders	64.9	42.0	151,000	30,000		
Public Sector Administration Intermediate Level	26.4	49.4	181,000	279,000		
Private Sector Administration Intermediate Level	26.5	44.2	558,000	967,000		
Technicians	5.3	8.6	285,000	690,000		
Foremen, Supervisors	4.9	6.2	350,000	517,000		
Total: Intermediate Occupations	33.9	41.2	210,000	394,800	11.3	18.5
Craftsmen	25.0	24.3	103,000	931,000		
Small Traders	48.8	48.7	941,000	824,000		
Businessmen Employing 10+ people	15.4	16.8	104,000	136,000		
Total: Craftsmen, Small Traders and Businessmen	35.3	33.7	208,400	189,100	10.8	8.9
Public Sector Clerical Workers	65.8	77.7	772,000	174,800		
Police and Armed Services	3.2	5.3	379,000	414,000		
Private Sector Clerical Workers	69.9	79.5	111,700	196,300		
Commercial Sector Employees	73.5	79.6	389,000	630,000		
Other White Collar Service Workers	87.5	83.2	809,000	869,000		
Total: Routine White-Collar Workers	66.4	74.0	353,500	553,800	18.5	25.9

TABLE 4.10

Distribution of Women in the Labour Force and Changes in Overall Employment Patterns, 1962–1985

	Women as % occupational groups		Total No. of employees in occupational groups		Sector as % of labour force	
	1962	1985	1962	1985	1962	1985
Skilled Industrial Workers	16.7	10.0	1,320,000	14,640,000		
Skilled Manual Workers	10.3	7.3	977,000	1,324,000		
Drivers	0.9	2.7	350,000	522,000		
Transport, Construction and Maintenance Workers	7.3	6.2	286,000	352,000		
Unskilled Industrial Workers	33.0	39.0	2,502,000	1,793,000		
Unskilled Manual Workers	15.0	32.2	1,132,000	717,000		
Agricultural Workers	11.6	13.0	809,000	237,000		
Total: Manual Workers	19.4	19.5	7,376,000	6,409,000	38.7	30.0
Farmers	38.4	37.9	3,045,000	1,475,000	16.0	6.9
Overall Total: Nos. in Labour Force			19,032,000	21,356,000	100.0	100.0
Overall Total: % Women in Labour Force				8,637,000		40.4

Source: *Données Sociales*, INSEE (1987) pp. 40, 42, 46, 52, 59 and 66.

qualifications held, the less chance there is in becoming unemployed. However, women are more likely to suffer unemployment than men with the same qualifications (cf., Coeffic, 1987). It is also important to avoid excessively optimistic judgements of the situation. Although uptake of patterns of study in secondary and higher education is strongly influenced by gender, it is the social class origins of pupils and students which still largely determine educational achievement (Oeuvrard, 1979).

As Table 4.11 clearly shows, participation in vocational education and training has been strongly associated with social class origins and in this sector children from working-class families have been disproportionately represented, while in higher education children from middle-class families have been greatly over-represented (cf., Bourdieu, 1989 for an analysis of attendance of the social origins of students of the "grandes écoles"). So, for example, in 1977–1978, 47.1 per cent of medical students were from a liberal professional background in comparison with only 7.4 per cent from a manual working-class background or 3.5 per cent from the agricultural sector, while 1.1 per cent of CEP holders were from a liberal professional background in contrast to 55 per cent from a manual working class background and 4.4 per cent from the agricultural sector. More recent figures are not readily available but the overall picture has changed little in this respect. For example, in 1986–1987, 31.2 per cent of university students were from a liberal professional and senior management background, 13.5 per cent were from a

TABLE 4.11

Social and Economic Background of Students in Vocational and Higher Education, 1977–1978

	% in Vocational Education				% in University Faculties						Technical Universities	% in the population aged 15–24 according to the occupational group of father
	CEP	CPA	CAP	BEP	Medicine	Law	Economic Sciences	Sciences	Arts	Total		
Liberal Professions and Senior Management	0.3	0.8	1.1	2.5	47.1	32.9	32.2	30.8	29.4	35.1	15.6	6.7
Middle Management	1.7	2.8	3.6	7.1	15.7	17.0	18.0	19.5	18.5	17.6	16.9	9.4
Industrialists and Wholesale Traders	0.2	0.5	0.5	0.8	[a]	[a]	[a]	[a]	[a]	[a]	[a]	[a]
White-Collar Workers	8.0	9.5	10.9	13.3	7.0	9.8	9.1	8.9	10.2	9.0	9.8	10.0
Craftsmen and Small Businessmen	2.4	7.3	5.4	7.1	10.7	11.0	12.0	9.5	10.7	10.9	11.8	7.0
Manual Workers	55.0	50.4	53.0	43.4	7.4	12.9	12.6	13.9	14.3	12.0	24.8	42.7
Small Farmers	4.4	6.3	4.5	6.8	3.5	5.3	5.9	6.9	4.8	5.1	10.3	7.8
Agricultural Workers	2.4	3.1	1.8	1.6	0.2	0.4	0.5	0.5	0.5	0.4	0.8	1.7
Service Workers	5.7	4.7	5.9	5.0	0.5	1.1	1.0	0.8	1.0	0.9	1.5	2.4
Others	19.9	14.6	13.3	12.5	7.9	9.6	8.7	9.2	10.5	9.0	8.5	12.3
TOTAL	100.0	100.0	100.0	100.0	100.0	100.0	100.0	100.0	100.0	100.0	100.0	100.0

[a] Figures conflated with those of craftsmen and small merchants.

Source: F. Oeuvrard (1979) "Démocratisation ou Elimination Différé" in *Actes de la Recherche en Sciences Sociales*, no. 30, pp. 94–96.

skilled manual background and 0.6 per cent had fathers who were agricultural workers (*Repères et Referénces*, 1988).

This indicates that although there have been some major changes for women in higher education and in the world of work, it still appears that social class origin is of major importance in the unequal distribution of opportunities in education and the job market. Again, no figures are available, to my knowledge, which would highlight the distribution of educational opportunities according to both social class and gender, but one can deduce that, as elsewhere in Europe, the expansion of educational opportunities in the 1970s largely benefited middle-class girls.

Although, as has been shown, a sizeable proportion of women have been able to improve their lot in the education system and in the job market, nevertheless inequality between the sexes in France is still strong. The Ministry of Education introduced some measures to combat sex discrimination in schools in 1982 with the twin objectives of reducing sex-role stereotyping in textbooks and in teaching materials and of stimulating interest in Science and Technology among young girls, in an attempt to encourage them to diversify their study patterns (UNESCO, 1983).[4] However laudable, it is still much too early to judge the effectiveness of such initiatives. All the evidence points to the conclusion that, given the effect of the sexual division of labour on the education system, changes in the educational sphere will have little chance of success unless the economic structure and the labour market also become similarly "desegregated". So it is highly likely that many more generations of women will have to be "sacrificed" before our collective social behaviour is sufficiently transformed for a just balance of power to exist between the sexes.

References

Baudelot, C. and Establet, R. (1971) *L'école capitaliste en France* (The capitalist school in France). Paris: Maspero.

Baudelot, C. *et al.* (1981) *Les étudiants, l'emploi et la crise* (Students, employment and crisis). Paris: Maspero.

Belloc, B. (1987) Le travail à temps partiel (Part-time employment). In *Données Sociales*, pp. 112–119.

Bourdieu, P. (1979) *La Distinction* (Differentiation). Paris: Editions de Minuit.

Bourdieu, P. (1989) *La noblesse d'état: grandes écoles et esprit de corps* (The nobility of the state). Paris: Editions de Minuit, Ch 1 and 2.

Bourdieu, P. and Passeron, J. C. (1964) *Les héritiers* (The inheritors). Paris: Editions de Minuit.

Bourdieu, P. and Passeron, J. C. (1970) *La reproduction* (Reproduction) Paris: Editions de Minuit.

Canceill, G. (1984) *Données Sociales*, INSEE, Paris.

Cacouault-Bitaud, M. (1985) *Des professeurs femmes a l'ére de la féminisation: positions, stratégies, 1960–1980* (Women Teachers in an era of feminisation: position, strategies 1960–1980). Thèse de 3 eme cycle.

Charles, F. (1988) *Instit ueurs: un coup au moral: genèse d'une crise de reproduction* (Teachers: a moral blow, genesis of a reproduction crisis), Paris: Ed. Ramsay.

Charlot, B. (1987) *L'école en mutation* (The school in transition). Paris: Payot.

Coeffic, N. (1987) Le devenir des jeunes sortis de l'école en 1983 (The future of young school-leavers in 1983). In *Données Sociales*, INSEE, Paris, pp. 120–126.

Données Sociales (1984) INSEE, Paris.

Données Sociales (1987) INSEE, Paris.

Durand-Pringborgne, C. (1988) *L'égalité scolaire par le coeur et la raison* (Educational equality in the hearts and minds). Paris: Fernand Nathan.

Duthoit, M. (1988) L'enfant et l'école. Aspects synthetiques de 20,000 élèves des écoles (The child and the school: a study of 20,000 school pupils). In *Education et Formation*, Misteré de l'Education Nationale p. 16.

Eurydice (1987) *Répartition par sexe des effectifs d'inspecteurs et des directeurs d'établissement* (Gender differences in the Inspectorate and in headships).

Féderation Nationale des Ecoles, de Parents et d'Educateurs (1988) Enfants et Parents en Question: L'Enfant de 7 à 11 Ans dans la Famille et Son Environment (Children and parents in question: The 7 to 11 year-old in his Family and Environment). In R. Sirota *L'école primaire au quotidien* (Daily life in the primary school). Paris: PUF.

Hurtig, M. F. (1982) Elaboration Socialisée de la difference des sexes (The Elaboration of Sex Differences) In *Enfance 4*, September–October.

L'Annuaire Statistique de la France (1985) Vol. 90, p. 290.

Lenoir, R. (1985) L'effondrement des bases sociales du familiarisme (The collapse of the social basis of the family). In *Actes de la Recherche en Sciences Sociales*, 57–58.

Mosconi, N. (1983) Des rapporte entre la division sexuelle du travail et inegalités des chances entre les sexes a l'école (The relationship between the sexual division of labour and inequality of opportunity at school). In *Revue Française de Pédagogie* (62), January–March.

Note d'Information (1988) Misteré de l'Education Nationale (M.E.N.) (88-17).

OECD (1979) *Les femmes et l'egalité des chances* (Women and Equal Opportunities), Paris.

Oeuvrard, F. (1979) Democratisation ou elimination différée. (Democratisation or deferred elimination.) In *Actes de la Recherche en Sciences Sociales*, 30, pp. 88–97.

Passeron, J. C. (1982) Differentiation: l'inflation des diplômes (Differentiation: the inflation of qualifications). In *Revue Française de Sociologie*, XXIII. no. 4.

Repères et Références Statistiques sur les Enseignement et la Formation (1988) Misteré d'Education, pp. 199 and 209.

Repères et Références Statistiques sur les Enseignement et la Formation (1988) Misteré d'Education. DEP M.E.N. p. 92.

Safilios-Rothschild, C. (1986) *Les differences selon les sexes dans la socialisation et l'education des jeunes enfants et leurs consequences sur leur choix des études et leurs résultats* (Sex differences in the socialisation and education of young children and the consequences on their choice of studies and their results). Paris: OCDE.

Sirota, R. (1988) *L'école primarie au quotidien* (Daily life in the primary school). Paris: PUF.

UNESCO (1983) *Etude sur l'image que donnent des femmes et des hommes les manuels scolaires et les livres pour les enfants en France* (A study of images of men and women in school textbooks and children's books in France), Paris.

Zazzo, B. (1982) Les conduites adaptives en milieu scolaire. Interêt et comparaison entre les garcons et les filles (Coping strategies in schools: boys and girls compared). In *Enfance 4*, September–October.

Notes

1. This increase in the representation of girls in the upper levels of education is not due to any demographic factors, but rather because in the lower levels of schooling boys have to repeat the year more often than girls and in upper secondary education the staying on rate is higher for girls.
2. It is interesting to note here that up until 1983, a quota was placed on the number of places for males and females in the école normale for primary teachers. This was discriminatory against girls since they applied in far greater numbers, so in 1983 a girl had a 7.2 per cent chance of getting into this level of teacher education, whereas a boy had a 19.5 per cent chance.
3. Here it is important to put the representation of girls in the engineering schools in context. On closer examination, it appears that girls have been far more concentrated in the less prestigious

engineering schools, where they constituted 83.2 per cent of students in 1975, than in the more prestigious schools, where they represented 26.8 per cent of students. (See Baudelot *et al.*, 1981.)

4. See Durand-Pringborgne C. (1988) *L'égalité scolaire par le coeur et la raison* (Educational equality in the hearts and minds). Paris: Fernand Nathan, for an account of measures taken by the Ministries of Education and Women's Rights to combat sexism in school. These included measures to promote information, research and consciousness-raising among careers officers, teacher educators, headteachers and deputy heads.

CHAPTER 5

Greece

GEORGIA KONTOGIANNOPOULOU-POLYDORIDES

THIS chapter examines the inter-relationship between the increasing participation of women in the Greek education system and continuing attempts at
educational reform, focusing particularly on this interaction process and also
on the unintended consequences of reform. The main points in the chapter are
the following:

— There is a plethora of analyses and explanations of women's participation
in the Greek education system. These are characterized by both differences
in the theoretical assumptions about the issue as well as in interpretation of
the empirical evidence and, therefore, in the conclusions which are
reached.
— The position presented in this chapter is that there has been a dynamic
development in women's educational participation in Greece, one which
shows a clear trend towards greater equality. This trend has emerged over
time, for the most part independently of educational policies aimed at
increasing equality of participation. An examination of recent educational
reforms and their consequences indicates that there are other broader
social factors related to the trend towards more equal educational
opportunities for women.

This chapter will review specific educational policies related to increasing
equality of opportunity for girls and women in Greece, concerning:

— structural changes;
— changes in the curriculum;
— tracking and options;
— counselling and guidance;
— access to higher education;
— subject choice in secondary and higher education.

These are placed within a time framework which does not support a wholly
causal relationship between the increase in women's participation in
education and wider social change. Further, the role of women in the labour
market will be reviewed and the issue of women's choice of employment will be
examined in relationship to expanding educational opportunities.

As in most European countries the development of the educational system in Greece has been characterized by (a) a massive increase in female enrolment in education since the 1970s, and (b) persistent but slowly diminishing inequality in subject choice at university level and in post-educational careers (OECD, 1986; Polydorides, 1985).

Recent reports and reviews of the issue have responded to various possible "commonsense" evaluations of the situation. These partly support the proposition that the law has been successful in guaranteeing equality of opportunity between men and women. Some writers argue that there has been no progress whatsoever, or, that even if there has been some progress within the educational system, it has not really affected the status of women in society at large (cf., Eliou 1978, 1988). Others assert that there is little point in demanding greater equality for girls in the education system but have rather opted to fight for equality in the status of women in the workforce and in academia (Kontogiannopoulou-Polydorides, 1987a). It is interesting to note that researchers in the area have often reached both similar as well as conflicting conclusions, questioning the relevance of achieving gender equality in education as an end in itself, as well as arguing that gender equality in higher education has not yet been achieved[1] (Eliou, 1987; Fragoudaki, 1985).

This discussion has been supported by empirical evidence which suggests that women are under-represented in academia, get less pay for equal work and are to be found in the lower strata of the occupational hierarchy in the workforce (Psacharopoulos, 1980; Eliou, 1988). However, a re-analysis of the same empirical evidence on a longitudinal basis leads to the argument that (a) although women's participation in higher education reflects overall inequalities in the education system, it also presents a dynamic development towards equality between the sexes, and (b) the increased rate of female participation in education does not reflect greater overall social equality, as had been argued, but, on the contrary, has simply drawn into higher education new entrants from the middle and lower middle social classes (Kontogiannopoulou-Polydorides, 1987a; Fragoudaki, 1985).

The argument presented in this chapter differs mainly in the sense that such accounts imply a *permanence* in the situation described, which does not stand up to evidence of the developments in the last twenty-five years. These developments have far from established an equal balance between men and women in society at large, but they have nevertheless reflected an interesting interplay between recent changes in the educational system and the evolution of patterns of women's participation in the labour market and wider society. This chapter will therefore outline educational policies related to gender equality and will present empirical data on changes in access to education by social origin and by gender. Finally, the chapter will try to analyse the interplay between changes in educational policy and changes in women's participation in education in order to identify the implications of such policy.

The Greek Education System

The Greek education system consists of nine years of compulsory education from the age of five and a half to fifteen and a half years old. All schools are now co-educational. About 5 per cent of pupils attend private schools.

The main sectors of the Greek education system consist of:

Pre-school education, from three and a half years old to five and a half years old, where attendance is voluntary.

Primary education from five and a half years old. This lasts for a minimum of six years. The curriculum is based on Greek Language, Mathematics, Environmental Studies, Art and Physical Education. In grades 3 to 6 the curriculum includes, in addition, Religious Studies, History, Geography, Civic Education, Physics and Chemistry and cultural activities. A programme in Foreign Languages has been introduced in 124 state schools since 1987 and a programme in Computer Studies is under consideration.

Lower secondary education in "gymnasia", from eleven and a half to fifteen and a half years old. This is aimed at preparing pupils for the demands of everyday life and at developing their potential. Here the curriculum includes Greek language and literature, Mathematics, the Sciences, History, Physical Education, Art, Home Economics, Classical Greek Literature and a foreign language. Transfer to and from lower secondary education does not depend on any selection or entry requirements.

Upper secondary education is provided by various types of "lycea", and by technical schools, which pupils attend from the age of fourteen and a half years.

Courses in technical schools last two years and aim to provide a broad general education, while training students in specific technical and vocational areas. Courses in lycea last three years and take place in general, comprehensive and technical and vocational lycea, all of which enjoy equal institutional status. These schools aim to help pupils make appropriate choices for further education or careers, and to enable them to develop their personalities, skills and aptitudes so that they can contribute to the economic, cultural and social development of the country.

Pupils are assessed on the basis of informal evaluation, as in lower secondary education, and annual written examinations. Schools are tracked or streamed and additional support is given to pupils with specific educational needs and those who are aiming at higher education.

The curriculum of the first two grades of the *general lycea* is based on Greek Language and Literature, Mathematics and Classical Greek Literature, together with Sciences and a Modern Language. The Social Sciences (History, Psychology, Religious Studies) are also studied at this level. In the twelfth grade, the core curriculum comprises mainly: Greek Language, a Modern

Language and Social Sciences and in addition, pupils must opt for one of four specialist areas, the first two in Mathematics and the Physical Sciences, the second in Greek Language and History and the last in the Social Sciences.

In the *technical and vocational* lycea, greater emphasis is given to vocational training. The first grade provides an even balance between general education and technical training, with emphasis given to Mathematics and Greek Language. The second two years are divided between general education and specialized vocational education.

Comprehensive lycea aim to integrate general education and vocational training, and to give pupils the opportunity to develop their own abilities and skills appropriate to national development.

The majority of pupils in upper secondary education take statewide national examinations and access to higher education is gained on the basis of rank order in these exams. Pupils are eligible to participate in the examinations provided they have followed one of the following general educational tracks in the twelfth grade:

(a) Mathematics and Science;
(b) Science;
(c) Language Literature and the Humanities;
(d) Social Sciences and Mathematics B.

Higher Education comprises universities and tertiary technical and vocational institutes. Specialization in the final year of lycea enables students to apply for one of the following areas:

(a) Mathematics, the Sciences, Engineering, Agricultural Science and Education;
(b) Biology, Dentistry, Medical and Veterinary Studies;
(c) Literature, Modern Languages, the Humanities, Law and Education;
(d) Sociology, Economics, Political Science and Education.

University education departments were created in 1985 and specialist Colleges of Agriculture, Industry, etc., with university status, were integrated into universities in 1989.

Overall policy and planning for universities and technical institutes are determined by central councils.

Educational Opportunities Policies

It must be stated at the outset that the issue of equal opportunities in education will be examined primarily at the level of higher education since girls and boys are equally represented in primary and secondary education, as can be seen from Table 5.1 below.

An analysis of the development of women's access to the different levels of the education system shows a familiar picture to other parts of the world and

TABLE 5.1

Rate of Enrolment by Age-Group and by Educational Level, 1960–1986

Educational level	1960		1970		1978		1986	
	Total % Age-Group	% Girls	Total % Age-Group	% Girls	Total % Age-Group	% Girls	Total % Age-Group	% Girls
Pre-school	14	13	30	30	43	42	48	46
Primary	110[a]	108[a]	107[a]	105[a]	107[a]	105[a]	107[a]	105[a]
Secondary: General	33	28	56	54	65	66	69	70
Secondary total (including technical and vocational)	39[b]	31[b]	68	57	77	70	80	75
Higher	4[c]	2[c]	13	9	19	14	24	23

[a] These figures represent the "actual" versus "expected" percentage of the age-range in primary education, including 12-year-olds who are repeating the academic year.

[b] Including all levels of technical and vocational education.

[c] Including only university education and teacher training.

Source: Ministry of Education, Directorate of Planning and Operations Research, provisional data 1986. Table adapted from Polydorides (1985).

to Europe in particular[2] (OECD, 1978; Polydorides, 1985). The gradual increase in educational participation, throughout the 1970s, has had important qualitative results for girls as well:

— Teachers have become, in general, more aware of the problem of role prejudice in education.
— Single-sex schools and classes were abolished in the 1970s.
— The influence of the women's movement has led to an awareness of the need to develop curricula and teaching materials which are less likely to encourage girls to restrict their educational choices.
— Tracking or streaming is relatively limited as a result of the traditional general curriculum as well as the inability of government policy in the mid-seventies to foster policies of segregation between the technical and vocational tracks.

For the purposes of the analysis a distinction needs to be drawn between (a) policies and changes which occur *within* the educational system, i.e. structural changes, changes in the curriculum, admissions policies and guidance, and (b) policies and behaviour *outside* the educational system, i.e. labour market policies, sex discrimination. All these influence girls' study choices, especially in higher education.We will deal here with recent educational policies geared explicitly or implicitly at fostering more equality of opportunity either by social origin or by gender.

Adopting the notion of equality of opportunity, as presented in international literature throughout the 1960s and 1970s, Greek educational policy theorists and critics succeeded in diffusing such ideas among academics and the politically active groups related in one way or another to the educational process. This they achieved by using some simple but convincing empirical data and theoretical arguments, which implied that Greek educational policy had been designed up to that point to have as at least one of its objectives, equality of educational opportunity. In reality, this specific issue had never been a part of implemented educational policy, but had rather been introduced, or imported, by educational theorists and advisers of international organizations, such as the OECD and UNESCO.

The reforms of the seventies had to counteract inequalities in the system which stemmed from, among other things, the dictatorship period of military rule from 1967–1974. Another task was to prepare the ground for the entry of Greece into the European Economic Community and in particular for the adoption of the 1975 Directive on the Equality of Treatment Between Men and Women Workers, which directly affected access to professional and vocational education. Changes within the educational system had already influenced the labour market by increasing the supply of women qualified to do jobs previously performed to a large degree by men. This had resulted in considerable pressure on employers to change existing hiring practices. The state responded by creating a measure of equal employment legislation in the public sector and the Council and the Secretariat for Women's Equality were set up in 1982 and 1985 respectively, as a direct result of the requirement to comply with EEC policies. As the issue of equal opportunities for women was still relatively new for the majority of the population in the early 1970s, it was not until the mid-1970s that legislation had any impact on the role of women in society. Since the mid-1970s governments have presented, within the framework of an overall policy of expansion of educational opportunities, the issue of equal opportunities for women as a major feature of educational policy, and have initiated measures designed to stimulate change with the stated objective of creating more opportunities for girls and women to further their educational careers. These have included the abolition of élite boys' schools, the imposition of co-education in all schools and the opening up of some formerly single-sex post-secondary institutions to women students.

Enrolment of both male and female pupils and students in education has increased continuously over this period, and policies which have increased overall participation have also promoted more equal participation by gender. Since the early 1970s, girls have begun to participate in equal numbers to boys at the level of secondary education and since the mid-1970s have increased their participation at the level of higher education. By the 1980s there were no substantial differences in access to either secondary or higher education, although strong divergences continue to exist in terms of choice of field of study or training, as will be explored later in the chapter. Indeed, in the Greek system, educational policy geared to promote equality in general has not been separated from specific policies addressed to promote women's participation, either through structural changes in the system itself or through influencing patterns of study. Substantive policies and statements of support for equality of opportunity have continued throughout the 1980s.

The current status of women in education suggests that overall equality of access and participation is now a "fait accompli" at all levels of education. However, even though equal participation rates for women have been virtually achieved, patterns of study mainly reinforce existing gender stereotyping and continue to contribute to occupational segregation.

Girls and Educational Achievement at School

The abolition of separate schools for boys and girls was considered extremely important in promoting equality of opportunity since separate schooling tends to contribute to sex-role stereotyping and to reinforce traditional social attitudes towards gender. The rapid introduction of co-education in the 1970s was therefore considered to be a crucial step in the reduction of sex-role stereotyping. The postponement of choice between academic or vocational and technical education until later in adolescence at the upper secondary level was also considered to be an important factor in broadening career and educational choices for both girls and boys.

The Curriculum

The curriculum is widely considered to be an important instrument in reinforcing or combating traditional sex roles in education. A unified curriculum in the compulsory years of education offered formally equal treatment of boys and girls at school up until the mid-1970s.

Curricular choice is very limited. Languages, Religious Education, Mathematics, Science, and a number of other subjects, are offered at all educational levels, and in all tracks of upper secondary education, differing only in the depth of the subject content. This uniformity, as well as the persistently general character of secondary schooling in the past, has protected girls from choosing or being encouraged to choose the kinds of subjects which would eventually channel them into streams and option tracks which would result in unequal access to higher education.

Curricular differentiation had been introduced for the first time in a number of schools in the large urban centres in the 1960s but this did not, however, attempt to distinguish between academic and vocational and technical education. It was not until after the mid-1970s that a differentiated stream was introduced in Greek schools. In 1982 a technical and vocational curriculum was designed for the country's technical and vocational upper secondary schools which was treated for the first time as an alternative within the state system, and not as a mainly private operation for those students who had failed in the mainstream system. The first differentiated technical and vocational streams did not attract girls on a large scale and they remained a rather limited 20 per cent of pupils in this sector (Polydorides, 1985). Both traditional views regarding women's social role, as well as the comparatively low prestige of the educational, and occupational orientation of these streams were the main reasons for this under-representation. Changes introduced in 1980 created two option tracks in Languages, Literature and the Humanities, and in Mathematics and Science in upper secondary education. These were replaced in 1983 by four option tracks in Mathematics and Science, Science, Language, Literature and the Humanities and in Social Science and Mathematics. This policy may have had the effect of reinforcing the over-representation of girls in the latter options and of boys in the Science and Technology options, with unforeseen consequences in terms of access to and subject choice in higher education, considered up until then as open and fairly equitable (OECD, 1978), but so far no data has been available which conclusively proves this point.

Patterns of Attainment and Curricular Choice

As is the case in other parts of the world, girls show a slight advantage in the early years of schooling compared with boys, a fact which is reflected in the overall data available in empirical studies as well as in national statistics (NSSG, 1980; Polydorides, 1985). A small-scale study of two schools in Athens in 1989, one in a middle-class and one in a working-class area, revealed some differences in attainment between boys and girls (Vernava-Stoura, 1989). Children were ranked on a three-point scale according to their acquisition of certain cognitive characteristics. Children in the more affluent school were found to be doing better than children in the less affluent school. Girls tended to be concentrated more than boys on the lower part of the three-point scale in the wealthier area, while they were found to be in equal proportion to the boys on the upper point of the scale in the working-class school. On the other hand, girls were concentrated more than boys on the lowest point of the three-point scale in the working-class school. These findings, coupled with teachers' observations, showed an early differentiation process which mainly favoured middle-class girls, placing them in the upper and average achievement levels, polarizing girls according to social class.

At the secondary level boys and girls exhibit divergent study patterns, whenever the system allows option choice and particularly beyond the age of compulsory schooling. For example, 57 per cent of fifteen to seventeen-year-old girls attended the general education track at the upper secondary level, compared with 44 per cent of fifteen to seventeen-year-old boys in 1985. On the other hand, boys were represented four times as much as girls in upper secondary level technical and vocational education (Ministry of Education, 1985).

It is clear that upper secondary general education has served a dual purpose for girls, since the reforms of the 1970s: as a stronghold and as an escape route. In the period up to 1982 girls were concentrated in the general education track simply because they were doing better than boys in the entrance examination at that level. This examination served as a mechanism for allocating students to the general and to the technical/vocational tracks. After the 1982 educational reforms, when this entrance examination was abolished, girls have remained largely concentrated in the general education track. Although one reason for this is to avoid training leading to private sector employment, upper secondary general education does provide an emphasis on the teaching of subjects which are prerequisites for university entrance. In this sense this track is a stronghold for girls, since it offers a direct opportunity to compete for a university place. On the other hand, it is an escape route because it does not provide specific training for a skilled job for those who do not finally gain a place in higher education. So this track protects girls and yet deprives them of the job-specific training provided by technical and vocational education as well as possible employment opportunities in the private sector. The crucial factor at this point is that personal choice now allocates boys and girls to the general and technical/vocational tracks in a largely similar fashion to the formal examination system prior to 1982, so what was once a product of the structure, is now seen as a matter of personal choice.

Teachers' Attitudes and the Hidden Curriculum

In the 1980s there have been a number of attempts to systematically revise curricula and textbooks, with the aim of eliminating gender-biased content, although this has not been matched by any systematic attempts to change day-to-day educational practices which would counteract traditional attitudes to gender roles, nor has there been any encouragement to introduce in class specific discussion topics to question differences that exist between men and women in many aspects of life. Researchers have also pointed to a number of aspects of the "hidden curriculum", which differentiate between boys and girls, some focusing in the past on the content of textbooks and especially primary readers, others on the interaction between teachers and pupils in the classroom and on the organizational features of schools. Although there are no longer uniforms or codes of dress for pupils, trousers are not allowed for girls in most schools and even today most schools have separate gymnastics classes and sports activities for boys and girls.

Teachers' responses confirm the general feeling that most teachers pay more attention to boys, both because of their potential disruptiveness as well as their belief in boys' potential achievement. They confirm that boys tend to dominate discussions in the classroom and research suggests that teachers tend to follow boys' interests more than those of girls. In primary schools, teachers prefer girls' obedience, but at the secondary school level teachers seem to divide their attention for different reasons, expressing a preference for boys as they feel that they respond more to the content of lessons, especially in Science and Mathematics, although girls largely gain a higher grade point average (Polydorides, 1984). In this context it is quite interesting to note that girls tend to develop a lower self-image compared with boys at the same level of achievement. In one study in an upper secondary school girls placed themselves lower than boys on a five-point self-ranking scale, even though they were subsequently found to have a higher grade point average. Boys evaluated themselves higher than girls before the results of their applications for places in higher education were known to them, although girls' assessment scores were higher. Girls rated themselves more highly once they knew that they had succeeded and had been admitted to higher education (Polydorides, 1985).

Although it is widely accepted that information on occupational careers should be provided at every level throughout school life, this has not been the case in practice. Little information on opportunities for girls in traditionally male-dominated areas is available, despite the important role which this could play in furthering girls' opportunities. The absence of a coordinated policy in this area may be one explanation for the divergent patterns of study which pertain at the levels of upper secondary and higher education.

Women and Higher Education

Admissions Policies and Access to Higher Education

Traditionally there has been some discrimination against girls in terms of admission to higher, as well as secondary, education. However, this has changed considerably in recent years. Higher technical and vocational education has been particularly characterized by a great increase in the participation of girls. In 1970 girls accounted for only 7 per cent of total student enrolments (OECD, 1980). Following the structural integration of higher technical and vocational education into tertiary education in the 1970s, combined with the introduction of a uniform admissions policy, girls' participation rose to 27 per cent in 1976–1977 (OECD, 1980). The figure for this sector is now 43.6 per cent. Representation of girls in university education has also risen rapidly in the past thirty years, from 23 per cent of the student body in 1960–1961 to 40 per cent in 1978–1979, to 48 per cent in 1986 (Kontogiannopoulou-Polydorides, 1987b and Ministry of Education, 1986), primarily due to changes in admissions policies and in the examination system, the one and only criterion for acceptance into higher education.

In 1964 the first major educational reforms which were explicitly concerned with equality of opportunity substantially changed the nature of the entrance examination for higher education (Polydorides, 1978). The essence of the changes introduced was twofold: examination subjects became more attuned to the content of the upper secondary curriculum and the administration of examinations became decentralized to the local authority level. Overall planning and subject distribution remained at the national level with the Ministry of Education.

By 1969 all university students were selected on the basis of the examinations which had been developed after 1974. Since that year, observed changes in the composition of the student body can be attributed to a large extent to the changes in the examination system, as shown in Table 5.2. This clearly shows a shift in the proportional representation of students from a professional/managerial background in relation to those from a blue-collar background. In 1980 a second major educational reform aimed at, among other things, greater equality of opportunity. Its main features were the introduction of an even stricter correspondence of examination subjects to the upper secondary curriculum and the upgrading of the matriculation examination as a school leaving certificate which meant that all pupils graduating from secondary schools had to participate.

In 1985, obligatory participation in the exam ceased with the introduction of a non-academic terminal track which has succeeded in enrolling up to 5 per

TABLE 5.2

Representation of Students in Higher Education by Father's Occupation, 1956–1985 Educational Opportunities Indices[a]

Father's occupation	1956–1957	1957–1958	1959–1960	1961–1962	1963–1964	1969–1970	1971–1972	1973–1974	1975–1976	1985–1986[b]
Professionals and self-employed	7.33	5.74	5.65	5.27	5.16	2.31	2.41	2.37	2.42	2.30
Managerial and administrative	2.00	0.89	1.96	0.83	1.89	1.83	1.32	1.19	1.01	0.71
Office personnel	5.53	4.09	3.60	3.77	3.90	2.78	2.60	2.77	2.96	2.55
Commerce and trade	1.63	1.44	1.48	1.55	1.58	1.65	1.52	1.53	1.54	1.60
Agriculture	0.41	0.45	0.48	0.51	0.49	0.61	0.59	0.58	0.52	0.48
Blue collar workers	0.37	0.98	0.90	0.95	0.88	0.87	0.92	0.95	1.00	0.90
Services and military personnel	0.90	0.82	0.70	0.63	0.65	0.84	1.22	1.06	1.21	0.95

[a] Percentage of students with father in occupational group over percentage of males over 45 in occupational group.

[b] 1985–1986 estimates are based on provisional data on students and the 1981 census.

Source: OECD (1980) Educational Reform Policies in Greece, p. 126; Ministry of Education, Directorate for Planning and Operations Research provisional data for 1985–1986.

cent of twelfth grade students. At the same time the establishment of four upper secondary tracks in 1983 gave rise to the fear that equality of opportunity might be at stake on two fronts. Firstly, because girls were most likely to choose, or to be forced to choose, the terminal track and, secondly, because the introduction of an increased number of options made it more likely that they would opt for the less prestigious of these fields of study.

Data available does not support the first of these fears. It is clear, for example, that the 1964 reforms greatly affected patterns of student recruitment by socio-economic background but the rate of change in women's participation in higher education, however considerable, was not equally affected (OECD, 1980; Polydorides, 1978). On the other hand, the 1980 reforms did not affect such patterns of recruitment, but did increase the overall rate of women's participation. Indeed these changes reversed the traditional proportion of boys and girls in higher education so that the success rate for girls in the entrance examination reached 54 per cent in 1980 (Polydorides, 1985). This was largely due to changes in admissions procedures to a system where acceptance is based on academic ranking in a uniform examination, which has helped increase women's participation in Greece, as in many OECD countries (OECD, 1978). Although the reforms clearly included the stated goals of improving educational opportunities for girls and working-class students, social reality emerged somewhat differently than expected. The reforms of the 1960s had not affected trends in women's participation to any great degree so that policy makers were not prepared for the extent to which this occurred in the 1980s. A Ministry of Education official, in charge of presenting the examination statistics to the public and the media, stated at an official meeting preceding the OECD examination of Greek educational reform policies, that it was not possible to publicize the increased success rate of women, "as people would laugh at the new examination system" (*sic*), and indeed such data were not presented in official publications at that time.

Patterns of Study and Attainment in Higher Education

Within higher education institutions, however, and universities in particular, access to some courses of study often embodies a more subtle form of differential treatment of male and female students. Of course women are never openly excluded from particular fields of education or training. Nevertheless there has been a pattern of organizing vocational and professional programmes so that the typical study choices of female students lead to the traditionally female-dominated occupations in the labour market. More importantly, the introduction of four secondary level tracks has not greatly increased women's participation in the high status fields of study such as Medicine, Technology and Science, since the distribution of female enrolments after 1985 merely intensified previous trends in subject choice as illustrated in Table 5.3 below.

TABLE 5.3

Distribution of Women Students in University Education and Teacher Training, by Sex and by Subject Area, 1986

Subject Area	Women as a % of enrolled students	Women as a % of first year students	Women as a % of graduating students
Humanities	73.96	77.56	79.03
Arts	52.45	60.31	53.65
Law	55.82	60.88	61.73
Social Science	56.55	61.19	69.25
Economics	44.23	47.08	40.79
Science	39.82	43.38	40.16
Technology	24.40	31.99	23.31
Health, Medicine	44.83	48.99	45.11
Veterinary Science	34.60	37.82	31.09
Education	53.86	54.81	60.24
Total	49.16	53.86	52.40

Source: Ministry of Education, Directorate of Planning and Operations Research. Provisional data (1986).

However, achievement patterns both in the entrance examination as well as during the first year of university study in fields dominated by men, show that girls do very well indeed when it comes down to actual performance. Data from 1981–1982 shows that slightly more women who decided to participate in the entrance examination for the science track did better than men, with 33.5 per cent ranking as very good and excellent, to 31 per cent of men, as illustrated by Table 5.4 below.

This situation pertained in the first year of studies where male and female students appeared to have the same overall achievement level, but where women were ranked as excellent by 6 per cent more than men. The pattern was not quite the same in the engineering entrance examination achievement

TABLE 5.4

Distribution of Results in the University Entrance Examination and in the First Year of University: Science Students 1981–1982

Achievement level	Entrance exam		University performance	
	% Women	% Men	% Women	% Men
Fair	16.0	19.6	0	0
Good	50.5	49.4	2.2	1.5
Very good	30.9	27.3	80.9	87.7
Excellent	2.6	3.7	16.9	10.8
% distribution of students by sex	47.3	52.7	41.9	58.1

Source: G. Kontogiannopoulou-Polydorides. *Achievement at university.* Research in progress, partially published in "The main characteristics of the entrance examination" in G. Kontogianno-poulou-Polydorides (1989) *The transition from secondary to tertiary education*, Athens: Vervakion Alumni Association.

levels, but first year results illustrated in Table 5.5 showed quite clearly that women performed slightly better at the university level in Engineering as well.

TABLE 5.5

Distribution of Results in the University Entrance Examination and in the First Year of University: Engineering Students 1981–1982

Achievement level	Entrance exam		University performance	
	% Women	% Men	% Women	% Men
Fair	3.3	0.7	10.5	18.2
Good	13.0	4.2	44.7	45.0
Very good	34.0	35.3	38.2	30.2
Excellent	49.7	59.8	6.6	6.6
% distribution of students by sex	26.9	73.1	28.3	71.7

Source: G. Kontogiannopoulou-Polydorides. *Achievement at university*. Research in progress, partially published in "The main characteristics of the entrance examination" in Varvakion Alumni Association (1989) *The transition from secondary to tertiary education*, Athens.

The above data shows that women can perform successfully in the entrance examination as well as in university studies in these fields. Their limited participation in the male-dominated fields of study, such as Science and Engineering, is due to "self-selection" or other processes operating independently of achievement patterns.

Women in the Labour Market

Patterns of Employment

Equal employment opportunity in the labour market, including equal pay for equal work, has had an influence on both the type of employment chosen by women as well as field of study. The existence of policies to ensure equal treatment of women in hiring and promotion is widely believed to have changed the aspirations of young women and therefore to influence the type of educational choices they make. But although educational policy has been successful in encouraging girls to enter various fields and vocationally oriented educational programmes, and despite more equitable admission policies at the secondary and higher education level, the fact remains that occupational opportunities for women are restricted in Greece. Indeed, while patterns of participation in education show a clear trend away from the division of "male" or "female" fields of study, there are no signs of similar developments in the employment sector. On the contrary, women's expectations regarding earnings after completion of secondary school studies are lower than those of men, and even more so after higher education. In 1977, the expected rate of return for female post-secondary degree holders was less than half the rate of return expected by men, as Table 5.6 shows. No research into relative earnings has been published since, but it may be supposed that although women are entering higher education in increasing numbers, their realistic expectations are less than those of men.

TABLE 5.6

Labour Market Perceptions by Selected Characteristics
Expected Earnings in Drachmas by Educational Level, 1977

	Secondary school graduates	Degree holders	Expected rate of return
Males	36,461	109,950	18.3%
Females	30,218	52,394	8.4%

Source: Papas, G. and G. Psacharopoulos (1987). The Transition from School to the University Under Restricted Entry: A Greek Tracer Study. *Higher Education*, **16** (4).

Analyses of employment data are complicated by the fact that it is outdated compared with educational data and that it refers to the previous generation while educational data refers to the incoming generation of an employable population. The effects of educational policies of the 1980s will not be fully realized in the labour market until the 1990s, so that arguments concerned with unequal qualifications should be treated with caution and will not be valid in the future.

The present characteristics of women in the labour market in Greece are similar to other European countries, namely:

— a lower level of pay compared with men;
— slower promotion in the private sector and mostly "non-activated promotion" in the public sector;
— vulnerability at times of economic crisis;
— discriminatory attitudes at the work place;
— unequal allocation to sectors of economic activity (Eliou, 1987).

Women have traditionally been concentrated in agriculture, they are absent from sectors considered "masculine" and they often work in unpaid jobs both at home or in family farms or small family enterprises. According to official statistics, about a half of Greek women work in agriculture and 17 per cent in manufacturing, while 40 per cent report that they are employed in family businesses. Census data indicate that women's pay is about 50 per cent of the rate of men's pay, and that this difference has not improved during the 1980s (NSSG, 1988). Data analysis indicates that only a small proportion of the differences in gross earnings between males and females can be explained by productivity-related characteristics. The rest, nearly 90 per cent of the gross differential, can be interpreted as due to a degree of sex discrimination (Psacharopoulos, 1980).

Women in Teaching

Women in the teaching profession are the largest group in public sector employment. Primary and secondary teachers are hired according to official procedures which stipulate that lists of applicants should be rank-ordered according to the date of university graduation. These procedures therefore constitute the best possible policy regarding equality of opportunity, enabling women to be recruited into Mathematics and Science, fields which constitute one of the least "feminine" fields of study, as well as in the more conventional fields of Foreign Languages, as illustrated by Table 5.7 below.

TABLE 5.7

Distribution of Teachers by Sex, Level and Selected Subject Area, 1983 and 1986

Level of education	1983		1986	
	% Women	% Men	% Women	% Men
Preschool education	94.1	5.9	94.7	5.3
Primary education	48.3	51.7	44.6	55.4
Secondary (total)	61.6	38.4	52.4	47.6
Secondary Greek language	78.4	21.6	n.a.	n.a.
Secondary Mathematics	35.1	64.9	n.a.	n.a.
Secondary Sciences	46.3	53.7	n.a.	n.a.
Secondary Foreign Languages	92.7	7.3	n.a.	n.a.
University (all grades)	8.2	91.8	23.7	76.3

Source: NSSG, Statistics of Education, Athens (1983) and provisional data, Ministry of Education, Directorate of Planning and Operations Research (1986).

The fact that female teachers dominate the lower levels of the educational system and male teachers the higher, especially in the fields of Mathematics and the Sciences, is considered to have an impact on the persistence of traditional attitudes towards educational and occupational choices of boys and girls. Moreover, if one compares the distribution of relatively new entrants into teaching with the distribution of teachers in 1983 a different pattern emerges. In 1980, 70 per cent of primary school teachers born in 1950 or later were women, showing a marked influx of young women in this sector. In upper secondary education, 57 per cent of teachers of Greek language and only 16 per cent of Mathematics teachers were women, a decline in the proportion in both subjects. At all levels almost 90 per cent of Foreign Language teachers were women. This shows, then, that in general the division of the teaching force by gender has actually increased in the younger age-group. There is no reverse discrimination policy which might reduce the number of women teachers at the lower levels, except in one-teacher schools in remote areas, where men are employed as a matter of policy, nor is there a positive discrimination policy which might increase the number of women teachers in Mathematics and Technology at the secondary school level. The number of women teaching at university level has increased in the years following the 1982 university reforms. These were aimed at facilitating increased access to aid promotion within university lectureships. Although without any specific reference to gender equality, the reforms have nonetheless had the effect of increasing women's participation at that level.

These advances have to be seen, however, as modest in the overall context; only 8.2 per cent of senior academic staff were women in 1986 and 38.5 per cent of junior academic staff, the latter figure much closer to the proportion of female university graduates. Needless to say, women's participation in the upper level faculty positions in Engineering, Veterinary Science and Science is

TABLE 5.8

Public Sector Employees and New Appointments,
1972–1978

	Women as % of all employees	Women as % of new appointments
1972	28	36
1974	29	37
1976	32	37
1978	31	40

Sources: Directorate General of Public Administration Census of Public Servants, Athens (1971); Statistics of Public Sector Employees (1973–1978).

very low. In contrast, women are better represented but are still less than 50 per cent of staff in Education, as illustrated in Table 5.9. So, even in teaching, where gender role stereotyping has not restricted women, stratified gender differentiation is to be observed at the school and university levels.

Women have also increasingly used their improved opportunities to gain professional qualifications to enable them to enter employment in the public sector during a time of expansion. Table 5.8 presents the increase in women's participation both in the public sector overall as well as in new appointments from 1972–1978.

The reasons for this are twofold: firstly, because access to such positions has been through connections or partisan politics which can favour women as well as men, and secondly, because promotion, maternity leave and equality in earnings are best guaranteed in public sector positions.

Equality of Educational Opportunity for Women: and Now What?

The overall evolution of women's participation in education in the last thirty years in Greece indicates that equality of opportunity in terms of access to, as

TABLE 5.9

Representation of Women in University Teaching, 1986

Subject area	% Women in upper grades	% Women in middle grades	% Women in lower grades
Humanities	15.45	33.77	58.79
The Arts	8.33	21.42	50.00
Law	11.62	23.07	64.23
Social Science	9.61	36.48	59.70
Economics	7.01	14.14	48.19
Science	4.48	18.45	27.33
Engineering	1.78	22.13	25.13
Health, Medicine	13.07	27.49	37.70
Veterinary Science	1.68	19.44	35.29
Education	33.33	19.60	0[a]
Total	8.20	24.16	38.55

[a] No new staff have been appointed in these newly founded university departments since 1982, and so are not represented on the lower grades.

Source: Ministry of Education, Directorate of Planning and Operations Research, Provisional Data (1986).

well as attainment in, education has been achieved so far at all levels. Inequality in terms of field of study at the university level persists, as is the case in many European countries, irrespective of the level of economic development (Eliou, 1987). In Greece, though, there is a significant rate of change which shows a clear trend towards a more equal representation of women in traditionally male-dominated fields. In 1985 I stated my conviction that "further research on, or demands for, equality of women's participation in the educational system are not justified . . . . The emphasis of researchers' and women's organizations' activity should be shifted towards equality in the status of women in the workforce and in academia", a point supported by earlier research by Psacharopoulos (Polydorides, 1985; Psacharopoulos, 1980). The evidence presented in this paper leads to the following conclusions:

(a) The issue of educational equality of opportunity for women has followed a different path in Greece than that followed by equality of opportunity by social origin, both in terms of timing as well as structural pattern of evolution.

(b) Reinforcement of sex role stereotyping and parental social attitudes as well as cultural socialization do not appear to have unduly hindered equality of opportunity by gender. Where these do play a role they can lead to more equality of access at the level of higher education.

(c) Although self-esteem tends to be lower in women, their better achievement levels counteract that fact, so that the only viable explanation of girls' choice of type of academic track, or young women's choice of university field of study or occupation is the existence of feedback from the division of labour and the division of sex roles in society.

(d) Labour market differences in promotion and earnings patterns are not justified either by the level of qualification or productivity, so that it is sensible to assume that discrimination influences occupational and, indirectly, educational choice to a large degree.

Before concluding, it is useful to summarize the evidence with respect to the four points above.

(a) Structural changes in the Greek educational system have concentrated on the reform of the selection process for admission to higher education in two instances in recent years. In both instances, the major stated goals of these reforms included promoting greater equality in educational opportunity between the sexes and social classes. The evidence presented has shown that in the first recent educational reforms of 1964 the result has been a dramatic change in the distribution of university students by father's occupation (as a measure of social origin) and is clearly presented in Table 5.2. Longitudinal data on the distribution of students by gender indicate that no important differences in women's participation in higher education were brought about by these policy changes. In the second case, the 1980 changes in the selection process led to the reversal of sex differences in higher education and to the proportional representation of women in terms of the application as well as graduation rate. No significant changes by social origin were identified at this time. Thus the entrance examination, managed centrally and uniformly for all and compulsory up to 1982 for secondary school graduates, had fostered by 1980 a pattern by which (i) more women have been successful and (ii) their distribution by field of study is more equitable than before.

(b) These changes have occurred despite the fact that there were no specific policies in the 1970s to encourage women to stay in the educational system, to re-enter education, to choose fields of education traditionally dominated by men, or to reduce stereotyping in the content of textbooks as well as in the division between general and technical/vocational education, measures usually considered of paramount importance by such international organizations as the OECD in promoting equality of opportunity (Fragoudaki, 1985).

Parental and social attitudes, in so far as they have any influence over girls' choices in upper secondary education, result in the channelling of girls into general education. Consequently, girls are oriented towards either public sector office employment or higher education as a result of the "compulsory" character of the entrance examination. Equality of opportunity is therefore fostered at this higher education level.

It is important to stress at this point that the educational and social dynamic which made possible the visible changes in women's participation in higher education was independent and preceded the institutional establishment of and legal support for women's equal rights in education, family and work, created after 1981 in response to the 1975 EEC Directive and which resulted in the creation of the Council for Equity and Women's Rights.

(c) The increased economic activity of women has been mainly limited to traditional areas, as indicated by their increasing participation in the public sector and the teaching profession. Although girls do better both in school as well as in such male-dominated fields of university study as Science and Engineering, their achievement patterns do not appear to increase their self-esteem and consequently their participation in these fields. On the contrary, the limited spectrum of female participation in economic life appears to relate to the decision of large numbers of women to enter teaching, which partly reflects and reinforces the ideas prevalent in society about gender roles. The problems related to inequality in employment by gender are intertwined with the issue of women's unequal access to certain fields of study. The only likelihood of changing further women's perception of the function of education is by fostering an increase and wider dispersion in their participation in employment: for example, in the sectors of Computer Science and Management Studies.

(d) The differences in the positions held by women and men in the labour market and the differences in pay for equal work show that there is strong discrimination by gender in Greek economic life. The chapter has shown that girls do better than boys at school, while boys do worse in the entrance examination for higher education. Girls do better than boys in (at least) the first year of university studies, even in male-dominated fields. These facts indicate strongly that the differences observed are not justified by the level of qualification. Research into relative earnings shows that they are not justified by productivity either, since the difference observed cannot be attributed to the measurable data normally explaining such differences. Further, more occupational sectors dominated numerically by women are dominated administratively by men, even in cases where there exists a standardized promotion policy, as is the case in the public sector and the school system.

At university level women academics occupy lower staff positions and, although represented in proportion to their representation in university studies, they do not gain promotion at the same pace as men into higher staff positions.

If differences in qualifications and productivity cannot justify the observed differences in the hierarchical positions of men and women in the Greek division of labour, then discrimination becomes the alternative explanation. Such discrimination, be it direct or indirect, cannot be overcome by mere individual "efforts" of qualified women to occupy "male-dominated positions", despite the educational gains which women have achieved in higher education as part of a broader social dynamic. Women in Greece are, at the moment, supported in the ideological sphere by women's organizations and some state agencies. More specific employment policies are needed to give them the necessary "push" in order to achieve more equality in the occupational division of labour. It is only specific labour policies and positive feedback from the labour market that will encourage women to compete for and achieve more desirable university fields of specialization leading to equal occupational choices.

References

Directorate General of Public Administration (1971) Census of Public Servants, Athens, mimeographed document.

Eliou, M. (1978) Those whom reform forgot. *Comparative Education Review*, 22 (1), Tables 4 and 5, pp. 68–69.

Eliou, M. (1987) Equality of the sexes in education and now what? *Comparative Education*, 23 (1).

Eliou, M. (1988) Gender equality in education. In M. Eliou, *Educational and Social Dynamic*, 2nd ed. Athens: Poria, Table 2, p. 212 (in Greek).

Eliou, M. (1988) Women and Education. In M. Eliou, *Educational and Social Dynamic*, 2nd ed. Athens: Poria, p. 224.

Eliou, M. (1988) Women in the academic profession: evolution or stagnation? *Higher Education*, 17, pp. 505–534.

Fragoudaki, A. (1985) Inequality in the Greek school. In A. Fragoudaki *Sociology of Education*. Athens: Papazisis, pp. 197–200 (in Greek).

Kontogiannopoulou-Polydorides, G. (1987a) Conceptual content, empirical data and theory in the Sociology of Education. *The Greek Review of Social Research*, 64 (in Greek).

Kontogiannopoulou-Polydorides, G. (1987b) Conceptual definitions, empirical data and theory in the Sociology of Education. *The Greek Review of Social Research*, 64, Table 2, p. 8 (in Greek).

Kontogiannopoulou-Polydorides, G. (1989) Achievement at university. Research in progress, partially published in "The main characteristics of the entrance examination". In Kontogiannopoulou-Polydorides, *The transition from secondary to tertiary education*. Athens: Vervakion Alumni Association.

Ministry of Education (1985) Directorate for Planning and Operations Research, provisional data.

Ministry of Education (1986) Directorate for Planning and Operations Research, provisional data.

Ministry of Education (1989) Directorate for Planning and Operations Research, provisional data.

National Statistical Service of Greece (1980) *Statistics of Education*. Athens: NSGG.

National Statistical Service of Greece (1983) *Statistics of Education*. Athens: NSGG.

National Statistical Service of Greece (1988) *Statistics of Education*. Athens: NSGG.

OECD (1978) *Policies for Equal Opportunity for Women in the Economy*. Manpower and Social Affairs Committee. Paris: OECD, p. 31.

OECD (1980) *Educational Policy and Planning: Educational Reform Policies in Greece*. Paris: OECD.

OECD (1986) *Girls and Women in Education*. Paris: OECD.

Papas, G. and Psacharopoulos, G. (1987) The transition from school to the university under restricted entry: a Greek tracer study. *Higher Education*, 16 (4).

Polydorides, G. (1978) Equality of educational opportunity in the Greek education system: the impact of reform policies. *Comparative Education Review*, 22, 1.

Polydorides, G. (1984) School-based evaluation and external examinations in the Greek educational system. ERIC report ED 247252, *RIE* December.

Polydorides, G. (1985) Women's participation in the Greek educational system. *Comparative Education*, **21** (3), Table IV, p. 232.

Psacharopoulos, G. (1980) *Sex discrimination in the labour market.* Paper presented at the Modern Greek Studies Association Symposium. Philadelphia, Pennsylvania, November 14–16.

Statistics of Public Sector Employees 1973–1978, mimeographed document.

Vernava-Stoura, T. Z. (1989) Cognitive development in primary school. In T. Z. Vernava-Stoura, *Issues in Cognitive Development, Learning and Evaluation.* Athens: Papazisis (in Greek).

Notes

1. Eliou questions the effectiveness of achieving gender equality by itself, while Fragoudaki queries (on the basis of 1978 data) whether equality has in fact been achieved within higher education, arguing that the educational system reproduces social inequality and gender inequality in society at large.
2. OECD (1988) *Policies for Equal Opportunity for Women in the Economy*, Manpower and Social Affairs Committee. Paris: OECD, p. 31. This report states: "Whether the success of women is measured by entrance into professional schools in industrialized countries or high school enrolment in development societies, women are now taking advantage of education to improve their social and economic positions in unprecedented numbers . . ."

CHAPTER 6

Republic of Ireland

KATHLEEN LYNCH

Formal education in the Republic of Ireland takes place in three separate phases. Primary education begins at the age of four and continues for a minimum of eight years until the age of twelve. From the age of twelve all pupils are entitled to enter the second-level system, although pupils may be over the age of twelve on leaving primary education. Second-level education is of five years duration, roughly from the age of twelve or thirteen to seventeen or eighteen. At seventeen, pupils who are suitably qualified may then enter third-level education (i.e. the universities and other institutes of higher education). Attendance at formal education is compulsory up to the age of fifteen. At present, approximately two-thirds of the age cohort complete second-level education (Clancy, 1989), while 25 per cent go on to higher education (Clancy, 1988, p. 71).

The position of women in Irish education is, in a number of respects, a contradictory one. While girls have attained higher aggregate grades in major public examinations than boys (Department of Education, 1983; Greaney and Kellaghen, 1984, p. 180; Clancy, 1987, p. 13) and while they are more likely to stay on to complete second-level education than their male counterparts – in 1966, for example, 55.7 per cent of seventeen and eighteen-year-olds in second-level education were girls (Department of Education, 1985–1986, p. 5, Table 3.2) – nonetheless, males slightly outnumber females in third-level education and greatly outnumber them in the increasingly expanding technological sectors of higher education (Department of Education, 1985–1986, p. 2; Clancy, 1988, pp. 17, 18).

To comprehend the contradictory position of women in education, one needs to examine their position within other social institutions within the state. The chapter begins therefore by outlining the economic and social position of women in Irish society. Following this an analysis of gender differences in educational participation is undertaken. Gender differences in curricular choice and educational attainment are then examined in detail. The chapter goes on to review the position of women teachers in Irish education; finally, it presents an analysis of gender differences in school ethos and highlights the need for further research on the relationship between gender and social class.

The Economic and Social Position of Women in Irish Society

Under the Irish Constitution a woman's place is clearly defined as being in the home. Indeed, it is implicit in the relevant article of the Constitution that womanhood and motherhood are synonymous:

1. In particular, the State recognises that by her life within the home, *woman** gives to the State a support without which the common good cannot be achieved.
2. The State shall, therefore, endeavour to ensure that *mothers** shall not be obliged by economic necessity to engage in labour to the neglect of their duties in the home. (Article 41.2) (*Emphasis by author.)

While there has been no legislation passed giving parliamentary expression to the aforesaid Article, the fact remains that only 26.4 per cent of married women were in the labour force, compared with an average of 41.6 per cent in other EC countries in 1986 (Blackwell, 1989, Table 3.8). Women's dependence on men within marriage is therefore not just a constitutional prescription; it is an economic reality. That dependency takes on an even more problematic meaning when one realizes that divorce is prohibited under the Constitution. With relatively high unemployment, at approximately 18 per cent of the population, no state-funded child-care facilities (McKenna, 1988) and no divorce, most married women with children are locked into a state of economic subordination to men, whether they wish it or not.

To suggest that the position of women in Irish society is one of unbridled subservience to men would, however, be far from true. Over the last twenty-five years major social and economic changes have occurred in Ireland which have advantaged women in several ways. The most obvious economic development which occurred was that Ireland changed from being a predominantly rural society, largely dependent on farming, to being an urban-industrial society, highly dependent on manufacturing and service industries. Industrial expansion led to increased job opportunities for women. Married women, in particular, became much more active in the labour force. From Table 6.1 below one can see that women comprised a noticeably larger proportion of the labour force in 1988 (30.5 per cent) than they did seventeen years previously (25.7 per cent). Also, married women's participation, though still low by international standards, was much greater in 1988 than it was in 1971: while married women comprised only 13.6 per cent of the female labour force in 1971 they constituted 41.3 per cent in 1988. With greater labour force participation came greater financial independence – at least for those who were in paid employment.

One cannot exaggerate the significance of labour force gains for women however. Women still dominate the part-time labour market: 69 per cent of all part-time workers are women (CSO, 1989, p. 13). Vertical segregation is also very much in evidence: a study by McCarthy (1988, Table 1) of forty-six companies in 1972 and 1983 found that only 11 per cent of senior management and professional posts were held by women in 1983. This represented a slight improvement from 1972 when 9.5 per cent of these posts were occupied by

TABLE 6.1

Changes in Women's Labour Force Participation from 1971 to 1988

Labour Force (LF)	1971	1981	1988
Total	1,125,400[a]	1,272,000	1,309,800
Total Women	289,300	370,000	399,500
Women as % of Total	25.7	29.1	30.5
Married women[b] in LF			
Total	39,200	112,000	164,800
As % of Female LF	13.6	30.2	41.3

[a] Figures are rounded.

[b] Includes separated and divorced women. In 1988, 9,200 (2.3%) of the total 399,500 women in the Labour Force were separated or divorced.

Sources: John Blackwell *Women in The Labour Force*, Dublin: Employment Equality Agency (1989), Table 3.1 and Central Statistics Office, *Labour Force Survey 1988*, Dublin: Central Statistics Office (CSO) (1989), Table 11.

women. In addition, few women are employers – 87.3 per cent of employers are men – yet women predominate in the employee sector at 68.4 per cent (CSO, 1989, Table 21). Men also control the land with 93.2 per cent of all agricultural workers, mostly farmers, being male, while women remain unpaid workers engaged in home duties – 99.5 per cent of those engaged in home duties are female (CSO, 1989, Tables 20 and 9). As is the case internationally, horizontal sex segregation also occurs in the labour market: 74.2 per cent of all clerical workers are female while men predominate in manufacturing as producers, makers and repairers at 83.1 per cent (CSO, 1989, Table 20). Indeed, recent data shows that two occupational groups account for over half the women at paid work in Ireland, 28.4 per cent of all women working are clerical workers, while 24.6 per cent are professional and technical workers, mostly nurses and teachers (CSO, 1989). Finally, as is true in many countries, women's earnings are considerably less than those of men. The average hourly earnings of women across all industry is 67.1 per cent of those of men (Blackwell, 1989, p. 48).

While labour market gains for women have been fairly slight in recent years, there have been some legislative advances. It was, however, the EC directives of the 1970s and Ireland's accession to a UN Convention which precipitated the enactment of legislative changes beneficial to women. The Anti-Discrimination (Pay) Act, 1974, the Employment Equality Act, 1977, the Unfair Dismissals Act, 1977, and the Social Welfare (No. 2) Act, 1985, were all passed in response to EC Directives (Department of the Taoiseach, 1987, p. 25). It was Ireland's accession to the 1985 UN Convention on the "Elimination of All Forms of Discrimination Against Women" that precipitated the enactment of the Irish Nationality and Citizenship Act, 1986 and the Domicile and Recognition of Foreign Divorces Act, 1986, both of which gave greater rights to married women. Were it not for EC membership in particular, it is doubtful if much of this legislation would have been passed; in 1975, for example, the Irish government sought a derogation from the Anti-Discrimination (Pay) Act and attempted to delay its implementation. This is not to deny the important work done by the Irish women's movement in pressing for social and political reform over the last twenty years. However, even members of the women's movement have admitted that many of their efforts to promote women's rights have met with limited success (Barry, 1988; Smyth, 1988).

One of the areas where there has been some advancement is in the establishment of structures and in the formulation of policies at a centralized government level to promote equal opportunities. A Commission on the Status of Women (1970) paved the way for the formation of the Council for the Status of Women (CSW) in 1973. The latter functions to co-ordinate the work of women's organizations, to examine and contest discrimination against women, and to consider legislative proposals concerning women. At present the CWS has almost fifty affiliated members. The Employment Equality Agency was established in 1977 and has done much to promote the awareness and practice of equal opportunities policies in the work place. A further encouraging development in 1982 was the appointment of a Minister of State at the Department of the Taoiseach (the Prime Minister) who is responsible for promoting action on women's affairs. At the policy level, the government has formally adopted policies for promoting equal opportunities between men and women in employment, legislation and education. The Department of Education, for example, has specific responsibility for the elimination of sexism and sex stereotyping in the education sector (Department of the Taoiseach, 1987).

While several legislative changes have guaranteed Irish women equal rights with men, these legislative changes have precipitated few changes in the socio-economic status of women: women still constitute a majority of those in the part-time labour market, and of those engaged in home duties. They are far less likely to be employers than men and those who are employees tend to earn less than their male colleagues. However, as the work of McCarthy (1988) and Blackwell (1989) shows, women have been making slight gains in recent years – there are considerably more married women working at present than there were in the early 1970s and women are also slightly more likely to be in senior management positions than they were then.

The Irish Education System

Patterns of Participation and Control

Figure 6.1 below gives an overview of the structure and control of the formal

Level	Duration	Age of Pupils/Students	Control and Type	Examinations	Fee/Non Fee
Primary (Compulsory)	8 years	4–12 years	National schools jointly owned by Church and State: all but 6 are denominationally managed, mostly by Roman Catholic (R.C.) authorities; 98.1% of all primary schools are state aided.	No formal examinations but records are kept of a pupil's performance over his/her primary career.	No fees in 98.1% of schools
Second Level (Compulsory up to age 15)	5 years	12–17/18 years	Four Types Secondary: privately owned and controlled (mostly by R.C. religious orders) but state aided (63.8% of 2nd level pupils). Vocational: entirely state owned and controlled (24.6% of pupils). Community: jointly owned by the state+R.C. religious orders. Controlled by a Board representing the state, religious orders, teachers and parents. Comprehensive: owned by the state and controlled by the state+religious representatives (the latter are Catholic or Protestant depending on the school). (C.+C. combined – 11.6% of pupils).	Junior Certificate[a] (after 3 years) Leaving Certificate (at the end of 2nd level – 5 years)	No fees in 92.7% of schools
Third Level	3 or 4 years for basic degree	17/18 years at entry	All state aided } Universities, Colleges of Education, Colleges of Technology, Regional Technical Colleges, Art Colleges	Variety of degrees and diplomas	All fee paying but grants for low-income students

[a] The Junior Certificate has replaced the Intermediate Certificate for 1989 onwards.

education system in the Republic of Ireland. From this one can see that almost all Irish primary school children attend publicly funded national schools, but that there are a few exceptions, such as denominationally managed schools run mostly by the Roman Catholic authorities. At second level, denominational education persists, particularly in the dominant secondary sector (64 per cent of all pupils are in the secondary sector). Not only is there a strong tradition of denominational education in Ireland, there is also a strong tradition of single-sex education. Just over half the pupils at second level are in single-sex schools and almost 40 per cent of those in primary are in either totally, or mostly single-sex schools (i.e. with co-education in infant classes only), as Table 6.2 below shows.

TABLE 6.2

Distribution of Pupils between Single-Sex and Co-Educational Schools at First and Second Level

Type of School Attended	First Level (Primary) (Age 4–12)		Second Level (Age 12–18)	
	No. of Pupils	% of Pupils	No. of Pupils	% of Pupils
Co-Educational	336,233	60.5	170,491	50.4
Single-Sex	156,332	28.1	168,042	49.6
Single-Sex but has co-education in infants (i.e. for the first 2 years)	63,555	11.4	Not applicable	
Total	556,120	100.0	338,533	100.0

Source: Department of Education, *Statistical Report* (1986–1987), Table 6, p. 15 and Table 6, p. 38.

Girls are, however, more likely than boys to attend single-sex schools at second level – 53.5 per cent of all girls in second level are in single sex schools compared with 45.6 per cent of boys (Department of Education, 1986–1987, Table 6, p. 38). This difference reflects a parental preference for single-sex education for adolescent girls, as Irish parents are free – within the limits of their income – to send their children to the school of their choice. There are no real gender differences in co-educational participation at the primary level. Girls are also more likely than boys to attend secondary schools, which are the least technically oriented schools in terms of curricula; 69.7 per cent of all girls at second level are in secondary schools compared with 57.6 per cent of boys (Department of Education, 1986–1987).

Gender differences are also evident in patterns of educational participation. From Table 6.3 we can see that while females have a higher participation rate at second level than males, this advantage is lost at third level where males outnumber females.

Recent research by Clancy (1988, p. 68) indicates, however, that the

TABLE 6.3

Female/Male Participation Rates at the three Major Education Levels

	Females		Males	
	No. of Pupils/ Students	% of Pupils/ Students	No. of Pupils/ Students	% of Pupils/ Students
First Level 4–12 years (approx.)	279,993	48.6	296,308	51.4
Second Level 12–17/18 years (approx.)	174,751	51.1	166.930	48.9
Third Level (17/18 and over approx.)	26,034	46.0	30,545	54.0
Total	480,778		493,783	

Source: Department of Education, *Statistical Report* (1986–1987), Table 1.

male/female balance is becoming more equitable as 48 per cent of the *entrants* to higher education in 1986 were women. His data comparing female participation in higher education over a thirty year period also gives some cause for hope. While women comprised only 27.4 per cent of full-time higher education students in 1955–1956 and 29.4 per cent in 1965–1966, by 1986–1987 they comprised 46 per cent – a very significant increase. He suggests that if present growth rates continue females will shortly constitute a majority of new entrants to higher education (Clancy, 1989, p. 1).

Curricular Options

All Irish pupils pursue the same curriculum at primary level. It comprises Irish, English, Mathematics, Social and Environmental Studies, Arts and Crafts, Music, Physical Education and Religion. This is not to suggest that boys and girls have identical educational experiences. Although no major research has yet been undertaken on pupils' experiences in primary schools, (such as research on textbooks and teacher behaviour), evidence from other countries would suggest that gender differences are likely to be common at the classroom level (Council of Europe, 1982; Marland, 1983; Stanworth, 1983). Evidence from the *Teacher's Handbook* for Primary Teachers certainly indicates that sexism is alive and well in the official guidelines given to teachers. With regard to the teaching of music the Handbook suggests that:

While a large number of songs are suited to both boys and girls, some songs are particularly suited to boys, e.g. martial, gay, humorous, rhythmic airs. Others are more suited to girls, e.g. lullabies, spinning songs, songs tender in content and expression. (p. 213).

Evidence of sexism is also clearly in evidence in the section dealing with Physical Education. In senior primary classes the Handbook suggests that:

. . . separate training in movement training may be made for boys and girls. Boys can now acquire a wide variety of skills and techniques and girls often become more aware of style and grace. Control and resiliency become more important. (p. 310).

At second level, pupils pursue a core curriculum up to the completion of the junior certificate examination, at the age of approximately fifteen years. The core varies slightly with school type. Irish, English and Mathematics are compulsory Junior Certificate subjects, in all types of second-level schools. In addition History and Geography are compulsory in secondary schools plus two other subjects from the prescribed list of twenty subjects. In community, comprehensive and vocational schools, students can take either Art, Commerce, Mechanical Drawing or Home Economics (in conjunction with Irish, English and Mathematics) plus two other subjects from the prescribed list. For the senior cycle Leaving Certificate Examination, Irish is the only compulsory subject out of a total of thirty-one subjects. One can see therefore that science is not a core subject for either boys or girls and that schools and pupils (depending on school size especially) have considerable latitude in their choice of subject options.

The freedom given to schools in curriculum provision and timetabling, especially at senior level, has resulted in very noticeable gender differences in both the availability and take up of particular subjects (Hannan *et al.*, 1983). As Table 6.4 below shows, technical subjects (such as Mechanical Drawing and Woodwork at junior level and Technical Drawing, Engineering and Construction Studies at senior level) are rarely available as options for girls: single sex girls' schools simply do not offer these, while timetabling within co-educational schools usually means that girls are excluded. Boys, on the other hand, are rarely given the option of doing Home Economics.

In terms of the Sciences and Mathematics gender differences have been reduced considerably in recent years. As can be seen from Table 6.5 below, 89.3 per cent of girls' schools offered higher course Mathematics at Leaving Certificate level in 1986–1987 and 72.6 per cent offered Physics compared with 73.9 per cent and 34.8 per cent offering higher Mathematics and Physics respectively in 1980–1981. The number of girls' schools offering Physics has more than doubled therefore in a short six-year period, while the proportion offering higher Mathematics and Chemistry is now almost equal to that of boys' schools. Within co-educational schools also, most schools now offer the Sciences and Mathematics equally to both sexes as Table 6.4 shows.

What has been happening to some extent is a certain levelling out of sex differences in subject provision apart from the provision of practical/technical subjects. From Table 6.5 one can see, for example, that boys' schools have increased their senior cycle provision of what may be defined as the more typically female subjects – Biology, Home Economics and History – while improving their science provision at the same time, though not at the same rate as girls' schools. The increased provision of subjects such as Biology and Home Economics (and within the year of 1989–1990, of German) in boys' schools shows that there has been some, albeit slight, movement of male schools into the "female subject world".

Changes in Irish second-level education are not confined to the area of

TABLE 6.4

The Relationship between the Gender Mix in Schools and the Availability of a Selected Range of Subjects

Subjects	Single Sex Schools Proportion Offering the Subjects		Co-educational Schools Proportion Offering Subjects		
	Boys' Schools	Girls' Schools	To Boys[a] only	To Girls only	To Both Sexes
At Intermediate Certificate Level	%	%	%	%	%
Mathematics (Higher Course)	89.8	95.1	2.6	0.0	97.4
French	96.8	99.5	0.8	1.3	97.9
German	13.9	48.0	0.0	5.5	94.5
Science A	94.1	89.7	1.9	1.3	96.8
Woodwork	56.7	0.5	54.3	0.3	45.4
Mechanical Drawing	75.4	1.0	37.3	0.0	62.7
Home Economics	1.6	97.5	0.0	46.5	53.5
At Leaving Certificate Level					
Mathematics (Higher Course)	92.0	89.3	11.9	1.0	87.1
French	96.6	100.0	0.3	5.4	94.3
German	16.1	46.7	9.1	12.7	78.2
Physics	93.1	72.6	13.7	0.0	86.3
Chemistry	92.0	88.3	4.4	0.5	95.1
Home Economics (Scientific and Social)	11.5	95.4	0.0	39.0	61.0
Technical Drawing	57.5	1.5	67.2	0.0	32.8
Engineering	13.2	0.0	85.9	0.4	13.7

[a] Management bodies in Irish second-level schools exercise a high level of autonomy in internal matters including timetabling (Hannan *et al.* 1983). They are free to offer a subject to one particular sex if they wish and some still do especially in the technical area and in home economics.
Source: Department of Education, *Statistical Reports*, Intermediate Certificate 1985–1986, Leaving Certificate 1986–1987.

curricular provision. As Table 6.6 shows many changes are also occurring in the uptake of particular subjects. Overall *both* boys and girls are moving out of the Arts, Humanities and certain languages into the Sciences especially and, to a lesser degree, into business subjects. Boys are moving into the practical/technological subjects as well (excluding Home Economics) but girls are not. The move out of the Arts and Humanities is especially noticeable among girls: in 1985–1986 only one-third of Leaving Certificate girls were studying Geography and only 28.7 per cent were studying History compared with 73.7 per cent studying Geography in 1972–1973 and 42.1 per cent studying History. The drop in the proportion of boys taking History and Geography over the same period was from 45.3 per cent to 35.3 per cent and from 70 per cent to 39.9 per cent respectively.

What is also interesting to note from Table 6.6, in terms of the breaking

TABLE 6.5

Proportion of Single-Sex Schools Offering Particular Subjects to Leaving Certificate Pupils in 1980/1981 and in 1986/1987

	Girls' Schools		Boys' Schools	
	1980–1981	1986–1987	1980–1981	1986–1987
	%	%	%	%
Mathematics (Higher)	73.9	89.3	91.7	92.0
Physics	34.8	72.6	79.2	93.1
Chemistry	73.9	88.3	83.3	92.0
Biology	100.0	98.5	75.0	88.5
History	95.7	99.5	84.0	95.4
Technical Drawing	0.0	1.5	33.3	57.5
Home Economics (Scientific and Social)	95.7	95.4	4.2	11.5

Sources: The 1980–1981 figures are taken from D. Hannan *et al.*, *Schooling and Sex Roles*, Dublin: Economic and Social Research Institute (1983), Table 5.7. The 1986–1987 figures are taken from the Department of Education *Statistical Report* (1986–1987), Table 14.5, p. 48.

down of traditional gender-specific subject choices, is the extent to which female participation in most of the business subjects has kept pace with that of boys from 1972 to 1986, while their rate of involvement in the sciences has grown dramatically – albeit from a low starting base – especially in subjects like Physics.

The reduction of gender differences in the provision, allocation and choice of Leaving Certificate subjects has not resulted, of course, in the elimination of gender differences in the take-up of particular sex-typed subjects. Boys still predominate in the Sciences (with the exception of Biology) while girls predominate in Art, Music and in the European languages of French, German and Spanish.

What Hannan *et al.* (1983, p. 154) observed from their major study of sex differences and education some years ago still holds true:

Although there are differences between the sexes in provision and allocation in the subjects we analysed, these differences are ... less than sex differences in the true rate of choice. In other words, the sex difference in pupils' own choices was greater than in either the provision or allocation of subjects to them. This finding suggests that simply increasing the provision or allocation of a subject to whichever sex ... will not automatically lead to a substantial reduction in the sex differences in take-up.

Overcoming the cultural barriers that discourage pupils from choosing non-traditional subjects for their particular sex is still a major task for those wishing to eliminate gender inequalities arising from curricular choices.

Given the pattern of subject take-up in second-level schools, it is not surprising to find that girls continue to dominate the entrants to the Arts and Humanities in higher education and are poorly represented in the technological fields. From Table 6.7 below we see that only 14.7 per cent of all entrants to the technological fields are female, while 63.9 per cent of entrants to the

TABLE 6.6

Changes in Subject Participation in The Senior Cycle Between 1972–1973 and 1985–1986: Proportion of the Leaving Certificate (L.C.) Cohort taking each Subject

Subjects	1972–1973[a]		1985–1986[b]	
	Girls	Boys	Girls	Boys
	%	%	%	%
Language Subjects				
Irish	97.9	96.5	90.1	89.1
English	99.6	97.8	91.8	90.1
French	58.6	33.0	72.1	47.8
Spanish	10.7	4.4	2.2	1.2
German	3.1	1.4	5.1	2.0
Italian	0.6	0.3	0.1	0.2
Latin	27.7	42.9	0.7	3.0
Greek	0.0	0.7	0.01	0.1
Hebrew	0.03	0.02	0.02	0.01
Arts, Humanities				
History	42.1	45.3	28.7	35.3
Geography	73.7	70.0	32.7	39.9
Art	29.1	14.9	22.7	12.3
Music	3.8	0.5	5.5	1.1
Classical Studies	– Not offered –		0.2	0.4
Practical/Technological				
Home Economics (general)	51.4	0.2	11.9	0.3
Engineering	0.0	5.1	0.2	14.0
Technical Drawing	0.001	8.6	0.5	28.6
Construction Studies	0.0	5.5	0.2	16.8
Sciences/Applied Sciences				
Mathematics	78.2	97.1	98.9	99.2
Applied Mathematics	0.05	4.4	0.4	4.0
Physics	1.9	22.3	9.4	33.0
Chemistry	7.6	30.5	16.0	25.3
Biology	28.6	21.1	65.5	37.4
Physics and Chemistry	2.0	7.4	2.3	4.4
Agricultural Science	0.1	4.3	1.1	7.0
Home Economics (Scientific and Social)	3.8	0.1	45.8	5.3
Business Subjects				
Accounting	21.0	17.6	27.4	24.3
Business Organization	23.0	19.1	34.8	29.3
Economics	12.3	21.9	11.2	21.1
Economic History	1.0	1.2	0.2	0.7
Agricultural Economics	0.0	0.9	0.3	1.1

[a] 1972–1973 Figures are based on the number who sat the Leaving Certificate Examination in 1973. They refer, therefore, to *one year's* cohort. In 1973, 13,449 girls and 11,831 boys sat the Leaving Certificate Examination.

[b] 1985–1986 Figures are based on the entire senior cycle student body studying for the Leaving Certificate. They refer, therefore, to the entire two year Leaving Certificate cohort. In 1985–1986, 53,948 girls and 48,817 boys were studying for the Leaving Certificate.

Source: Department of Education, *Statistical Reports 1972/73 and 1985/86*. Dublin: Government Publications Office.

TABLE 6.7

*Distribution of All New Entrants to Higher Education by Gender and Representation
of Women within Each Field of Study in 1986*

	Males	Females	Total		Representation of Women
	%	%	No. of Students	% of all Students	%
Humanities (including Arts)	10.9	21.2	2,720	15.9	63.9
Arts and Design	2.4	5.7	683	4.0	67.9
Science	12.9	16.6	2,531	14.8	54.2
Agriculture	2.3	0.7	265	1.5	23.0
Technology	40.4	7.6	4,240	24.7	14.7
Medical Sciences	3.2	4.1	626	3.7	53.8
Education	2.8	8.1	916	5.3	72.6
Law	1.4	1.8	273	1.6	53.5
Social Science	1.8	5.9	639	3.7	75.0
Commerce	20.7	24.0	3,817	22.3	51.5
Hotel, Catering and Tourism	1.2	4.2	449	2.6	76.8
Total %	100.0	100.0	–	100.0	47.8
No.	8,964	8,195	17,159	–	–

Source: Clancy (1989), Table 5.

Humanities and Arts and 75 per cent of entrants to Social Science are female. What is interesting to note from this table however, is that women now constitute a higher proportion of entrants to the Sciences (including the Medical Sciences) than men. Given that the entry requirements for these faculties are not dissimilar from those required from the technological fields, namely, a good mathematics and scientific background in the Leaving Certificate, it is clear that girls are eligible for many of the technological courses on offer. Few choose to opt for these. It must be borne in mind, however, that while female participation in the technological field is still very low, it is considerably higher now than it was in the past. Nine per cent of university students in the field of technology were female in 1980, while there were no females in this area in 1950 (Clancy, 1989, Table 4). Similarly, 14.8 per cent of new entrants to engineering were female in 1984–1985 compared with 5.1 per cent in 1975–1976 (Higher Education Authority, 1975–1976, 1984–1985).

Educational Attainment

In accordance with their child-centred philosophy, Irish primary schools do not require pupils to sit any major public examinations. There is therefore little known about gender differences in educational attainment up to the age of twelve. A recent study of 2,000 thirteen-year-olds in the fields of Mathematics and Science only was conducted by the US-based Educational

Testing Service (ETS) in conjunction with the Educational Research Centre (Dublin). It found no significant difference between boys and girls in Mathematics performance but there were significant differences in the field of Science, boys performing significantly better (ETS, 1989, pp. 19, 40). Data available from second-level public examinations (Leaving Certificate, 1983) also suggested that boys out-perform girls in certain science subjects notably in the higher courses in Physics and Chemistry. However, girls performed better in the lower courses in these subjects, in higher course Mathematics, and in both higher and lower courses in combined Biology and Physics and Chemistry, as Table 6.8 below shows.

TABLE 6.8

Gender Differences in Performance in a Selected Range of Science Subjects and Mathematics in the Leaving Certificate Examination 1983

Subject	Higher Course % Awarded Grade C or higher		Lower Course % Awarded Grade C or higher	
	Girls	Boys	Girls	Boys
Mathematics	67.9	62.2	43.4	49.9
Physics	54.4	62.6	65.3	50.8
Chemistry	61.2	66.5	74.3	50.1
Physics and Chemistry combined	76.8	69.3	46.7	38.1
Biology	59.0	55.3	43.4	42.6

Source: Department of Education (1983) Published Leaving Certificate Results.

The problem with these figures, of course, is that they only apply to one particular cohort of students. Earlier research by Hannan *et al.* (1983, pp. 290, 291) for example, suggested that at the intermediate level (higher courses) girls tend to perform less well than boys in both Mathematics and Science. Girls' aggregate score (namely, combining ordinary and higher level papers) in Leaving Certificate Mathematics was also lower than that of boys in 1981 – the year in which Hannan *et al*'s study was undertaken (Brennan, 1986, p. 134). A more systematic analysis of student performance in the Mathematics and Science areas would need to be undertaken, therefore, before one could say definitely what the precise gender differentials are. The indications to date seem to be, however, that boys perform better in Science and, but to a lesser degree, in Mathematics.

Girls perform more highly than boys however in the languages area. Brennan's (1986) analysis of Hannan's data shows girls performing more highly than boys in Irish and English in the Leaving Certificate in 1981. The 1983 Leaving Certificate results show a similar pattern in a range of language subjects, with the exception of higher course German, as Table 6.9 illustrates.

In terms of aggregate performance in public examinations, research

TABLE 6.9

*Gender differences in Performance in a Selected Range of Languages in the Leaving
Certificate Examination 1983*

Subject	Higher Course % Awarded Grade C or higher		Lower Course % Awarded Grade C or higher	
	Girls	Boys	Girls	Boys
Irish	68.2	61.4	49.4	34.3
English	58.1	50.2	36.9	33.7
French	56.4	50.0	56.0	49.6
German	63.0	69.2	66.1	59.7
Italian	79.2	75.0	71.4	44.4
Spanish	69.8	60.1	38.8	34.4

Source: Department of Education, Leaving Certificate Results (1983).

indicates that girls tend to do better overall. In his analysis of the Leaving
Certificate results for 1980 Clancy found that a higher proportion of girls
obtained Grade C or higher in sixteen of the twenty-nine subjects taken by
both sexes (1989). In my own analysis of the Leaving Certificate results of 1983
I also found that girls got higher grades in more subjects than boys; while there
were fourteen higher course subjects in which more boys obtained Grade C or
higher, there were fourteen other higher course subjects in which more girls
attained Grade C or higher. In the lower courses, however, girls attained high
grades (C or higher) in considerably more subjects than boys, seventeen
compared with eight among the boys. Clancy (1989) has also observed that the
girls entering higher education in 1986 had performed more highly on the
Leaving Certificate than boys, while an earlier study by Greaney and
Kellaghan (1984, p. 180) found girls' aggregate score on the Leaving
Certificate to be higher than that of boys.

If one is to take the level of degree awarded as a measure of performance in
higher education, then women do not achieve quite as highly as their male
colleagues, although the differences are not great and appear to be declining.
In 1983, 1984 and 1985 women constituted 37.9 per cent, 38.1 per cent and 39.6
per cent of those obtaining first, upper second or undifferentiated second class
honours degrees although they comprised 44 per cent, 44.1 per cent and 44.3
per cent of those obtaining degrees in the respective years (Clancy, 1989,
Table 6). Women also constitute a minority among masters degree and
doctoral graduates: only 36 per cent of masters degree graduates and 29.2 per
cent of doctoral graduates were women in 1985 (Clancy, 1989, Table 6).

Overall, the pattern of performance which we observe among women in
education is an uneven one. While girls perform more highly than their male
colleagues in the Leaving Certificate and have higher grades on entering
higher education, they do not seem to retain this advantage within higher

education. In particular, they are considerably less likely than males to pursue higher degrees despite their favourable academic record. It would seem, therefore, that women "choose" (for whatever reasons), not to maximize their educational potential, rather than being forced out of the system due to low performance.

Women in Education: The Teachers

When examining the position of women in the teaching profession in Ireland, it is important to distinguish between lay and religious female and male teachers. Religious teachers, i.e. nuns, priests and brothers, do not compete for posts in the open labour market. Due to their controlling interest in a majority of secondary, and a number of primary schools, religious are given senior positions within these without having to compete with outsiders.

When one excludes religious women, one can see that women are seriously under-represented at the most senior management levels in schools, the position of women in second-level schools being particularly bad.

Table 6.10 below shows that while 75.5 per cent of primary teachers are women only 37.9 per cent of principalships are held by women. Women are, however, well represented in the less senior posts of vice-principal and privileged assistant. In second-level, although lay women comprise 46.4 per cent of teachers in secondary, community and comprehensive schools, they only hold 6.2 per cent of principalships (see Table 6.11); in the vocational sector they comprise 41.2 per cent of the teaching force and 4.8 per cent of the principals. While women in secondary, community and comprehensive schools are reasonably well represented in vice-principalships and A posts, they are very poorly represented in these posts in the vocational sector.

What causes particular concern about these figures is that there does not appear to be any major change in the distribution of male and female teachers occurring. Data collected by Kellaghan, Fontes, O'Toole and Egan (1985) in 1981 shows that the proportion of men and women holding primary school principalships has not changed over the eight years in between: in 1981 7.8 per cent of women and 38.7 per cent of men were principals (Kellaghan *et al.*, 1985, p. 25); the corresponding figures in 1988–1989 were 7.6 per cent of women and 38.3 per cent of men. At second-level, data on the community and comprehensive schools *alone*, which have been the most rapidly expanding schools for the last fifteen years, shows that very few women have been appointed at senior level in these schools since they opened. In 1985–1986, 95 per cent of principalships in these schools, 79 per cent of the vice-principalships, 69 per cent of the A posts and 56 per cent of the B posts were held by men, although women constituted 48 per cent of the staff at the time (Answer to a Parliamentary question given to the Teachers' Union of Ireland). One of the major known problems at primary level, at least, is the low proportion of female applicants for principalships. In 1985 and 1986 only 31.5

TABLE 6.10

The Distribution of Senior Posts between Men and Women in Primary Schools in 1988–1989

Gender[a]	Principalships (Both Types)		Vice-Principalships		Privileged Assistants[b]		A Posts[c]		B posts[c]	
	N	%	N	%	N	%	N	%	N	%
Female	1092	37.9	1481	83.2	268	80.7	176	65.9	1218	73.8
Male	1788	62.1	298	16.8	64	19.3	91	34.1	433	26.2
Total	2880	100.0	1779	100.0	332	100.0	267	100.0	1651	100.0

[a] These figures refer only to lay teachers as these comprise 95% of the teaching force. In all there are 19,077 lay teachers, of whom 14,404 (75.5%) are female and 4673 (24.5%) are male.
[b] These were posts created when small schools were amalgamated. The dominance of women shows that the men got the principalships in the new schools while the former female principals became privileged assistants.
[c] In primary schools these are allocated largely on the basis of seniority.
Source: Department of Education (1989).

TABLE 6.11

The Distribution of Senior Posts between Men and Women in Second Level Schools Secondary and Community and Comprehensive Schools
1988–1989

Gender		Principalships N	%	Vice-Principalships N	%	A Posts[b] N	%	B posts[b] N	%
Female	Lay	35	6.2	222	39.8	890	42.1	2049	48.5
	Religious	235	42.0	8	1.4	37	1.7	110	2.6
Sub-Total Female (%)			(48.2)		(41.2)		(43.8)		(51.1)
Male	Lay	151	27.0	324	58.1	1171	55.4	2019	47.8
	Religious	139	24.8	4	0.7	17	0.8	46	1.1
Total		560	100.0	558	100.0	2115	100.0	4224	100.0

Total number of Teachers in 1988–1989 = 14,035 comprising 6511 (46.4%) female lay, 992 (7.1%) female religious, 5,964 (42.5%) male lay, 568 (4.0%) male religious.

Vocational Schools 1985–1986[a]

Gender	Principalships N	%	Vice-Principalships N	%	A Posts[b] N	%	B posts[b] N	%
Female	12	4.8	31	12.6	158	22.8	522	36.2
Male	238	95.2	216	87.4	534	77.2	921	63.8
Total	250	100.0	247	100.0	692	100.0	1443	100.0

Total number of teachers = 4,940, comprising 2,906 (58.8%) males and 2,034 (41.2%) females.
[a] Separate data for lay and religious teachers in vocational schools was not available, however, almost all teachers in these schools are lay persons.
[b] Allocated largely on the basis of seniority.
Source: Department of Education for Secondary, Community and Comprehensive schools (1989); Teachers' Union of Ireland (TUI) for Vocational Schools (1989).

per cent of the applicants for principalships were women. In both these years however, women who did apply for principalships fared well: 42 per cent of the posts were given to women in 1985 and 44.9 per cent in 1986 (Irish National Teachers' Organisation, *Central Executive Committee Report 1988*, p. 154). No published research has been conducted on the relationship between the gender of applicants and the distribution of senior posts in second-level schools.

The under-representation of women in senior posts at first and second level is even more exaggerated at third level. Smyth (1984) found that only one in every seventy-four university professors is a woman although women comprise 16 per cent of the full-time teaching staff in the university sector. Women are equally poorly represented at senior level in most other colleges of higher education: at the time of Smyth's study there were no female principals or senior lecturers in the eight surveyed higher education colleges controlled by the Vocational Education Committees (Smyth, 1984).

What must also cause concern is the male/female balance among new teacher appointees. Despite the fact that females constituted the great majority of graduates in education in 1987, 20 per cent of male graduates in both the primary and second-level sectors got permanent jobs in Ireland compared with 9 per cent of female graduates. By contrast 81 per cent of women graduates in primary and 82 per cent in second level got part-time or temporary jobs, the corresponding figures for men being 64 per cent and 65 per cent respectively (Higher Education Authority, 1988, Tables C and 4.1). Not only are women not getting senior posts, but they are less likely than their male colleagues to get one of the few permanent jobs available.

The low representation of women in senior positions in schools, particularly in what are the most publicly controlled schools in the country, namely the vocational (especially) and the community and comprehensive schools, merely reflects their subordinate position in public life generally. In 1986, out of a total of twenty-one secretaries or deputy secretaries in any of the government departments, none were women; only one (1.1 per cent) of the ninety-five assistant secretaries was female and twelve (4.5 per cent) of the 266 principal officers. Only six (7.2 per cent) of the eighty-three judges in the country are female, while women constitute only 10.4 per cent of the national/central executive members of the four main political parties (Department of the Taoiseach, 1987, pp. 52, 55, 57).

The Ethos of Schools

There are a variety of sociocultural and political factors which explain why women do not advance as well as men in schools – either as students or as teachers – despite their high performance. Hannan *et al.* (1983) have shown how girls in schools suffer adversely from low teacher expectations while Kellaghan *et al.* (1985) show how female teachers are adversely affected in their promotional prospects by multiple role responsibilities, lack of child-care services, negative self-images and discriminatory selection procedures.

Many of the factors which help explain women's seemingly contradictory location in education (high academic performance combined with low representation in technological courses and in the more prestigious programmes and posts) have, however, little to do with schooling *per se*. Where schools do seem to play a role is in the ethos they provide for their male and female pupils.

In a national study of the hidden curriculum of second-level schools Lynch (1989a, 1989b) found that boys' and girls' schools differ considerably in their social climates. In the extracurricular sphere, Lynch found that the aesthetic, moral/religious and sociopersonal development of pupils were higher priorities in girls' schools than in boys'. Furthermore, girls' schools placed greater emphasis on developing qualities such as caring for others, sincerity, gentleness, "refinement" and self-control, than their male counterparts.

Table 6.12 below gives some quantitative evidence of the ways in which male and female schools differed in the extracurricular sphere. It shows in particular how artistic and religious/moral activities are generally more central to the agenda of girls' schools than of boys'.

Lynch's data (1989a, 1989b) also showed how girls' schools give considerably more time on the daily timetable to the teaching of religion, how

TABLE 6.12

Differences Between Boys'[a] and Girls'[a] Second-Level Schools in Extracurricular Provision in the Arts and in Religious-Related Societies and Activities

Type of Activity	Name of Activity	Girls' Schools $N=21$	Boys' Schools $N=20$	Statistical Significance
		%	%	
Religious-Related	Temperance Society	76.2	40.0	P < .05
	Legion of Mary	28.4	5.0	—
	Vincent de Paul	19.0	25.0	–
	Charitable Events	33.0	15.0	–
Arts	Debating/Public Speaking	100.0	75.0	P < .05
	Drama	85.7	40.0	P < .01
	Arts/Crafts	71.4	25.0	P < .01
	Dancing	14.3	0.0	–
	Musical Activities	100.0	55.0	P < .01
	School Magazine	57.1	50.0	–
	Board Games (esp. chess)	33.3	60.0	–
	Irish Club (cultural club)	23.8	10.0	–
	Photography	19.0	20.0	–

[a] All the girls' schools and all but two of the boy' schools were managed by Catholic authorities. Both girls' and boys' schools were fairly similar in social class intake.

Source: Lynch, Kathleen "The Ethos of Girls' Schools" *Social Studies*, Vol. 10, Nos. 1/2 (1989), pp. 11–31.

they allocate more time to personal development and pastoral care and how strict control of dress and behaviour is more likely to be a feature of girls' schools than of boys'. In their statement of aims, for example, Lynch (1989a) found that the development of self-discipline and/or self-control were cited as school aims in all thirteen girls' schools which made their prospectuses available as policy statements. None of the twelve boys' schools which made their prospectuses available, made any reference to the desirability of developing self-discipline or self-control.

Boys' schools, on the other hand, were found to place a high priority on the development of physical prowess and motor skills. In their prospectuses and school magazines, boys' schools highlighted both the quality of their sports' facilities and their sporting achievements. A number of the school magazines and reports from boys' schools displayed pages upon pages of teams which participated or succeeded in sporting events. No such display existed in girls' schools' magazines. Photographs of girls playing the harp or piano, or reading quietly in the library, replaced the male images of physical prowess on the sports field.

An important finding from Lynch's data, however, is that girls' schools did not sacrifice academic achievement for the sake of moral, religious or sociopersonal goals. She found that girls' schools had a strong achievement ethos in the academic sphere – measured in terms of the frequency and compulsoriness of assessments, and the extent of prize giving. Indeed, the achievement ethos in girls' schools was frequently stronger than in boys'. It seems therefore that:

Girls' schools tend to present girls with two seemingly contradictory role models: on the one hand they are educated to compete and succeed within the formal educational system . . on the other hand they are socialised to be guardians of the moral order, to be unselfish, non-assertive and appreciative of the cultural rather than the purely material products of the age. (Lynch, 1989a, p. 27).

Boys are not presented with these dichotomous models to the same degree; instrumental goals, such as labour market success, are encouraged therefore in a much more singular manner among boys. To understand why women do not realize their potential as much as men at the more advanced stages of education and in the labour market generally, one needs to examine the hidden curriculum of schools more closely. Girls are constantly reminded that labour market involvement is only one of their many responsibilities in life; boys do not receive this message to the same degree. Girls are socialized into subordination in subtle ways that cannot always be measured in statistical terms. A considerable amount of research needs to be undertaken to elicit what these precise mechanisms are so that policies can be devised to overcome them.

Gender and Social Class

Throughout this paper women and men have been treated as singular undifferentiated entities. This is a rather simplistic representation of both gender groups, albeit necessary in a chapter of this kind. However, as class inequalities are, if anything, even more conspicuous in Irish education than gender inequalities one must point to the interface between social class and gender at this point. Although no major study has yet been undertaken of the differences in educational opportunity for working class and middle class women *per se*, the research available on all working class students, indicates that working class women are much more disadvantaged in education than their middle class sisters. Working class students, including girls, are considerably more likely to leave school earlier than middle class students (Breen, 1984, p. 32). Female under-representation in higher education is also most noticeable among working class women (Clancy, 1988, p. 73).

The experience of working class girls in schools is frequently very different to that of their middle and upper class sisters as well. This is particularly evident when one compares fee-paying secondary schools with publicly controlled schools. Fee-paying schools have far better extracurricular facilities, relative to their size, than public schools (Lynch, 1989b, pp. 112–115). Girls attending fee-paying schools also have access to a culture and ethos which emphasizes social confidence, artistic accomplishment, and styles of behaviour which anticipate power: the same does not obtain for girls attending public schools (Lynch, 1987, 1989a). To fully comprehend the position of women in Irish education further research is necessary particularly research which examines the relationship between social class, ethnicity and gender in education.

While women's retention and performance rates within Irish education are quite satisfactory in many ways, much remains to be done. Women are still largely absent from the technological programmes which offer some of the best employment opportunities at present. They do not undertake higher degrees as often as men despite their adequate undergraduate performance. Men's higher degrees give them a competitive labour market edge in a society which strongly emphasizes the use of credentials in selecting for all types of jobs.

Most importantly of all, women are frequently socialized in schools into the attitudes which facilitate their subordination: docility, compliance and caring for others. While caring for others, being considerate and sensitive are undoubtedly highly valuable social qualities, they become social millstones for women when men are not socialized into them as well.

References

Barry, U. (1988) Women in Ireland. In A. Smyth (Ed.) *Women's Studies International Forum*, Vol. II, No. 4, 317–322. New York: Pergamon Press.

Blackwell, J. (1989) *Women in the labour force*. Dublin: Employment Equality Agency.

Breen, R. (1984) *Education and the labour market*. Dublin: Economic and Social Research Institute (ESRI), Paper No. 119.

Brennan, M. (1986) *Factors affecting attainment in the Irish Leaving Certificate Examination*. University College, Dublin. Unpublished M. Ed. thesis.

Central Statistics Office (1989) *Labour Force Survey, 1988*. Dublin: Government Publications.

Clancy, P. (1987) Does school type matter? The unresolved questions. *Sociological Association of Ireland Bulletin*, **49**, April 12–14.

Clancy, P. (1988) *Who goes to college? A second national survey of participation in higher education.* Dublin: The Higher Education Authority.

Clancy, P. (1989) Gender differences in student participation at third level. In C. Hussey (Ed.) *Equal opportunities for women in higher education.* Dublin: University College Dublin.

Council of Europe (1982) *Sex stereotyping in schools.* Lisse: Swets and Zeitlinger.

Department of Education (1971) *Primary school curriculum: Teacher's Handbook.* Dublin: Government Publications Office.

Department of Education (1972–73) *Statistical Reports.* Dublin: Government Publications Office.

Department of Education (1985–86) *Statistical Reports.* Dublin: Government Publications Office.

Department of Education (1986–87) *Statistical Reports.* Dublin: Government Publications Office.

Department of Education (1983) *Leaving certificate examination results.* Athlone: Department of Education.

Department of Education (1989) Personal Communication by author with Department of Education.

Department of the Taoiseach (1987) *United Nations convention on the elimination of all forms of discrimination against women: first report by Ireland.* Dublin: Government Publications.

Educational Testing Service (1989) *A world of difference: An international assessment of mathematics and science.* New Jersey: Centre for the Assessment of Educational Progress.

Government Publications (1937) *Constitution of Ireland.* Dublin: Government Publications Office.

Greaney, V. and Kellaghan, T. (1984) *Equality of opportunity in Irish schools.* Dublin: The Educational Company.

Hannan, D., Brean, R., Murray, B., Watson, D., Hardiman, N. and O'Higgins, K. (1983) *Schooling and sex roles.* Dublin: Economic and Social Research Institute, Paper No. 113.

Higher Education Authority (1975–76) *Accounts and student statistics.* Dublin: Higher Education Authority.

Higher Education Authority (1984–85) *Accounts and student statistics.* Dublin: Higher Education Authority.

Higher Education Authority (1988) *First destination of award recipients in higher education* (1987). Dublin: Higher Education Authority.

Irish National Teachers' Organisation (1988) *Central executive committee report.* Dublin: Irish National Teachers' Organisation.

Kellaghan, T., Fontes, P., O'Toole, C. and Egan, E. (1985) *Gender inequalities in primary school teaching.* Dublin: The Educational Company.

Lynch, K. (1987) The universal and particular: gender, class and reproduction in second level schools. *Women's Studies Form, UCD,* Working Papers No. 3.

Lynch, K. (1989a) The ethos of girls' schools: An analysis of differences between male and female schools. *Social Studies,* **10**, 1/2 Spring, 11–31.

Lynch, K. (1989b) *The hidden curriculum: reproduction in education, a reappraisal.* Lewes: Falmer Press.

McCarthy, E. (1988) *Transitions to equal opportunity at work in Ireland: problems and possibilities.* Dublin: Employment Equality Agency.

McKenna, A. (1988) *Child care and equal opportunities.* Dublin: Employment Equality Agency.

Marland, M. (Ed.) (1983) *Sex differentiation and schooling.* London: Heinemann.

Smyth, A. (1984) *Breaking the circle: the position of women academics in third-level education in Ireland.* Dublin: EC Action Programme on the Promotion of Equal Opportunities for Women, 1984.

Smyth, A. (1984) The contemporary women's movement in the Republic of Ireland. In A. Smyth (Ed.) *Women's Studies International Forum.* Vol. II No. 4, 331–341. New York: Pergamon Press.

Stanworth, M. (1983) *Gender and Schooling.* London: Hutchinson & Co.

CHAPTER 7

Poland

HENRYK SZYDLOWSKI AND GRAZYNA DUDZIAK

CONTEMPORARY patterns in the education of girls in Poland are a consequence of changes which occurred after Independence in 1918 and in particular after the Second World War. The position of women in Polish society improved as a result of socio-economic changes and the principle of sexual equality was enshrined in the Constitution of the Polish Republic in 1921. This granted women equal rights with men in all spheres of the state and in political, economic, cultural and educational life.

Despite such changes in the formal constitution, however, many more men than women continued their education in high schools and universities in the interwar years. With high levels of unemployment, employers often preferred to hire men in preference to women and wage rates often differed according to sex and age. At this time industry in Poland was not well developed, and 70 per cent of people lived in rural areas, where men traditionally undertook manual work and women housework.

Gradual changes in perception of the traditional role of women between 1921 and 1939 paved the way for a rapid improvement in real equality of opportunities between the sexes after the Second World War. This was a consequence of accelerated social change, following the change in political system as well as of consistent government policies, which have sought to realize the principle of equality of opportunity in the Polish education system. At present all schools are co-educational, except for theological and military academies, and since the 1960s only one subject, Physical Education, has been taught separately to boys and girls.[1]

This chapter will firstly outline the structure of the Polish education system. It will then outline the position of girls and boys in secondary education and in post-compulsory education and present data on women in the labour market, concentrating in particular on employment in and attitudes of men and women to the area of Science and Technology.

The Polish Education System

Education in Poland is free and compulsory from 1 October of the year in which a child is six years old until the end of the school year in which the child has completed elementary school at the age of fifteen. Elementary schools, which offer an eight-year programme, are the basic unit of the Polish educational system. Table 7.1 below gives the number of pupils and students enrolled at each level in the academic year 1984–1985.

TABLE 7.1

Distribution of the School Population, 1984–1985

Institution	% age group
Kindergarten (3–6 years)	84.0
Kindergarten (6–7 years)	100.0
Elementary schools (7–15 years)	98.2
Special elementary schools (7–15 years)	1.8
Music and Art schools (7–15 years)	0.1
Vocational schools (15–18 years)	51.0
Vocational schools for the handicapped (15–18 years)	1.7
General high schools (*liceum*) (15–19 years)	17.0
Technical high schools (*technicum*) (15–19 years)	20.0
Institutions of higher education (19–23 years)	10.0
Vocational training for high school graduates (19–20 years)	6.0

Source: Annual Publication of Statistical Data, Warsaw (1986).

Nursery Education. A child can be admitted to a day nursery at the age of four months and leaves the nursery as soon as he or she is three years old. Children can attend kindergartens from the age of three to seven years. Monthly payments depend on family income and children can stay for six to eight hours a day, five days a week, while parents are at work. Part-time nursery education is compulsory for all six-year-olds and is free of charge when children attend nursery schools.

Elementary Education is compulsory from 1 October of the year in which a child reaches the age of seven and lasts eight years. All elementary schools are co-educational and all subjects are compulsory. All schools are supported by the state and the curriculum and syllabi are set centrally for the whole country. Pupils who do not satisfactorily complete a school year are required to repeat the year.

There are no private schools in Poland. In rural areas schools are organized on the basis of districts (*gmina*), in which the distance between the settlements is up to seven kilometres. In sparsely populated areas, there is usually only one school to serve a wide area. In larger settlements in such areas, younger children either attend classes which are affiliated to a central school or have to use public or school transport to attend the central school.

The curriculum comprises Polish, Environmental Studies, Music, Mathematics, Art, Physical Education and Technology in grades 1–3, with the addition of History, Biology and Geography from grade 4 on, Physics from grade 6 and Chemistry and Social Science from grade 7. Compulsory Russian for all school pupils and university students has now been abolished and other European languages, in particular English, substituted.

There is no religious instruction in elementary schools, but children can attend special classes organized by the church authorities in every parish once or twice a week. In larger towns, some pupils can attend elementary schools which specialize in Music and Art in addition to the normal school curriculum. Children who are mentally or physically handicapped can attend special elementary or vocational schools, located in larger towns and there is some boarding school provision for children from remote rural areas.

Upper Secondary Education. About 90 per cent of all children attend upper secondary education after the age of fifteen. The two major types of secondary school in Poland are high schools and vocational schools. High schools are subdivided into two further types: *technikum* (technical high schools), offering a five-year curriculum, and *liceum* (general high schools), offering a four-year curriculum. Access is determined by a locally administered entrance exam in Polish, Mathematics and two other subjects, and on the basis of the applicant's final elementary school report.

General high schools comprise the following faculties: General, Classics, Mathematics and Physics, Biology and Chemistry or the Humanities. The basic general programme comprises Polish, History, Mathematics, Physics, Chemistry, Biology, Geography, Physical Education, a Western European language, Work and Technology, Music and Defence Instruction in grades 1 to 4 with Social Science in grades 3 to 4, and Religious Education in grade 3. Chemistry, Music, Work and Technology and Defence Instruction are dropped in grade 4. All pupils follow the basic programme, opt for one of the other faculties, and may in addition take an option in one of the following subjects in the general faculty: a Modern Language, Geography and Astronomy, Technical Training, Gymnastics, or Teaching Studies. There are also some vocational high schools which offer the basic four-year general high school programme and vocational training for a single profession, and some general high schools which specialize in Music and the Fine Arts. There are also a few general high schools under the control of the Catholic authorities, which are obliged by law to follow the same curriculum as the state schools. Pupils at all high schools matriculate by taking a final examination which is a prerequisite for university entrance. Those who do not wish to continue their studies at university level may go on to two years' vocational training for high school graduates.

Technical high schools offer, as a rule, a similar curriculum to general high schools, but with additional vocational training. There are several different kinds of technical high schools which specialize in such areas as Agriculture, Economics, Chemistry, Energy Studies, Telecommunications, Engineering, and Health, etc. Technical high schools offer pupils the opportunity to complete matriculation, necessary for entrance into higher education, but it is not obligatory. As a rule pupils take a diploma which is a certificate of their vocational specialism, and 50 per cent of them complete matriculation at the age of nineteen.

Vocational schools offer several general subjects, some vocational subjects and work placements in factories, farms, laboratories, and also in private workshops. Most of the vocational schools provide a transfer route to technical high schools after the third year.

Higher Education. At the level of higher education, there are three kinds of institution in Poland. Universities usually comprise the faculties of Humanities, Law, Natural Science and Educational Studies. Technical universities provide training in various Engineering disciplines, such as Civil and Mechanical Engineering. Academies provide training in Medicine, Commerce, Theology, the Fine Arts and Military Studies. There are some institutions of higher education, such as colleges of education and engineering academies, which, although offering the university or technical university curriculum, have fewer faculties, research facilities and well qualified staff. Besides state-financed university education, the Catholic church also runs some institutions, such as the Catholic University at Lublin, and the Academy of Theology at Krakow, and theological seminaries organized in every diocese.

Most courses in higher education last five years, with the exception of Medicine and Theology, which last six years or longer, and lead to a Masters degree. Every institution has its own admissions procedures. Candidates need to have obtained successful results at matriculation and in the entrance examination, and other criteria, such as military training or work experience, may also be taken into account. If there are too many qualified candidates for places available, a competitive examination may be organized. Some conditions for admissions, such as to the medical academies, are centrally determined and the number of places limited.

In addition to the student's main subject, other compulsory subjects such as Russian, other Modern Languages, Sports, Military Training, and Economics, Politics, and Philosophy, used to comprise about 20 per cent of the university curriculum.

Since 1973 all teachers have had to complete a degree in higher education. Teachers of children under the age of ten may still be graduates of colleges of education, but in the main elementary school and special education teachers have to be graduates of university faculties of Educational Studies, while specialist secondary teachers are trained by their appropriate faculties.

However, there is now much more freedom for universities to set their own study programmes, with the exception of military training. A measure was introduced in 1980 to combat teacher shortages, which required students of Languages, History, Physics, Chemistry, Mathematics, Biology and Geography to take courses in "Pedagogical Studies".

An Overview of the System

The Polish education system contains many positive features. The curricula of all elementary and secondary schools are unified for the whole country. All subjects at elementary school are compulsory and therefore pupils are able to choose the kind of secondary education which is most suited to their needs. A variety of schools provide the possibility of continuing studies to a higher level. All schools are free of charge and a system of scholarships is available for students on a low family income to compensate for potential loss of earnings. Opportunities for adults to return to study are also available.

However, there are also a number of negative features. Firstly, the system has undergone frequent changes, especially at the university level. Secondly, there is still a shortage of fully qualified teachers, as teaching has for many years been one of the most underpaid and undervalued professions in Poland. This shortage is being relieved by the employment of unqualified teachers who are required to complete their studies on a part-time basis, but this often takes many years and can be a drain on work and family life. Since 1989 the profound political changes in Poland have left the country with an unprecedented need for teachers of English and other European languages. Thirdly, there is a shortage of school buildings in newer urban areas which means that some schools have to work on a shift basis. Fourthly, many elementary schools are badly equipped for scientific activities and there is an acute shortage of modern instruments, such as personal computers. Finally, the proportion of young people going on to higher education in Poland at 16 per cent is low in comparison with many OECD countries.

Girls and Educational Achievement at School and in Higher and Further Education

Upper Secondary Education

At upper secondary school level there is a marked difference in the types of school which boys and girls attend. Girls make up the major proportion of pupils in general high schools and are in a minority in vocational schools. This is illustrated by Table 7.2 below.

TABLE 7.2

The Distribution of Pupils in Post-Elementary Schools by Sex and Type of School, 1985–1986

Schools	Distribution of pupils % in types of school	% Girls	% Boys
Vocational	43	38	62
Technical high	36	55	45
General high schools	21	72	28

Source: Annual Publication of Statistical Data, Warsaw (1986).

Of those who attend *technika* (technical high schools), girls have tended to be concentrated in certain areas such as medical schools, art schools and schools of economics, where they make up the majority of students. Girls are in an overall minority in technical high schools, as illustrated by Table 7.3 below.

TABLE 7.3

The Distribution of Pupils in Technical High Schools by Type of School and by Sex, 1985–1986

Types of schools	% Girls	% Boys
Medical	98.9	1.1
Economics	88.7	11.3
Arts	59.6	40.4
Technology	22.8	77.2

Source: Annual Publication of Statistical Data, Warsaw (1986).

At the *liceum* (general high school), girls have tended to opt for the basic programme or to specialize in the Humanities, Classics, Biology and Chemistry and Physical Education, as illustrated in Table 7.4 below. This pattern of subject choice influences, although does not ultimately determine, their future field of study at university. Those who opt for the basic programme are either undecided as to the pattern of their future studies or go on to specialize in such subjects as Theology, the Fine Arts, etc., which are not offered as study programmes at school.

More boys than girls attained the matriculation certificate at general high school, which enables them to enter university. In 1983–1984, 84 per cent of boys at general high schools were successful at matriculation, in comparison with 76.2 per cent of girls. At technical schools just under half of school leavers matriculated and there was no significant differences between the sexes.

TABLE 7.4

The Distribution of Pupils in General High Schools by Programme and by Sex, 1985–1986

Faculty	% Girls	% Boys
Humanities	82.9	17.1
Classics	78.0	22.0
General	77.9	22.1
Biology and Chemistry	76.2	23.8
Mathematics and Physics	53.5	46.5

Source: Annual Publication of Statistical Data, Warsaw (1986).

Sex Differences in School Performance

In Poland so far no other research has been carried out into the comparative achievements of boys and girls at school. The only examination taken by the majority of young people in Poland is the high school leavers certificate. This cannot, however, be regarded as an objective measure of educational attainment as the only subjects which are a uniform part of the examination are Polish Literature and Mathematics. The oral part of the examination consists of five subjects, two of which are optional to students, and is set by local committees with local teacher participation, so the demands as well as the scope of questions may vary considerably.

In the 1980s, however, there were some attempts to compare performance in the Natural Sciences and in Geography, although no comparisons have been made with other subjects. A representative nationwide sample of eighth grade elementary school pupils was drawn up and data analysed by sex and by rural or urban background (Zaborowski and Karpinczyk, 1985). Tests administered included both national and international test questions, the former aimed at evaluating Polish curricula. A total of seventy items were tested, covering skills acquisition in Biology, Chemistry, Geography and Physics. Boys appeared to perform significantly better overall in both rural and urban areas. The best results in all cases were obtained by boys in urban areas, followed by boys in rural areas and then by girls in urban areas. This may indicate that rural disadvantage can combine with sex differences to create further disparities in school attainment.

Girls in Tertiary Education

About a third of pupils from technical and general high schools go on to higher education and a similar proportion of pupils from general high schools go on to two or three year vocational courses. Overall 58.4 per cent of students in tertiary education and 52 per cent of students at university are female. In the tertiary sector, the majority of girls specialize in such subjects as Medicine and Economics, which prepare them for such jobs as kindergarten teachers, social workers, laboratory technicians, accountants, etc. Table 7.5 below illustrates the distribution of students in this sector, showing clearly the low proportion of girls in technical tertiary education.

At the university level the majority of students of the Humanities, Linguistics, Psychology, the Natural Sciences and Mathematics, Educational Studies and Medicine are women. Within Medicine, Pharmacy, Dentistry and Paediatrics are especially popular among women. Many young women also specialize in the Sciences, where they make up over 60 per cent of students overall and 80 per cent of students of Biology and Chemistry. Physics is less popular but here young women still constitute 40 per cent of students. As Table 7.6 illustrates, 61.4 per cent of Mathematics students were female in

TABLE 7.5

The Distribution of Students in Vocational Training for High School Graduates by Programme and by Sex, 1985–1986

Faculty	% Females	% Males
Medicine	88.9	11.1
Economics	81.7	18.3
Art	50.4	49.6
Technology	21.4	78.6

Source: Annual Publication of Statistical Data, Warsaw (1986).

TABLE 7.6

The Distribution of Students in Higher Education by University Faculty, by Sex, 1985–1986

Faculties	% Females	% Males
Humanities	74.3	25.7
Medicine	61.9	38.1
Natural Sciences and Mathematics	61.4	38.6
Economics	56.9	43.1
Fine Arts	47.4	52.6
Agriculture	46.6	53.4
Law and Administration	46.0	54.0
Physical Education	35.6	64.4
Technology	20.4	79.6

Source: H. Szydlowski and G. Dudziak (1985).

1985–1986, which compares favourably with the 20.4 per cent of female Technology students at university. Gender balance was more equal in the areas of the Fine Arts, where 47.4 per cent of students were female, in Agriculture, where 46.6 per cent of students were female and in Law and Administration, where 46 per cent of students were female in 1985–1986. A slight majority, at 56.9 per cent, of Economics students were female in that year.

As outlined earlier, most teachers in Poland are required to hold Masters degrees. Among Physics graduates, about twice as many women as men choose teaching as a career and a similar pattern may be observed for graduates in Mathematics, Chemistry, Biology and Geography (Szydlowski and Dudziak, 1985). Teaching has traditionally been a popular choice among women graduates because of the relatively short working hours and long holidays in teaching. The Polish educational system also provides the opportunity for working people to continue their studies at a post-Masters degree level on 1–2 year vocational courses. Here it appears again that the majority of women opt to continue their studies in the educational field and a lower proportion opt for Agriculture, Economics, and Physical Education than at Masters degree level, as illustrated by Table 7.7 below.

TABLE 7.7

The Distribution of Post-Masters Degree Students by Sex and by Programme, 1985–1986

Programme	% Females	% Males
Education studies	67.5	32.5
University faculties (total)	57.9	42.1
Fine Arts	45.5	54.5
Agriculture	31.8	68.2
Economics	26.9	73.1
Physical Education	26.3	73.7
Technology	19.3	80.7

Source: Annual Publication of Statistical Data, Warsaw (1985).

Sex Differences in University Attainment

In order to estimate the influence of sex differences on the acquisition of knowledge among Science students at university level, we have analysed the results of 178 Physics students at A. Mickiewicz University in Poznàn from 1978 to 1983. A one to five scale, from unsatisfactory to very good, was employed to analyse university examination results, and matriculation results in Physics and Mathematics were also taken into account (Szydlowski and Dudziak, 1985).

Table 7.8 gives the average results of 102 male Physics students and 76

TABLE 7.8

Test Results of Knowledge Acquisition in Physics Students

Group of subjects	Average results on a 1–5 scale	
	Men	Women
Matriculation results	4.34	4.25
Entrance examination results	3.73	3.78
Mathematics	3.41	3.42
Experimental Physics	3.75	3.64
Theoretical Physics	3.62	3.48
Foreign languages	3.76	3.62
Humanities	4.05	4.15
Physics laboratory work	3.48	3.43
Weighted mean overall	3.72	3.66

Source: H. Szydlowski and G. Dudziak (1985).

female students by subject group. From the data the following patterns emerged:

— overall students appeared to perform better at matriculation than at university entrance;
— students obtained their best results in the Humanities rather than in Physics in the main;
— the average results of female students were only significantly different than the average results of male students in the area of theoretical Physics;
— in laboratory work, the results of male and female students were almost the same.

These findings suggest that those girls who take up Physics and scientific studies at university are probably the most able in these subjects. Scientific aptitude was more common among men but the majority of men choose to study Technology. For those reasons the results presented here are not representative of the whole population of university undergraduates.

Sex Differences in Attitudes towards Technology

As part of an international research project carried out by the University of Eindhoven in the Netherlands in 1985, a study was carried out on the general differences in attitudes towards Technology between the sexes in Poland (Szydlowski and Dudziak, 1985). A questionnaire was administered to 342 fourteen to fifteen-year-old pupils in the Poznàn district, representing the last grade in Polish elementary schools. Pupil responses to eighty-two questions were recorded on a five point scale from (1) strong agreement to (5) strong disagreement. A summary of results of the average responses of boys and girls are set out in Table 7.9 below. In general it appears that:

TABLE 7.9
Sex Differences in Attitudes Towards Technology

Sample of questionnaire responses	Mean on Scale 1–5 From (1) Strong agreement to (5) Strong disagreement	
	Boys	Girls
I would like to work in technology later	2.46	3.77
A person in a technological job does interesting work	1.95	2.37
I like to read magazines about technology	2.15	3.49
I like repairing things at home myself	1.98	3.31
Technology is too difficult for me	3.79	3.02
A girl can have a technological profession as well as a boy	2.48	2.05
Boys are able to repair things better than girls	1.99	2.37
Boys know more about technology than girls	1.99	2.25

Source: H. Szydlowski and G. Dudziak (1987).

— girls were generally less inclined to choose a career in technology, despite the fact that they claimed to find such work interesting;
— girls appeared to be less interested in technology than boys, were less interested in reading articles about technology and in repairing domestic equipment;
— girls found technology more difficult and unpleasant than boys, although they were more convinced that girls could work in this field than boys were;
— girls were less in agreement than boys with the view that boys have a better practical and theoretical knowledge of technology than girls.

Women and Employment

Women Graduates in the Labour Market

The main employer in Poland has been the state. The Polish state still controls most of industry, together with education, science, the health service, architecture and other sectors of employment. In the agricultural sector, three-quarters of agricultural land is farmed by private family enterprises and the remainder by state and co-operative farms. A private sector also exists in small factories and workshops, which co-operate with state-controlled industry. Private enterprises employ just over a quarter of the total workforce, with private agriculture employing 80 per cent of this figure.[2]

In Poland women now account for 44 per cent of the total labour force. Table 7.10 below illustrates the employment of graduate women in state sector employment in 1985–1986.

As can be seen from the data, a number of Polish women graduates are

TABLE 7.10

Percentage of Women Graduates in the Main State Employment Sectors in Poland, 1985–1986

Graduate occupation	% of women	Graduate occupation	% of women
Pharmacists	86.6	Mathematicians	49.2
Librarians	86.1	Lawyers	45.0
Dentists	82.1	Agronomists	39.7
Biologists	79.0	Architects	39.0
Psychologists	78.2	Civil engineers	38.2
Teachers	71.2	Physicists	29.9
Philologists	69.2	Road-building engineers	26.4
Chemists	62.7	Metallurgists	16.5
Food industry engineers	59.0	Veterinary medics	16.0
Economists	58.1	Electronics engineers	15.6
Medics	54.7	Electrical engineers	10.9
Textile engineers	50.8	Mining engineers	9.2
Geographers	51.1	Mechanical engineers	7.1

Source: Annual Publication of Statistical Data, Warsaw (1985).

employed in light industry, mainly in laboratory work in the food, chemical and textile industries. Fifty-nine per cent of food industry engineers and 50.8 per cent of textile engineers were women in 1985–1986, for example. The majority are engaged in employment which requires patience and accuracy, such as dentistry, teaching, pharmacy and librarianship, or which involves working with people or nature, such as psychology, teaching, medicine or biology. For example, 82.1 per cent of dentists and 86.8 per cent of pharmacists were women in 1985–1986. Fewer women graduates are employees in heavy industry, such as mining, at 9.2 per cent of mining engineers, mechanical engineering, at 7.1 per cent of engineers, or metallurgy, at 16.5 per cent of metallurgists. Fewer women than men enter those occupations which demand creative design skills, such as architecture or civil engineering. Thirty-nine per cent of architects were women in 1985–1986 and 38.2 per cent of civil engineers. So, in general, although Polish women graduates reach comparable occupational levels as men, they tend to be concentrated in the "women's professions". There is also a reluctance on the part of employers to appoint women to executive or senior posts. Absentee rates are similar for men and for women but one explanation for this reluctance is the right of women to maternity leave of 2–3 years, followed by reinstatement in post.

Women in Science and Technology: a Case-Study

In order to analyse the participation of women in postgraduate studies and research work, we carried out an investigation into 1,500 students and 608 members of staff on science courses at the A. Mieckiewicz University in Poznàn and 3,700 students and 955 members of staff at the Technical University in Poznàn (Szydkowski and Dudziak, 1987). Table 7.11 below gives comparative data on the two institutions.

An analysis of this data shows that the proportion of women staff in the Sciences at A. Mieckiewicz University, at 29.7 per cent of staff, was almost double the proportion at the Technical University, at 15.3 per cent. The proportion of women students on Science courses at A. Mieckiewicz University, at 68 per cent of students, was nearly five times as high as the proportion of women Science students at the Technical University at 15.3 per cent of students. In both institutions the proportion of women staff and research workers in the Sciences was less than that of women Science students. This disparity was particularly marked at A. Mieckiewicz University, where the proportion of women Science students was over twice the proportion of women members of the Science departments. Paradoxically, in some departments where women students were in a substantial minority, such as in Electrical or Mechanical Engineering, the proportion of women members of staff was relatively high.

Overall it was apparent that the "feminine" options of Biology and

TABLE 7.11

*Percentage of Women in Science and Technology at A. Mieckiewicz
University, Poznàn, and the Technical University of Poznàn,
1985–1986*

Faculty	% Female staff	% Female students
Mathematics	25.2	65.0
Physics	25.5	40.0
Chemistry	32.9	80.0
Biology	42.6	86.0
Geography	29.3	70.0
Total: A. Mieckiewicz University	29.7	68.0
Civil Engineering	16.6	16.0
Mechanical Construction	10.2	19.0
Mechanical and Auto Engineering	2.6	2.4
Electrical Engineering	13.0	10.0
Chemistry	37.2	48.0
Total: Technical University	15.3	19.0

Source: H. Szydlowski and G. Dudziak (1985).

Geography attracted the highest proportion of women students, but that their representation in Chemistry and Mathematics was higher than in many West European university departments. In the more "applied" areas of Construction and Engineering, the proportion of women students was conspicuously low.

Table 7.12 presents data on the number of women research employees in Science and Technology at both institutions in 1985. This shows that there was a higher proportion of women employees among research assistants and lower grade lecturers than among professors and senior lecturers. Women staff were again slightly better represented in the "feminine" areas of Biology and Chemistry. At the Technical University a similar pattern is to be observed within the university hierarchy, where women were particularly badly represented in senior posts.

A Case-Study of Attitudes to Employment among Male and Female Scientists and Technologists

A further investigation into the attitudes of members of staff in the faculties of Science and Technology at the A. Mieckiewicz University in 1987 was carried out by means of a seventy-five item questionnaire (Szydlowski and Dudziak, 1987). Respondents were asked to grade items on a five-point scale from strong agreement to strong disagreement; 118 responses were completed, 40

TABLE 7.12

Occupational Levels of Male and Female Members of Staff at A. Mieckiewicz and Technical Universities, Poznán, 1985

Faculty	Professors		Assistant professors		Assistant lecturers		Faculty total
	% Males	% Females	% Males	% Females	% Males	% Females	
Mathematics	11.6	2.9	44.7	16.5	18.5	5.8	100
Physics	16.3	2.1	41.1	18.4	17.0	5.0	100
Chemistry	16.8	7.7	35.7	17.4	14.7	7.7	100
Biology	20.9	9.5	17.6	18.2	18.9	14.9	100
Geography	28.4	3.0	28.4	10.4	20.9	8.9	100
Total: A. Mieckiewicz University	18.8	5.0	33.5	16.2	18.0	8.5	100
Civil Engineering	17.8	0.0	35.6	9.2	30.0	7.4	100
Mechanical Engineering	12.9	1.4	50.3	6.1	26.6	2.7	100
Mechanical and Auto Engineering	23.5	0.0	48.7	0.9	25.2	1.7	100
Electrical Engineering	13.5	1.0	41.0	6.5	31.5	6.5	100
Chemistry	15.4	1.3	34.6	23.1	12.8	12.8	100
Total: Technical University	16.6	0.7	42.1	9.2	25.2	6.2	100

Source: Szydlowski, H., Dudziak, G. Contributions to the Third GASAT Conference, London (1985).

by female and 78 by male members of staff. Responses were analysed by the sex of the respondent and the following conclusions reached:

— *Involvement in Professional Work.* The majority of respondents were convinced of the value of scientific work for technological development, were interested in their work and experienced a high degree of job satisfaction. The majority took a respectful interest in the work of their colleagues, appreciated the need to keep up to date in their knowledge and did not work out of pure necessity. There were few significant sex differences in these views. Men appeared to be slightly more interested in their work, to be more actively involved in following the latest scientific achievements and to consider their work to be a lifetime objective.

— *Attitudes towards Women in Professional Research Work and Towards Teaching.* In general it was considered that men and women should enjoy parity of status in research work and that the present number of women in employment should be supported. There were no significant sex differences in opinion over such questions as to the competence and supervisory capacity of women in research. Slight differences occurred in attitudes towards the desirability of a high uptake of women of professional work, particularly scientific research. More men also rated the performance of male Science students as better. Although teaching was not seen as a preferable area of employment to research, in general it was found to be a pleasurable activity by both sexes.

— *Experimental, Practical Skills and Creativity.* Although generally positive attitudes towards co-operative work were expressed, women were less willing to mend minor failures in equipment at home or in the laboratory. Women also rated themselves as less creative in their work and to be less interested in supervisory promotion.

— *Reconciliation of Professional Work and Family Commitments.* There were few sex differences in response to the item concerned with the difficulties in reconciling family duties to research work. The majority of researchers of both sexes found it difficult to keep up their studies but more women had delayed entry into research work because of family commitments. Men were also found to be less active in family duties. Both sexes were positive about the number of friendships which their work engendered, but women were less involved in activities with colleagues.

— *Evaluation of Experimental and Theoretical Work.* The majority of the respondents of both sexes were working as experimenters and were aware of the difficulties involved in theoretical work.

— *Social Value of Work and Positive Evaluation of Work.* The majority of respondents were dissatisfied with the quality of their work and most experienced shortages of equipment, time and relevant reading matter. This did not vary according to sex.

Men were more convinced that their work was not harmful to the environment than women were and more interested in the aesthetic form of their products. Both men and women were somewhat in doubt as to the usefulness of their work, although more women expressed this view.

These findings suggest that some positive changes have occurred. In many areas sex differences, attitudes and experience did not appear to be strong. However, other results give more cause for concern, particularly those which revealed ambivalent answers from women about the usefulness of their work to society and their reluctance to take up supervisory positions.

In general we are of the opinion that the Polish education system does not formally discriminate against girls, except in military schools or theological seminaries. On the other hand, there is a strong tradition that girls are not educated for occupations that demand physical strength, such as construction or mining, or involve long absences away from home, such as aviation. Girls predominate in those areas of the education system which lead to occupations connected with health, catering, economics and the humanities, and this pattern is replicated in the labour market. Since young people in Poland are formally free to choose their future training and employment specialisms, we feel that the existing situation must be a product of biological, social and psychological differences reinforced by traditional attitudes. It would be necessary to conduct further detailed studies in order to explain the existing situation, for example into choices made at the general high school and into the effect of differences in family wealth on such choices.

References

Szydlowski, H. and Dudziak, G. (1985) Women in the natural sciences at A. Mieckiewicz University and Technical University at Poznàn. In *GASAT 3 Congressbook*. London:

Szydlowski, H. and Dudziak, G. (1985) Remarks about women's employment in science and technology in Poland. In *Congressbook of the Women Challenge Technology Conference*. Elsinore.

Szydlowski, H. and Dudziak, G. (1987) Research work of men and women in science and technology. In *GASAT-4 Congressbook*. Ann Arbor.

Zaborowski, I. and Karpinczyk, P. (1985) *Students achievements in Physics: results from an all Polish inquiry 1981–1988*. Warsaw: IKN.

Notes

1. Political changes in Poland in 1990 have not changed the legal position of women, but may have economic effects on the employment situation of women.
2. This description of the Polish economy refers to the situation at the end of 1989. The current economic changes underway in Poland in 1990 will clearly transform this picture considerably, for example the reduction in state sector employment will have a disproportionate effect on women's employment levels.

CHAPTER 8

Spain

ISABEL ALBERDI AND INES ALBERDI

The Spanish Education System

Research into the issue of girls and educational equality is of comparatively recent origin in Spain. This chapter will first briefly outline the structure of the Spanish education system and changes in access to all forms of education. It will then summarize quantitative research into the attainment patterns of girls in education and review the position of women in teaching and in higher education. Finally, quantitative research into the image of women in textbooks and into the area of teachers' attitudes and the development of girls' self-image will be presented.

Education in Spain went through significant changes in 1970. In that year the Ley General de Educación (General Education Act) transformed the structure of the education system, establishing compulsory attendance at school between the ages of six and fourteen, and introducing a policy of co-education for the first time. This marked a significant change from the previous system in which parents were under no legal obligation to send their children to school at all or beyond primary education. Co-education had also been declared illegal in 1938. The 1986 OECD review of education in Spain described the 1970 reforms as a "more spectacular expansion than in any other OECD country". The reforms involved the deliberate transfer of responsibilities from the centre to the regions, an intensive school building programme and the employment of thousands of new teachers.

The 1970 Act stated that "all Spaniards have the right to basic education and vocational training to fit them for a job that would be both useful to society and personally fulfilling". The Act therefore proposed a universal model of education open to all and began a process of integrating both sexes within the same educational establishments, starting at the primary level.

All new state schools and colleges are now co-educational and single-sex state schools were given the deadline of 1985–1986 to open access to all pupils. At present the Spanish education system consists of:

Pre-school education, divided into kindergartens for children under four years old and infant schools for children of four to five years. Eighty-five per cent of four-year-olds were in pre-school education in 1985 and it is the government's aim to supply a place on demand for all two to five-year-olds.

Primary or basic education (educación general basica), which is compulsory and free of charge, consists of two stages from six to eleven years and from eleven to fourteen years. Substantial reforms in 1981 and 1984 were aimed at standardizing opportunities and results in primary education, introducing measures to avoid early selection and to compensate for social and individual inequalities. A policy of maintaining small schools in rural areas was introduced to counter rural depopulation and rural-urban disparities;

Upper secondary education is subdivided into an academic programme, leading to the Bachillerato (pre-university course), and Formación professionel (vocational education). Access to the academic programme is determined by successful completion of the Graduado Escolar (matriculation certificate) at the end of primary education. A third of pupils leave primary education with the Certificado de Escolaridad, an attendance certificate, which only entitles them to enrol in vocational education. This lasts two years, with a possible extension of two to three years. Pupils are enrolled on a specific vocational programme out of about fifty-six options, of which Administration and Electronics are the most popular. About a third leave with no qualifications and many parents and employers equate this sector with failure.

The academic programme lasts three years with a fourth year for university preparation (Curso de Orientación Universitaria). The curriculum includes traditional secondary school subjects, with a strong emphasis on the Arts, Social Sciences and Technology;

Controversial reforms proposed in 1990 aim to raise the school leaving age from fourteen to sixteen and reorganize the structure of compulsory education to bring the system into line with Europe. Primary education will run from six to twelve years, secondary education from twelve to sixteen and the Bachillerato from sixteen to eighteen. Vocational education will also begin at sixteen, in an attempt to raise the status of this area, secondary education is to be organized in terms of bands of knowledge rather than specific subject titles, and it is proposed that religious education is voluntary (Evans, 1990).

Higher education comprises universities, polytechnics, and higher technical schools, offering courses of one to three years' duration and university schools, which offer one-year courses. Access to higher education is virtually on demand, subject to the availability of places and successful completion of the Bachillerato and COU, although quotas exist for medical and primary education students. Selection is stricter after the first year exams and 40 per cent of students repeat the year. Degree courses at universities can often take five to six years.

The university schools are considered to be of lower prestige and there is a much greater demand for academic rather than technical qualifications in what the OECD describes as "title-fever" (OECD, 1986).

Adult education is still a priority in a country where 8 per cent of the population is illiterate and an estimated further 23 per cent functionally illiterate.

A parallel private system of schools exists, the majority of which are Catholic. These receive substantial state aid, and are required to follow the same curriculum. In 1985, 36 per cent of Spanish schools were private (OECD, 1986).

In the case of post-compulsory secondary schooling, vocational training and tertiary education, attendance is voluntary and depends very much on social origin. Women now have formal legal access to all such educational establishments.

Girls and Educational Achievement

As can be seen from Table 8.1 below, there has been an enormous increase in the number of pupils and students since 1970 and the most remarkable feature of this increase has been the influx of women into all levels of education. Between the academic years 1961–1962 and 1981–1982 the total number of students in post-compulsory secondary education rose by 1.5 times and the total number of students in higher education 6.5 times, an increase more due to educational policy than to demographic factors.

The ratio of boys to girls at the primary level has been approximately the same since the early 1960s. There has been a significant rise in the number of girls staying on for the Bachillerato and for the pre-university course in the academic programme of upper secondary education, although not matched by a similar rise in girls on the vocational programme.

There is also a higher proportion of women students at university today. In the academic year 1984–1985 women represented 48.4 per cent of registered university students, which is a spectacular increase from the 23.4 per cent of twenty years earlier. By the academic year 1985–1986 there were as many women as men at university.

Primary Education

Primary education is very different today to what it was twenty years ago. The separation of sexes into different schools and classrooms has become very rare and the curriculum is the same for both sexes throughout, although in some schools boys and girls are taught separately for Physical Education and Crafts. Up until the late 1960s many children were not expected to study beyond primary level, especially in rural areas. The curriculum was differentiated according to the sex of the children. Girls went to school mainly to learn domestic skills and the boys to become literate enough to find some sort of non-agricultural job.

TABLE 8.1

Distribution of Students by Educational Level and Sex, 1961–1982

	1961–1962[a]		1975–1976		1981–1982	
	Males	Females	Males	Females	Males	Females
Higher Education	72,693	22,206	307,668	175,205	352,604	277,045
Middle Schools and other vocational courses / Upper Secondary Schools:	154,150	59,650				
Secondary Schools / Academic education	363,877	229,723	419,068	399,317	520,890	603,439
Vocational education			217,190	88,064	375,251	243,839
Primary and pre-school education / Primary Schools	1,684,392	1,725,308	2,791,413	2,682,055	2,888,043	2,741,831
Pre-school education			448,809	471,437	600,417	597,480

[a] Pre the 1970 reforms which substantially altered the structure of the system.

Source: Informe Foessa (1975) and authors.

Mixed or co-educational schools have been gradually established in Spain since 1970. Co-education at primary level is considered to be a positive change by the majority of teachers, though there has been no public debate about its advantages and disadvantages (Subirats, 1985). The question of its validity in a social context which strongly emphasizes different social roles for each sex has only been posed from a feminist perspective, which argues for a more active encouragement by schools of a genuine integration of girls and boys in the classroom. The literature on this subject often draws a distinction between nominally mixed schools, which have pupils of both sexes, and co-educational schools, in which a positive effort to integrate both sexes takes place (Instituo de la Mujer, 1988).

It is of interest to note that girls do better than boys throughout primary education. Under the Spanish education system pupils who do not achieve a minimum level at a particular grade have to repeat the academic year. At every grade, more boys than girls are kept back to repeat the year. The examination results of girls on completion of the eighth grade of primary education tend to be better on average than those of boys. More girls attain the Graduado Escolar (the school graduation certificate), which allows them to enter the academic programme of upper secondary schooling, than the Certificado de Escolaridad (ordinary school certificate) at the end of their compulsory education. A large-scale survey carried out by the CIDE (Centro de Investigación y Documentación Educativa) in 1985 among eighth grade primary pupils showed substantial differences between girls and boys with respect to their educational performance, aptitude, and attitude to education and society (CIDE, 1988). Girls attained slightly better marks in all subjects on average. They were better at Arithmetic, Reading, Spelling and Comprehension. However, boys achieved better results in aptitude tests, except for abstract reasoning.

Upper Secondary Education

As stated before, girls have tended to opt for the academic rather than the vocational programme in upper secondary education, as illustrated by Table 8.2 below. This may be related to their greater success rate in the Graduado Escolar and may also reflect a measure of choice.

TABLE 8.2

Distribution of Pupils by Sex at Secondary School Level, 1986

	Academic course	Vocational training
% Boys	46.49	57.32
% Girls	53.51	42.68
Total	100.00	100.00

Source: Estadisticas Ministerio de Educación y Ciencia, Madrid (1986).

Although it might be thought that the academic courses in upper secondary education have more prestige attached to them, this pattern of choice may also be to the disadvantage of girls, given that it is vocational training that leads more directly to the labour market.

In the last year of upper secondary education, students must take four options within either the Science programme or the Arts Programme. At this level girls have shown a marked preference for Languages and Literature rather than for the Sciences, as illustrated by Table 8.3 below, a pattern which is repeated at the level of higher education.

TABLE 8.3

Distribution of Pupils in Upper Secondary School Options, 1983–1984, Selected Subjects

	% Girls	% Boys
Science options	45.5	54.5
Biology	54.0	46.0
Chemistry	46.0	54.0
Geology	40.0	60.0
Technical drawing	24.0	76.0
Arts options	64.8	35.2
Latin	67.5	33.5
Greek	69.5	30.5
Art	64.5	35.5
Mathematics	56.2	43.8

Source: CIDE, Encuesta a los alumnos de COU (1983–1984).

Among the other possible options, the most popular choice for girls is Modern Languages, followed by Classics and the Humanities, and Social Sciences. Of the Natural Sciences, Biology is the most popular option and Physics the least popular, followed by technical subjects. As at primary school, female pupils attain better academic results in general and more boys than girls are kept back in the same grade to repeat the academic year. More girls than boys complete the "Bachillerato" and this difference has increased in the last few years.

In the vocational programme, where girls are generally under-represented, there is also a strongly differentiated pattern in the options taken by boys and girls. The former have tended to favour the options of Electronics, Administration and Motor Mechanics, while girls have tended to choose Administrative, Health and Hairdressing options (as illustrated by Table 8.4 below). Girls' performance in vocational education is generally better than that of boys, especially in Administration, where they outnumber boys.

Higher Education

Although university education has been formally open to women in Spain

TABLE 8.4

Distribution of Vocational Education, by Subject,
1984–1985

	Boys	Girls
Administration	21.00	56.00
Agriculture	2.00	1.00
Graphic Design	0.50	0.20
Motor Mechanics	14.00	0.20
Draughtmanship	5.00	2.00
Electronics	39.00	1.00
Hotel and Catering	1.00	0.70
Carpentry	1.00	0.10
Maritime Studies	0.70	0.01
Metalwork	9.00	0.10
Fashion and Dressmaking	0.04	1.00
Mining	0.04	0.00
Hairdressing	0.80	9.00
Beauty therapy	0.09	0.20
Chemistry	0.90	1.00
Textiles	0.03	0.10
Health	1.00	15.00
Sound and Image	0.60	0.20
Glass and Ceramics	0.01	0.00
Domestic Science	0.02	6.00
Construction	0.10	0.01
Others	2.10	3.20
Experimental/Undecided	1.00	3.15
Total	100.00	100.00

Source: Estadísticas Ministerio de Educación y Ciencia, Madrid (1986).

since 1920, there have been implicit barriers against the admission of women until the 1960s.

Since the 1970 reforms the number of women students in higher education has increased dramatically to the point where the numerical representation of the sexes is virtually equal in university schools and faculties. During the academic year of 1984–1985, 48.2 per cent of university students were women. The biggest surge in the growth of women studying at university occurred between 1980–1985, when the number of female students increased by 33 per cent while the number of male students grew by 12 per cent, as illustrated in Table 8.5. The proportion of female students at higher technical schools remains, however, low at 16.5 per cent of students in 1988–1989.

The pattern of polarization of subject choice is repeated at this level as well. Women generally enrol on courses considered to be traditionally more suited to them, such as Humanities, Fine Arts, Teaching and Pharmacy. Few women set their sights on such subjects as Engineering and Architecture. Nevertheless, one significant development has been the recent increase in the numbers of women enrolling for Veterinary Science, Medicine and Law, subjects which

TABLE 8.5

Changes in the Composition of the University Student Body by Sex, 1980–1985

	No. of males (000s)	% Males	No. of females (000s)	% Females	Total (000s)
1980–81	363.4	56.0	285.6	44.0	649.0
1981–82	365.5	54.6	304.3	45.4	669.8
1982–83	368.3	53.0	323.9	47.0	692.2
1983–84	386.4	52.0	357.8	48.0	744.2
1984–85	406.1	51.8	380.8	48.2	786.9

Source: Estadísticas Ministerio de Educación y Ciencia, Madrid (1986).

offer good career prospects but which have traditionally been the preserve of men. This is illustrated by Table 8.6 below.

The Position of Women in Teaching

The proportion of women in the teaching profession varies according to the level of education, the subject taught, and the level of responsibility. In primary schools, children are taught by maestros (general teachers), who enjoy a far lower status and level of pay than secondary school subject specialists (profesores). Under the proposed reforms for 1992, these divisions will remain but it is envisaged that teaching becomes an all-graduate profession (Evans, 1990). At the primary level, there are far more women teachers than men overall and as Table 8.7 shows, the proportion of women teachers decreases inversely with the level of education. The under-representation of men is particularly marked at the level of nursery education.

The proportion of women occupying the post of school principal or headteacher also shows how men predominate in the world of education. Although 61 per cent of primary teachers were women in 1985–1986, only 46 per cent of school managers and 39 per cent of headteachers were women. Male teachers also tended to predominate in Mathematics and the Sciences while women predominated in the Social Sciences.

At the level of upper secondary education women represented 48 per cent of teachers on the academic programme and 32 per cent of those responsible for vocational training in 1985–1986. At the post-compulsory level, as at the primary level, fewer women hold tenured posts while the majority of school directors are men. On the vocational programmes, women are in the minority in tenured posts (heads of department, etc.) and the majority in other positions, such as technical assistants.

As Table 8.8 below shows, the majority of university lecturers are men. The number of women in higher education increased between 1979 and 1984 when there was a spectacular growth in the number of university teaching staff overall. However, there is still little parity between men and women at this

TABLE 8.6

Distribution of Student Enrolments by Subject Area in Pre-University Colleges, Higher Technical Schools and Universities, 1984–1985

	% Female students	% Male students		% Female students	% Male students
1. Primary Teacher Training	18.80	5.98	28. Industrial Studies[a]	0.37	3.54
2. Law	13.60	14.46	29. Optical Science[b]	0.31	0.23
3. Philology	7.31	2.77	30. General Science	0.29	0.96
4. Geography and History[b]	6.45	4.21	31. Interpretation and Translation[b]	0.29	0.09
5. Business Studies	6.17	8.37	32. Geology	0.28	0.40
6. Nursing	5.17	1.31	33. Librarianship[b]	0.21	0.19
7. Economics and Business Studies	4.8	7.8	34. Agronomy[a]	0.19	0.51
8. Medicine	3.71	3.15	35. Telecommunications[a]	0.13	0.90
9. Philosophy and Education	3.67	1.68	36. Tech. Eng. Telecommunications	0.11	1.69
10. Psychology	3.57	1.35	37. Forestry	0.08	0.25
11. Biology	3.00	2.92	38. Mining Engineering[a]	0.07	0.40
12. Pharmacy	2.84	1.26	39. Physiotherapy[b]	0.07	0.02
13. Chemistry	1.99	1.92	40. Statistics[b]	0.06	0.06
14. Social Work[b]	1.85	0.28	41. Estate Management[a]	0.05	0.15
15. Information Science	1.57	3.56	42. Publishing	0.05	0.45
16. Veterinary Science	1.24	1.82	43. Topography[b]	0.04	0.27
17. Philosophy and Humanities	1.18	0.62	44. Aeronautics[a]	0.03	0.40
18. Mathematics	1.17	1.38	45. Mining Engineering	0.03	0.49
19. Fine Arts	1.16	0.89	46. Chemistry[b]	0.03	0.07
20. Information Science	0.94	1.46	47. Technology	0.02	0.32
21. Civil Engineering[a]	0.80	0.71	48. Theology	0.02	0.06
22. Politics and Sociology	0.73	0.60	49. Canon Law	0.01	0.01
23. Architecture[a]	0.67	1.65	50. Aeronautical Engineering	0.01	0.41
24. Technical Engineering	0.67	9.53	51. Shipbuilding	0.01	0.12
25. Physics	0.64	1.62	52. Tech. Eng. Shipbuilding	0.01	0.12
26. Agricultural Engineering	0.64	1.94	53. Electronics	0.00	0.21
27. Technical Architecture	0.54	1.95			
Total	100%	100%		100%	100%
					N = 86,648

[a] Higher technical school courses.
[b] Pre-University College courses.
Source: Ministry of Education and Science Statistics, Madrid (1986); Estadísticas Ministerio de Educación y Ciencia.

TABLE 8.7

Distribution of Women in Primary Education, 1985–1986

	Public schools % women	Private schools % women	Total % women
Nursery	93.0	96.0	94.0
First stage	78.0	86.0	80.0
Second stage	65.0	68.0	66.0
Third stage	41.0	55.0	46.0
Total	60.0	66.0	61.0

Source: Estadísticas Ministerio de Educación y Ciencia, Madrid (1986).

TABLE 8.8

University Teachers by Sex, 1979–1980 and 1984–1985
(Total numbers and percentages)

	Total Nos.	1979–1980		Total Nos.[a]	1984–1985	
		% Men	% Women		% Men	% Women
Professors	1,656	95.5	4.5	—	93.0	7.0
Lecturers	1,848	91.5	8.5	—	89.0	11.0
Associate Lecturers	4,924	82.0	18.0	—	77.0	23.0
Course Tutors	3,594	81.0	19.0	—	76.0	24.0
Research Assistants	7,735	70.0	30.0	—	64.0	36.0
Others	64	82.8	17.2	—	70.0	30.0
Total	19,821	79.2	20.8	44,981	75.0	25.0

[a] Representation by grade not available.
Source: Estadísticas Ministerio de Educación y Ciencia, Madrid (1986).

level of education. Women tend to occupy the posts at the bottom of the academic hierarchy although there have been some improvements in this respect in recent years. The proportion of women professors nearly doubled between 1979 and 1984 and the proportion of tenured lecturers rose from 8.5 to 11 per cent. The same pattern is evident in educational administration where women, again, are seldom to be found in senior positions. Although 57 per cent of teachers are women, there are no women in the higher echelons of the Ministry of Education.

The Other Face of the Reality

Though growing in confidence, female pupils and students still come up against a series of obstacles to their full acceptance as equals. Women are treated with less respect by male teachers; the textbooks used give a traditional and pejorative image of women; and the structure of authority in education is weighted in favour of men. This section will focus particularly on the areas of textbooks and classroom interaction, where most research into sex discrimination in education has been carried out in Spain, particularly since the establishment of the Instituto de la Mujer (Institute of Women's Affairs) in 1983.

In the wider labour market, women are increasingly active. About 30 per cent of women work and there is an increasing recognition of the importance of women's labour market participation in Spanish society (Alberdi and Escario, 1987). This has had profound repercussions on the role of women within the family (Conde, 1984). However, these changes have seldom been reflected in schools.

The Image of Girls and Women in Textbooks

One of the most important obstacles to the erosion of sex stereotyping in education is the content of textbooks used at all levels of the school system. The most detailed and systematic study in this area to date was carried out in 1984 (Heras y Trias, 1987). Other authors have reached similar conclusions but have treated the subject in a more superficial way (Alvaro and Monge, 1984; Careaga, 1987; Garreta, 1984).

The 1984 research looked at two aspects of the problem: the role played by women in the writing and production of textbooks and the stereotypical images of men and women presented in textbooks. In terms of the publishing world, the researchers found that it was principally the male sex which was responsible for the writing, supervision, editing and illustration of books. In terms of content, the study found that textbooks were heavily influenced by the notion of women as being inferior to men, especially with respect to jobs and careers. In particular, the authors studied the following aspects:

— The frequency with which women appeared in the text and in the illustrations.
— The vocabulary employed when referring to men and women.
— The portrayal of women in various contexts – family, school, political participation, professional life, etc. – both in the text and in illustrations.

With respect to the first of these points, there was clearly a much stronger representation of men than women in textbooks. Women figured in 26.2 per cent of book illustrations that showed individuals and 35.5 per cent that showed groups of people. The figures for men were 73.7 per cent and 61.4 per cent respectively. Combining the two sets of figures, it was found that men were depicted twice as often as women in textbook illustrations (65.6 per cent as against 34.4 per cent).

Secondly, a detailed breakdown of the vocabulary was undertaken to analyse content in terms of the names, adjectives and verbs used. A frequency count of names cited revealed who were the main characters in the books. This clearly showed that women did not play a great role in the "reality" presented by the books and, indeed, were often only mentioned in passing. The female sex accounted for 26.2 per cent of the total number of names cited in the textbooks studied. It could be argued that male names are used more frequently in a generic way in the Spanish language. However, when only the names of actual characters were analysed, female names still accounted for only 28.4 per cent of names, illustrating how "invisible" women are in textbooks.

The study found that although many of the adjectives employed in textbooks applied equally to both sexes, several adjectives were used to apply specifically to one sex or the other, especially when referring to attitudes, ways of reacting and character traits. There was also a marked difference in the adjectives used to describe appearance, age, etc. Both men and women were often described as "tall" and "blond", but women were "pretty", "fair", "clean", "kind", "homely", while men were "cheerful", "courageous", "wise", "famous", "respectable". These examples support the more common stereotype of men as playing a more important and active role in society generally while women are seen to be confined to a more domestic and passive role.

When depicted at home, men were usually to be found having a wash or brushing their hair, in contrast to women who were depicted cleaning the house and looking after the children in conformity with their traditional role of wife and mother. Women were represented as focusing their aspirations on marriage while men were represented as being more careerist, more materialistic and as having greater imagination. Women were seldom portrayed as having the initiative to act and to participate. They appeared to be more submissive, they did not say much, or understand much. Men were rarely depicted as showing emotion, they gave the orders, they conquered, they took on responsibility, etc. All professional and occupational activities were portrayed as being inherently masculine.

Thirdly, within the domestic sphere, the study found that the nuclear family was invariably the family model presented. Family conflict was absent, there was no divorce and there were no alternative models portrayed such as one-parent families. Girls were depicted as being brought up to follow the same path as their mothers, that is to say, to stay at home and do the housework. Although the textbooks analysed showed both sexes studying and playing together at school, it was the boys who, in 84 per cent of the cases noted, were the main characters and leaders.

Illustrations to material referring to events and situations in the political world showed women in only 10 per cent of cases. It is especially significant that women accounted for only 13.2 per cent of the total of 2,549 references (illustrations and text) to people at work. Approximately one-third of the jobs carried out by women were in commerce, at 31.5 per cent, and 30.5 per cent of women illustrated appeared as secretaries or administrative assistants in public administration and business. Women appeared in only 11.3 per cent of the examples in which the liberal professions were cited. Most teachers were depicted as women but women were never portrayed as professors, scientists or researchers. In industry, women scarcely figured. Where they did, it was in the less qualified jobs.

The study concluded that it was in Humanities textbooks that discrimination against women was strongest. Deprived of their collective identity in History books, women were portrayed as powerless and as having no historical role to play. They always belonged to someone and the only importance they had was in relation to men or in relation to their reproductive function. Although sexism was inevitably less immediately evident in Physical Geography textbooks, the same old theme was still present. It was men who were portrayed tapping the earth's riches and as being responsible for making the economy function.

In language textbooks, women made their appearance as wives, housewives and mothers in reasonably well-off social environments. These women did not appear to have any life of their own. They dedicated their existence to the well-being of the family and the organization of the household. Older women, single women, widows, divorcees (with or without children) did not exist as far as these books were concerned. Women employed outside the home made the occasional furtive appearance, but always carrying out the more menial and less qualified jobs in the labour hierarchy. If a women appeared occupying a responsible position at work or in a career not traditionally followed by women, it was shown as something exceptional and not as a possible role model for girls.

Sexism was even found in the pages of Mathematics textbooks, despite the apparently neutral and technical character of the subject. Stereotyping of male and female roles occurred in the examples, exercises and problems set by the writers. Mothers and housewives were shown as the people responsible for buying the basic necessities, food, clothes, etc. Men, on the other hand, appeared as professionally competent people who did less shopping but who were responsible for purchasing a wider variety of goods, including the more "important" and costly consumer items, such as cars.

This study showed how much textbooks are permeated through and through by sexism. They either ignore women altogether, play down their qualities and attributes or describe their role in society in a very restrictive way. No attempt is made to do justice to the multiple and changing roles of women in the present time and indeed in the past. Textbooks used by primary schools give children a limited view of the world, a view that does not conform to reality, and a view that clearly discriminates against the female sex. They paint not just a partial, but also a false, picture of reality.

The models portrayed in these textbooks are assimilated by boys and girls who grow up believing that they are natural and therefore justifiable. Boys then expect girls to be sweet, submissive, fragile and interested in their own little domestic world. Girls are encouraged to modify any educational or professional ambition they might have so that they may better play the role traditionally reserved for them. Boys expect to be the dominant figure in any situation and try to live up to their strong and decisive role in all circumstances. The nuclear family model and the sexual stereotypes that the textbooks tend to have as their only point of reference run the risk of provoking a dangerous dissonance between what the child is taught and what he or she experiences as the reality of his or her own home: working mother, unemployment of the father, one-parent family, sharing of household tasks, etc.

While it is true that men and women begin to be influenced by sex role stereotyping from the day they are born, and that both the family and the media have an important function in this respect, it is clear that school textbooks can either reinforce traditional stereotyping or try to counteract sexism in Spanish society. The content of textbooks currently used in schools goes against the objectives of the education system in that it is often contrary to the aims of linking the school environment to reality, of helping the children to develop a critical understanding of society, of nurturing tolerance and of reducing prejudice and above all, sexism. Instead, textbooks play a negative role in the education process. In their distortion of reality, they help to perpetuate the domination of women by men.

Teachers' Attitudes and the Development of Girls' Self-Image

Another important aspect of the internal dynamics of the education system that must be studied in order to understand the social behaviour and occupational aspirations of adolescent students is the attitudes of teachers, which have such a profound influence on pupils' perceptions of society.

A study of the attitudes of secondary school teachers based on action research with a small sample of secondary teachers in Madrid in 1986, showed that the teachers concerned generally accepted that boys and girls were equal (Alberdi, 1987a). They claimed that they treated all children alike, irrespective of sex. However, responses began to take on more complex hues when deeper questions were asked. In general, the teachers showed little awareness of the persistence of sexism. They tended to believe that it had ceased to be an issue after the establishment of co-education. On closer questioning they accepted that sexism continued to be a problem in school, but they tended to duck the issue by claiming that this was simply a faithful reflection of society. The education system was sexist because society was sexist.

The teachers generally accepted that girls work harder than boys in secondary school and tend to be more academically able as a group. They did question, however, the long-term commitment of girls to certain careers. Such conclusions can only be reached by teachers on the basis of their understanding of the role of women in society, given the proven ability of the girls in school. Teachers, like parents, anticipate the problems that girls are likely to face in the labour market. They discourage girls from following certain careers, knowing that they will experience discrimination, and often abdicate responsibility to parents by claiming that it is the job of the family to advise the child. Although based on a small sample, it seems clear that these pressures do have an effect on the direction which female students take.

According to recent research the family still exercises a very strong influence on education and career aspirations and can be an even more conservative influence on children than the teacher (Alberdi, 1987b). Because parents want to make sure that their children get on in life, they may encourage their daughters to work hard at school but, in reality, they see marriage and the subsequent raising of a family as the main priority. Nevertheless, since girls are now faced with more varied futures in their personal and occupational lives, there is some evidence that parental attitudes are slowly changing.

In school little formal discrimination exists in terms of the separate treatment of boys and girls. One study found that only toilets, cloakrooms and changing rooms were separate for boys and girls (Subirats, 1985). However, at the level of the hidden curriculum, more recent research has shown that teachers address themselves to boys more than to girls during classes (Subirats and Brullet, 1988). This study calculated the number of words addressed to the pupils over a certain period and found that the proportion was 100:74 in favour of the boys. However, it was also found that this ratio changed, according to the behavioural context. Those words and sentences which were directed at controlling behaviour or organizing the class were addressed to girls less often than the average number of overall words addressed to them. The number of verbs of movement directed to the girls was also less than the average number of words directed to them overall. A very low level of verbal interaction was observed during manual work classes and group activities.

Analysis of the interviews with teachers involved showed the persistence of sex stereotyping on their part, but also some change in perception of the place of women in society. The teachers talked about the girls in a way that would suggest a departure from the point of view traditionally held by their profession about the role of women in society, although boys continued to be thought of as playing the traditional masculine roles.

The conclusions of this study were that there is a tendency for the education system to develop a more consistent treatment of girls and boys, irrespective of their sex. However, this tendency is based on the universalization of the masculine model rather than on the fusion of the feminine and the masculine. The system as a whole continues to assume the existence of natural differences between male and female and to condone the predominance of men as part of the natural order.

In a pilot project for action-research into the issue of girls and new technology, funded by the Spanish Ministry for Education and the European Commission in 1987–1988, we found that sexism is still prevalent in Spanish society but that teachers are beginning to show greater commitment to the principle of equality. Sexism persists because it is rarely challenged. Once the issue is brought up there are few voices who defend the status quo in the face of a greater ideological commitment to equality of opportunity.

Equal Opportunities Policies

Until the law which created the Instituto de la Mujer (Institute of Women's Affairs) of the Ministry of Culture was passed in October 1983, there were no national institutions charged with the task of promoting the equality of women in education. This was despite the political changes initiated in 1975 and constitutional changes in 1978, which established equality of all Spaniards before the law and the illegality of sex discrimination. Before then, anti-sexism activity was largely the province of unofficial women's groups in Spanish society.

Since 1983, the Instituto de la Mujer has tried to encourage a change in attitudes within the education system with the objective of eliminating sex discrimination in the labour market. Working together with the Ministry of Education and Science and through a policy of financial and moral support to groups working in the area, the Institute has begun a process of consciousness-raising aimed at combating discrimination against women in education. This process has been furthered by holding seminars, public debates and by publishing research findings.

Since Spain became a member of the European Economic Community in January 1986, and within the framework of its equal opportunities policies, the Institute has taken a more positive and concrete role in, for example, teacher training, school and careers counselling and new technology. The Institute has just completed a campaign aimed at changing attitudes in the media. This campaign, which was directed towards opening up further occupational opportunities for girls and women, also tried to put over the message that domestic work and family responsibilities should be shared between men and women. Although results are hard to evaluate, the campaign has succeeded in identifying sexism as a problem in the education system among a wider audience and in creating wide agreement that it should be combated.

A three-year action plan on equal opportunities for women proposed by the Spanish government in 1986 has given a high priority to education and training on the assumption that discrimination in society needs to be fought through the education system. Twenty thousand copies of a handbook on equal opportunities have been distributed by the Ministry of Education to schools, colleges of education and in-service training centres for teachers throughout the country, along with an extract from the government's published policy on equal opportunities. This gives statistical data on the educational disparities between men and women in Spain and lists objectives in the areas of education and training to overcome such inequalities, drawing on the experience of other European countries. Governmental, regional and municipal authorities are urged to publish lists of recommended teaching materials and textbooks and to make parents aware of educational and vocational opportunities available to their daughters, especially in the sciences and in new technology. Schools are urged to teach domestic skills to boys as well as to girls (Council of Europe, 1988).

This action plan opens up the possibility of a better education for women and raises hopes that the biological differences between men and women will cease to result in inequality of opportunity.

References

Alberdi, I. and Alberdi, I. (1984) Mujer y educación, un largo camino hacia la igualdad de oportunidades (Women and education, a long road to equality of opportunity). *Revista de Educación*, **275**, Madrid.

Alberdi, I. (1987a) Coeducación y sexismo en la enseñanza media (Co-education and sexism in secondary education). In *La Investigación en España sobre mujer y educación* (An investigation into women and education in Spain). Madrid: Instituto de la Mujer.

Alberdi, I. (1987b) El gasto en educación y la participación de los padres y las madres en la tarea educación (Educational expenditure and the participation of mothers and fathers in the task of education). Documentos de Trabajo. Madrid: FIES.

Alberdi, I. and Escario, P. (1987) Attitudes of women towards familial change. In Shamgar-Handelman and Palomba (Eds.) *Alternative patterns of family life in modern societies*. Rome: IRP.

Alvaro, I. and Monge, I. (1984) La familia en los libros de texto de lectura infantil (The family in infant school textbooks). *Revista de Educación*, 275.

Careaga, P. (1987) Modelos masculinos y feminos en los libros de texto de EGB (Masculine and feminine role models in primary school textbooks). In *La investigación en España sobre mujer y educación* (An investigation into women and education in Spain). Madrid: Instituto de la Mujer.

Centro de investigación y documentación educativo (1988) *La presencia de las mujeres en el sistema educativa* (The presence of women in the educational system). Madrid: Instituto de la Mujer.

CIDE (1984) Encuesta a los alumnos de COU 1983–1984 (An enquiry into COU students 1983–1984). In J. Carabana Modesto intento de interpretación de las tasas femininas de escolaridad (A modest attempt at the interpretation of the results of girls at school). *Revista de Educación*, **275**.

Conde, R. (1984) (Ed.) *Familia y Cambio Social* (The family and social change). Madrid: Centro de Investigaciones Sociológicas.

Council of Europe (1988) *Council of Europe Bulletin*, February.

Evans, S. J. (1990) Catholics oppose reform proposals. *Times Educational Supplement*, April 6, 1990.

Fundación Foessa (1975) *Informa Foessa*. Informe sociologico sobre la situación social de España (Sociological review of the social situation in Spain). Madrid: Euramerica.

Garreta, N. (1984) *La presencia de la mujer en los textos escolares* (The presence of women in school textbooks). *Revista de Educación*, **275**.

Heras y Trias, P. (1987) El papel de la mujer en la ensenañza y en los libros de texto de Cataluna (The woman's role in education and in textbooks in Catalonia). In *La Investigación en España sobre mujer y educación* (An investigation into women and education in Spain). Madrid: Instituto de la Mujer.

INE (1986) *Estadísticas del Ministerio de Educación y Ciencia* (Statistics of the Ministry of Education and Science). Madrid.

Instituto de la Mujer (1985) *Mujer y Educación* (Women and Education). Madrid: Instituto de la Mujer.

Instituto de la Mujer (1988) *La presencia de las mujeres en la sistema educativo* (The presence of women in the education system). Madrid: Instituto de la Mujer.

OECD (1986) *Review of National Policies for Education: Spain*. Paris: OECD.

Subirats, M. (1985) Mujer y educación: de la enseñanza segregada a la coeducación. (Women and education: from single-sex education to co-education). *Mujer y educación*. Madrid: Instituto de la Mujer.

Subirats, M. and Brullet, C. (1988) Rosa y azul. La transmisión de los géneros en la escuela mixta (Pink and blue. The transmission of sex-roles in the co-educational school). Madrid: Instituto de la Mujer.

CHAPTER 9

Sweden

INGA WERNERSSON

IN ANY discussion of gender equality and education in Sweden the concepts of equality of access to education and educational achievement on the one hand and the notion of the school as an instrument for changes in sex role attitudes on the other need to be separated. If education is viewed as a "commodity", gender equality in education can be defined as an even distribution of educational resources, regardless of the pupil's gender, with the expectation that all pupils should reach largely similar results on the basis of fair competition. However, the school is also an agent of socialization and, at least in theory, can be used to change ideological images and social attitudes. Since the late 1960s official Swedish policy has not only been concerned with a redistribution of educational resources, but has also stressed the importance of changing the content of education to actively promote new ideas of gender roles and relations.

This chapter will firstly give a brief history of the educational system of girls in Sweden and an outline of the current Swedish education system. It will then compare female and male participation and achievement at different levels in the education system and present and discuss Swedish research on gender differentiation and sex differences in the classroom. The position of women in teaching and in the labour market will be briefly reviewed. Finally, the effects of Swedish government policy towards gender equality in education since the 1970s will be discussed and to some extent evaluated.

Historical Background

In 1842 compulsory elementary schooling was introduced in Sweden. In the debates preceding this decision the issue was raised as to whether girls ought to have the same education as boys, or for that matter, whether ordinary girls needed any formal education at all. In the actual legislation girls were included on the same terms as boys. There was, however, a loophole called the "minimipensum", which enabled poor children, children deemed unintelligent, and girls to leave school after a very short period if the parents so decided.

By the early 1800s a system of private secondary schools for girls had started to develop. A system of public secondary schools for boys had been long established and the consequences of this dual system was that girls' education was more expensive than boys', so that the social selection of girls to secondary education was much narrower than that of boys. The content of girls' education was directed towards preparing them for the tasks of wife and mother, and for a very narrow range of occupations (e.g., teacher, nurse, office worker). The demand for secondary education for girls stemmed from economic and demographic factors. One consequence of industrialization was that fewer women were needed for production in the home. There was also a surplus of women in the population and many women never got married. Working-class girls got jobs in the new industries but the growing middle classes were anxious to support secondary education for girls to ensure that their daughters would have some means of financial support to protect them against having to take up factory work and so sinking into the proletariat. It was not until 1927 that the state took the same responsibility for the secondary education of girls as for that of boys.

In the 1940s two government commissions developed the outlines of a democratization and expansion of the school system. In the intense debates which took place during the 1940s and 1950s the need for special educational arrangements for girls was one issue, although not a major one. The position of the separate girls' schools was also discussed. Defenders of single-sex education for girls argued that a special and valuable form of education had developed in this type of school. Since the girls' schools had not offered formal examinations there had been more room for experimentation in teaching methods and individual learning methods, and it was argued that single-sex schools should be retained for both boys and girls who needed a calmer pace of study and more individual attention. However, single-sex schools disappeared between 1962 and 1972 when comprehensive schools gradually replaced the differentiated school system.

The Swedish Education System

The Grundskola (Compulsory Comprehensive School)

In Sweden children start school at the age of seven. For six-year-olds a voluntary year in preschool education is available. The compulsory school years are organized in three "stages": grades 1–3 for seven to nine-year-olds ("lower stage"), grades 4–6 for ten to twelve-year-olds ("middle stage") and grades 7–9 for thirteen to fifteen-year-olds ("upper stage"). Until now teacher education has followed the three "stages" of education with two types of classroom teachers, teaching grades 1–3 or grades 4–6, and subject teachers certified for teaching in grades 7–9 and in upper secondary schools ("gymnasieskolan"). This is now changing. In future, all compulsory school teachers will be qualified to teach pupils at two overlapping "stages" – grades 1–7 or 4–9 respectively.

In Sweden compulsory education is organized under central state control with very few private alternatives to the public system. In 1986 only 0.7 per cent of children of school age attended private schools. The educational aims, content and methods of state education are set out in a curriculum common to the whole country. Three such curricula have been drawn up – in 1962, 1969 and 1980 – since the introduction of comprehensive schools. Within the broad framework of the common curriculum a system of decentralized decision making is now being developed.

The Gymnasieskolan (Integrated Upper Secondary Education). The different types of upper secondary education are integrated under one system, offering three to four year academic course programmes, two year academic course programmes and two year vocational education programmes. There are also shorter specialized courses. All programmes, which include two year courses in Swedish and English, give pupils a general qualification for university studies.

Higher Education. Undergraduate university education is organized in five sectors, which lead to employment in the technical professions, in administrative, economic and social professions, in nursing and medicine, in teaching and in jobs in the sphere of culture and information. A student can be admitted to a fixed course programme leading to an examination for a specific profession in one of these sectors or to single courses of varying length. In all programmes and courses, admission to universities is restricted. In addition to marks gained in upper secondary education, work experience also gives credit when applying for higher education.

Adult Education. The most important ideological motives for the reform of the education system in Sweden have been those of social equality and democratization. By the early 1970s it had become apparent that there had been a discrepancy in educational opportunity between different age groups because many older people had missed out on the reforms of the early 1960s and a system of adult education at different levels was developed to meet this problem. Adult education is an important part of the Swedish education system, and is to some extent designed to compensate for failure and unfairness in other parts of the education system. There are several forms of adult education. "Kommunal vuxenutbildung" (municipal adult education) is designed to give a general education at the compulsory or upper secondary school level. "Arbetsmarkhadsutbildung" (labour market training) is organized at the national level and gives vocational training to combat unemployment. A third form of adult education consists of shorter and specialized courses, "Studiecirkel" (study circles) which can have very different content – ranging from general educational or skills-based courses to leisure

courses. Several forms of financial aid for adult education exist to encourage
student take-up.

Girls and Educational Achievement at School and in Further and Higher Education

At Compulsory School Level

The Swedish "Läroplan" (National Curriculum) is central to the issue of
gender equality in and through education. All schools are co-educational but
in the National Curriculum of 1962 traditional sex roles were taken for
granted. In 1969 and 1980, however, radical goals were formulated to enable
schools to take an active part in the struggle for gender equality. The National
Curriculum of 1969 stated explicitly that:

— educational content should be identical for boys and girls;
— individual pupils should be encouraged to make non-traditional educational and occupational choices;
— the compulsory school should be an example of good practice, showing
  that it is possible to treat members of both sexes in a fair and equal manner;
— the historical background of traditional sex roles should be highlighted
  and current practice should be debated and criticized.

The National Curriculum of 1980, which is still in force, has similar broad
aims.

At the level of compulsory education there is officially no formal sex
differentiation and action to promote gender equality in the "Grundskolan" is
prescribed, but actual practice may be at variance with these aims. Sex
differences in achievement at the age of compulsory education tend to be in
favour of girls. In a study of relative achievement in the sixth grade published
by Svensson in 1971, it was shown that in terms of language skills girls
performed better than boys with the same level of intelligence, but in terms of
numerical and spatial skills the picture was more complicated (Svensson,
1971). At this level boys tended to perform better overall than girls, even
though the differences were small, but at the same level of achievement girls
tended to get better marks. A replication of the study published by
Emanuelsson and Svensson in 1985 showed that the picture had changed
somewhat. By 1985 girls were achieving better test results in verbal skills and
there were no significant sex differences in numerical and spatial tests. There is
a possibility that changes in school organization have played a part in the
positive development of girls' test performance. Girls still tend to attain a
better grade average. Boys also tend to be in receipt of special (compensatory)
education more often than girls. In 1986, for example, 24 per cent of boys in
grades 3 to 6 compared with only 14 per cent of the girls received

compensatory education for learning problems (Statistika meddelanden U, 1986).

During the first six years in school there are no optional subjects. Traditionally sex-typed subjects like Woodwork, Typing, Home Economics and Needlework are compulsory for both boys and girls, and Physical Education is also taught in mixed classes. During the last three years of compulsory education some subject options are introduced, such as a second foreign language (French or German) or the "home language" of immigrant students. Although there is a great deal of local autonomy in the organization of the optional courses, the National Curriculum states that: "Courses shall have such aims that a very skewed sex distribution of uptake cannot be predicted" (Läroplan för Grundskolan, 1980).

Both boys and girls tend to choose a second language as an optional subject at this level, although a higher proportion of girls do so. About 30 per cent of the boys but only 2–3 per cent of girls choose courses in the Natural Sciences and Technology. In other areas there are no great sex differences. In grades 7 to 9 there is also a choice between courses of different degrees of difficulty in ordinary or advanced English and Mathematics. About as many girls as boys (about 75 per cent) choose to take advanced Mathematics. More girls than boys (80 per cent compared with 70 per cent) choose to take advanced English (Statistiska meddelanden U, 1986).

Studies by Wernersson (1982) and Einarsson and Hultman (1985) showed that teacher-pupil interaction in the classroom follows the same general patterns as described in British and American studies, reviewed by Kelly (1986) and Brophy (1985). According to studies of classroom settings from kindergarten to upper secondary school level, boys seek and get more attention from the teacher than girls. The general pattern seems to be the same regardless of the age of the pupil, but the tendency for boys to receive more teacher attention is more pronounced in the early and later school years. In a study carried out by Kärrby in 1987 of preschool education it was found that in a part-time nursery school six-year-old-boys had more frequent contact with adults than girls. In the full-time day-care centres, however, girls had more frequent contact with adults than boys.

Other studies by Wernersson (1977) and Wernersson and Lander (1980) of pupils of compulsory school age showed that pupil–pupil interaction is, to a large extent, restricted to the same-sex group. Very few sociometric choices of "friends" were made between the sexes despite the co-educational setting. Boys and girls tended to exist in two separate groupings that are relatively closed to each other. The same pattern has been demonstrated at the preschool level. Gunnarsson (1978) found that children who spent all their time at home had more contacts with children of the opposite sex than children in day-care centres who played more in same-sex groups. This can be explained by the fact there are more children to choose as playmates in the day-care centres while at home children have to play with those available, regardless of sex. In the 1987 study by Kärrby mentioned above, it was found, however, that children in the day-care centre tended to integrate themes for play typical of the opposite sex into their own fantasy play. Moreover, in a study of sex differentiation in the school setting play and learning activities tended to be far less sex-typed than activities in other settings (Wernersson, 1977).

Efforts have been made to find ways of changing sex role attitudes among teachers and pupils. However, it has proven very difficult to integrate the notion of equality into the teaching of different subjects (Wernersson, Lander and Öhrn, 1984). Teachers, in general, have an ambivalent attitude towards gender equality, accepting some aspects such as a commitment to developing the same skills in boys and girls, but at the same time expressing doubt about some of the consequences of equal opportunities policies, such as a greater demand by women for equality at home as well as at work.

In conclusion it can be said that at the level of compulsory education:

— there is no formal organizational sex differentiation in Sweden;
— girls and boys tend to make sex-stereotyped option choices;
— girls tend to achieve a slightly higher level of academic attainment;
— boys are more disruptive in class and receive more teacher attention;
— the positive development of the achievement of girls may partly be attributed to changes in school experience;
— boys and girls tend to form separate friendship groups.

Upper Secondary Education

Around 90 per cent of each cohort leaving the Grundskolan (compulsory schools) go on to "Gymnasieskolan" (integrated upper secondary schools) for a further two to three years of study, where there are places available for all who complete compulsory education. Overall, female pupils constitute slightly less than half of the school population at this level. Even though the stated goals of gender equality are the same at this level as at the lower level, the reality is quite different. Here, the division of labour between men and women in society is clearly mirrored, since boys and girls show very different patterns of educational and occupational choice. In practice there is one "female" and one "male" branch in upper secondary education. This is especially true of vocational education programmes. Table 9.1 below shows the distribution of male and female pupils in educational programmes of different lengths and degrees of vocational specialization.

Over the ten years illustrated in the table it is apparent that female study patterns have become more similar to those of males. In 1976 the majority of girls opted for vocational programmes and in 1981 the majority opted equally for academic and work-related programmes. By 1987 a clear majority of girls opted for the longer academic programmes, in a largely similar proportion to boys.

TABLE 9.1

Distribution of Female and Male Pupils in Upper Secondary School Courses,
1976–1987

	1976		1981		1987	
	% Girls	% Boys	% Girls	% Boys	% Girls	% Boys
Academic 3–4 year programmes	33	45	42	51	53	44
General 2 year programmes	14	11	16	11	11	12
Vocational 2 year programmes	53	44	42	38	36	42
Total	100	100	100	100	100	100

Source: Statistisk Årsbok (1977, 1982–1983, 1989).

In Table 9.2 a detailed picture of the uptake of different course programmes from 1976 to 1981 by female pupils is presented. We can see that in the three to four year theoretical courses there was an increase in the percentage of girls in all areas, smaller in the traditional female areas and somewhat greater in traditional male and gender-neutral areas. In the two year academic and work-related programmes few changes occurred over the period described. All of the changes were inside traditional female or gender-neutral areas. Upper secondary education in Sweden has in all twenty-six different course programmes and of these only a handful have a balanced sex distribution, that is 40–60 per cent of each sex. In practice education at this level consists of, more or less, single-sex courses and much of the teaching is carried out in single-sex settings.

If sex differences in achievement are examined at this level girls again often appear to outperform boys. In 1986, for example, girls had a higher mean grade in all course programmes but one (Statistiska meddelanden U, 1987). In work-related courses there is a clear tendency for the predominant sex to receive the highest marks in those, often practical, subjects that are characteristic for each programme. In Literature, Composition and Foreign Languages and Chemistry female pupils attained better results than males, while male pupils attained better results than females in Physics. In Mathematics females sometimes "out-performed" males and vice versa.

These official data clearly demonstrate that upper secondary education is sex-differentiated as a result of sex differences in option choices. It is less easy, however, to discern whether this is the result of some form of sex discrimination and there are no studies of sex differentiation in the classroom at this level of education in Sweden, to my knowledge. Many classes at this level are effectively single-sex. The situation when one sex comprises a small minority presents special problems and different measures have been taken to

TABLE 9.2

*Distribution of Girls in Upper Secondary Education Programmes, by Subject,
1976–1981*

	1976	1981	1987	% Change between 1977 and 1985
3–4 year academic programmes:				
Economics	51	59	62	+11
Humanities	83	87	87	+4
Natural sciences	40	45	50	+10
Social sciences	65	70	70	+5
Engineering	7	11	21	+14
2-year general programmes (examples):				
Economics	56	60	58	+2
Social work	71	65	61	−10
Technology	3	2	6	+3
2-year work-related programmes (examples):				
Clothing and textiles	84	88	96	+12
Building and construction	1	1	2	+1
Distribution and clerical work	80	81	71	−9
Motor mechanics	2	2	3	+1
Agriculture	39	39	41	+2
Food technology	47	49	55	+8
Forestry	2	3	1	=0
Metalwork	2	3	4	+2
Nursing	92	91	91	−1

Source: Statistisk årsbok (1977, 1982–1983, 1988).

meet these, such as clustering minority sex members together and using different teaching techniques. Although girls' educational performance is generally superior to that of boys, girls also seem to have a higher drop-out rate (Reuterberg, 1986). At this level it could be argued that both girls and boys "lose out" in the educational system, in different ways. However, when post-school outcomes are examined, the picture changes. Table 9.3 below shows the occupational destinations of school-leavers who completed vocational education programmes in upper secondary education in 1982–1983.

These data illustrate the argument that it seems to be easier for young men to break into traditionally female occupations than for young women to break into male occupations. More young women than men experience periods of involuntary unemployment, especially where they have entered male-dominated occupations. Overall women tend to secure jobs in the occupational area for which they are educated more often than men. However, the reverse is experienced by those women who have entered male-dominated

TABLE 9.3

Occupations in 1985 of those who Graduated from Vocational Education Programmes in Secondary School 1982–1983

	% Working in occupation for which they were qualified		% Out of work at any period	
	Men	Women	Men	Women
Female-dominated spheres of education	75	74	34	42
Male-dominated spheres of education	58	43	45	58
All types of education	62	69	43	48

Source: Statistisk årsbok (1986).

occupations while those men who have tried to enter female-dominated occupations have been relatively successful.

In upper secondary education the situation of girls can be summarized as follows:

— girls comprise about half of the student body;
— the pattern of educational choice is very different for boys and girls;
— patterns of educational choice for girls are, however, changing.

Higher Education

Since the university reforms of 1977, when several forms of post-secondary education, such as teacher education and nursing education, were integrated into the university sector, women have constituted the majority of university students. In higher education, as in post-compulsory upper secondary education, there is a strong pattern of sex differentiation according to subject area. Table 9.4 below shows the sex distribution of students pursuing different lines of study.

TABLE 9.4

Distribution of Students in Higher Education by Sex and by Area of Study, 1986

	Male students		Female students	
	Nos.	%	Nos.	%
Science and Technology	23,375	77	6,982	23
Administrative, economic and social studies	15,556	47	17,542	53
Nursing and medical studies	4,898	23	16,398	77
Teacher education	4,737	24	15,000	76
Arts and cultural studies	2,356	39	3,685	61
All university students	71,394	44	90,365	56
Qualifications awarded	11,073	36	19,686	63

Source: Statistisk årsbok (1989).

Of the five educational sectors in higher education women predominate numerically in two sectors, men dominate one and the two other sectors show a more even distribution. However, different lines of study within the sectors vary a great deal. In the technical sector, Architecture and Chemistry, and a few other areas, an even distribution of men and women is shown. Despite the female dominance in the nursing and medical sector there are still more men than women training to be doctors. In Sweden, no distinction has been drawn between degrees and diplomas since the university reforms of 1977. However, it must be underlined that even if women are in a majority at the universities, men still dominate the "prestige" areas leading to the most well-paid jobs. That so many more women than men are awarded qualifications can partly be explained by the fact that more women choose to take shorter vocational courses.

In postgraduate education women comprised 31 per cent of registered students and 23 per cent of those awarded doctorates in 1985–1986 (The Swedish Institute, 1987). A similar variation in subject choice as in undergraduate studies can be seen. At the technical universities 13 per cent of postgraduate students are women compared with 47 per cent in arts subjects.

Adult Education

In adult education the majority of students are women. Table 9.5 below illustrates the distribution of men and women in some of the different forms of adult education.

Apart from "labour market training", where more men are found, women predominate in the various forms of adult education. This is partly as a result of the need of many women to update skills after a career break for child-rearing, but another reason is that men more often get different types of "on the job" training in their different occupations. However, a paradoxical effect

TABLE 9.5

The Distribution of Men and Women in Different Forms of Adult Education, 1987

	Men		Women	
	Nos.	%	Nos.	%
Municipal adult education ("second-chance education")	51,830	36	93,940	64
Basic literacy and numeracy	5,440	45	6,520	55
"Arbetsmarknadsutbildung" (Labour market training for the unemployed)	15,100	63	8,970	37
"Folkhögskola" ("Folk high school")	6,130	40	9,140	60

Source: Statistisk årsbok (1987).

of the fact that fewer women are the main bread-winner in the family is that it is easier for women to obtain funds for adult education. State funds are available to compensate for an eventual loss of income for those in part-time employment or for those at work in the home, and child-care is counted along with other forms of work experience in obtaining grant aid, as a measure to promote gender equality. For those on higher incomes, usually men, it is more difficult to take up adult education, at least on a full-time basis (Lundquist, 1986).

The Position of Women in Teaching

Women comprise 62 per cent of all teachers. However, women teachers are clustered at the lower end of the education system and at the lowest salary levels. In 1987, 68 per cent of the teachers at compulsory school level were women compared with 44 per cent in the post-compulsory upper secondary school (Statistiska meddelanden U, 1987). In the category with the highest pay only about 10 per cent are women. Table 9.6 shows the percentage of women at different levels of the teaching profession.

TABLE 9.6

Distribution of Women in the Teaching Profession, 1987

	Total No. of Teachers	No. of Women Teachers	% Distribution of Women Teachers 1987	% Distribution of Women Teachers 1977
Headteachers	2,173	277	13	(7)
Assistant headteachers, directors of studies	3,074	978	32	(19)
Elementary teachers (for 7–9-year-olds)	23,094	22,730	98	(99)
"Middle school" teachers (for 10–12-year-olds)	22,359	14,819	66	(61)
Secondary teachers (for 13–19-year-olds)	39,222	18,404	47	(45)

Source: Statistisk årsbok (1987).

Although this table illustrates a classic hierarchy in the teaching profession, there has been a small increase in the percentage of female headteachers and directors of studies, following a 1977 Government Commission into the situation, which put forward measures to promote women in school leadership roles. In other influential positions women are still under-represented, although this is changing. In 1977, for example, 33 per cent of the members of the local school boards were women, a proportion which had risen to 41 per cent by 1983 (SOU, 1980).

Another aspect of sex differentiation in the Swedish labour market is part-time work. One-third of the teachers work part-time and of those about 80 per cent are women, meaning that two in five female teachers work part-time compared with one in seven male teachers.

Teaching is traditionally a female occupation. At the same time it is a profession with more prestige than most other traditional female jobs. For the pupils women teachers may have a double image, as both authority figures and "mothers". Yet the hierarchical structure of the school with, typically, a male headmaster and female class teachers, mirrors the situation of gender differentiation in the labour market and in society as a whole.

Women in the Labour Market

In comparison with many European countries, the Swedish government has played a strong role in the promotion of equal opportunities in the labour market since the 1970s, and, in particular, after the passage of the Equal Opportunities Act of 1980. All government ministers are required to pay attention to aspects of policy concerning equality between men and women in the fields for which they are responsible. Overall responsibility rests with the Ministry of Civil Service Affairs through its Equality Affairs Division (Jamstalldhetsenheten) and through the Council on Equality Issues (Jamstaldhetsradet), an advisory body representing women's organizations, political parties and employer and employee organizations. A formally independent agency, the Office of the Equal Opportunities Ombudsman, was established in 1980 to ensure compliance with the Equal Opportunities Act and a Commission for Research on Equality between Men and Women was set up in 1983 to initiate and publicize research work in this area.

About 82 per cent of all Swedish women are in paid employment and their numbers in the labour force increased significantly during the 1970s. Nearly all women in Sweden carry on working until their first child is born and more and more women are returning to work within a year of having a child. Since 1974, both the father and mother of a child have been entitled to substantial benefits enabling them to take care of their children without loss of income. Leave of absence is provided for a total of twelve months in connection with childbirth with parental benefit at 90 per cent of gross income for nine months. Leave may be taken at any time up to the child's fourth birthday and parents can decide how to divide time off work between them. Very few fathers, however, use the opportunity to take time off work to look after their young children, in part because of discouragement by employers. Benefits can be used either to take time off work full-time or part-time over a long period. Parents of children under the age of eight have the right to reduce their working day by two hours, but with a corresponding reduction in pay. Child-care provision for children under six has also been rapidly expanded. In 1986, 47 per cent of all preschool children were cared for in day-care centres run by local authorities. The Swedish Government has committed itself to increasing day-care for all children aged eighteen months to six years by 1990. However, there is currently a critical shortage of preschool teachers in several locations, partly because of the relatively low rates of pay. Use of relatives, childminders and one parent working irregular hours are common strategies to combat this problem.

Despite such progressive policies, women are still employed in a more restricted sector of the labour market, where different rates of pay and hours of work prevail, although this is not as strong a difference as in many other European countries. Women have been recruited largely into the expanding areas of the public services, but have entered the industrial, technical and economic sectors to a far smaller degree. It is estimated that women predominate in 56 occupations, while men do so in 161 occupations, despite governmental efforts to change this. In addition, women still tend to take the lion's share of domestic work and often work part-time for this reason. Forty-four per cent of women work part-time compared with 6 per cent of men, which explains to some extent the disparity in wages.

Representation of women in decision making and advisory bodies has, however, increased substantially in the past ten years. In 1985, 31 per cent of members of the Swedish Parliament were women and about 28 per cent of seats in the influential Parliamentary Standing Committees were held by women. In 1986 the Cabinet consisted of five women to sixteen men and 37 per cent of county councillors were women. Although women have made progress in quantitative terms here, they tend to be concentrated in those areas connected with health, social welfare and cultural affairs, and are much less well represented on indirectly elected bodies and in central and regional government administration. In 1986 only 26 out of 251 senior government officials were women (The Swedish Institute, 1987).

Equality in Education and Equality Through Education

For more than two decades the official goals of the Swedish school system have explicitly included gender equality as an important issue. This chapter has attempted to describe the situation of girls and women in the Swedish education system. From an organizational and formal point of view, the Swedish education system is now fairly free from sex differentiation. Reforms of the education system at different levels since the late 1960s have stressed the importance of gender issues and measures have been taken to guarantee gender equality and fairness. It has been difficult, however, to judge to what extent the different measures taken have been successful. The current official strategy is to be more precise in formulating goals. In a five-year plan proposed to promote equality between the sexes in the 1990s, a central objective is the even distribution of boys and girls in all branches of education, expressed in terms of quantifiable targets. One such target is that within the next five years at least 10 per cent of applicants for upper secondary training programmes should belong to the minority sex in those areas where boys or girls now constitute less than 5 per cent of trainees. The long-term goal is that in no course of study at upper secondary level should the minority sex fall below 40 per cent of students. It remains to be seen whether this strategy will be effective. So far, however, it is obvious that deep-seated cultural patterns as well as the economic reality of the surrounding society make females and males use education in different ways. The division of labour in society is clearly visible in choice of subject area in upper secondary and higher education. Sex differences in behaviour in the classroom are also apparent. It is hard to say, though, to what extent this situation is caused internally in the education system and to what extent this has been brought about by socialization in the family and by the structure of the labour market.

At the beginning of the chapter the importance of defining two different aspects of gender equality in relation to education was stressed, namely equality *in* education and equality *through* education. Education, especially at the level of compulsory education, has been perceived in Sweden as a very important tool in changing attitudes and ideologies of sex and gender. Organizational changes have been made and have had demonstrable results. Data presented in this chapter show that girls and women have roughly equal access to education as boys and men, and that girls, at least in the compulsory and upper secondary level, tend to achieve slightly higher marks than boys. Official data show that some of the patterns of educational choice are slowly changing. However, it is also clear that many more men than women use the educational system to "get the cream of the cake" through participation in the more prestigious forms of education which lead to the well-paid power positions. There has been change, change which is still going on, towards gender equality in the educational system. Social change in other areas, such as the increase in participation of women in the labour market, and the more modest increase in the participation of women in legislative bodies at different levels would not have been possible without changes in the education system. However, at the same time sex differentiation in the classroom still reinforces the traditional patterns of female subordination. Education is a tool for long-term social change in the role of men and women in society. This change, however, often consists of adjustment of the needs and wishes of the individual to the demands of the labour market, supported by the rhetoric of fairness and equality between men and women. When, for example, there is an increase in the demand for manpower in the industrial sector, girls are urged, in the name of equality, to become engineers and technicians. This may be viewed as a measure towards real gender equality or it can be viewed as another example of the use of women as a "reserve army of labour" in times of specific skills shortages. In Sweden there has been a remarkable stability in the basic patterns of gender relations and yet also a substantial change in social sex roles. The educational system contains the same contradictions as the rest of society.

References

Brophy, J. (1985) Interaction of male and female students with male and female teachers. In L. C. Wilkinson and C. B. Marrett (Eds.) *Gender influences in classroom interaction.* New York: Academic Press.

Einarsson, J. and Hultman, T. (1985) *Godmorgon flickor och pojkar?* (Good morning girls and boys?). Stockholm: Liber.

Emanuelsson, I. and Svensson, A. (1985) *Does the level of intelligence decrease? A comparison between thirteen-year-olds tested in 1961, 1966 and 1980.* (Report no. 1985: 02.) Department of Education and Educational Research, University of Göteborg.

Gunnarsson, L. (1978) Children in day care and family care in Sweden: a follow-up. In *Research Bulletin no. 21.* Department of Educational Research, University of Göteborg.

Kärrby, G. (1987) *Könsskillnader och pedagogisk miljö i förskolan.* (Sex differences and the pedagogical environment in the preschool.) (Report no. 1987: 02.) Department of Education and Educational Research, University of Göteborg.

Kelly, A. (1986) *Gender differences in teacher-pupil interaction: a meta-analytic review.* Department of Sociology: University of Manchester.

Lundquist, O. (1986) Vuxenstudiestödet som rekryteringsinstrument – perspektiv bakat och framåt. (Financial study aid for adults as a tool for recruitment – perspective back and forth) in K. Abrahamsson and K. Rubenson *Den "nya" utbildningsklyftan: 90-talets utmaning.* (The "new" education gap: The challenge of the 90s.) *Vad säger forskningen?* Liber Utbildnings förlaget, F 84: 4.

Läroplan för Grundskolan 1980 (Curriculum for the compulsory school 1980.) Stockholm: Skolöverstyrelsen.

Reuterberg, S.-E. (1986) Orsaker till studieavbrott och linjebyten i gymnasiaskolan. (Reasons for leaving school and changing study courses in the upper secondary school.) *Publikationer från institutionen för pedagogik,* **17.**

Statens Offentliga Utredningar (SOU) (1980) *Fler kvinnor som skolledare: Betankände av utredningen om kvinnliga skolledare.* (More women in school leadership roles: A report from the Governmental Commission on women principals and headteachers.) Stockholm.

Statistisk årsbok (1977) (Statistical yearbook.) Stockholm: Statistiska Centralbyrån.

Statistisk årsbok (1982–83) (Statistical yearbook.) Stockholm: Statistiska Centralbyrån.

Statistisk årsbok (1987) (Statistical yearbook.) Stockholm: Statistiska Centralbyrån.

Statistisk årsbok (1988) (Statistical yearbook.) Stockholm: Statistiska Centralbyrån.

Statistisk årsbok (1989) (Statistical yearbook.) Stockholm: Statistiska Centralbyrån.

Statistiska meddelandan U. (1986) Stockholm: Statistiska Centralbyrån.

Statistiska meddelanden U. (1987) Stockholm: Statistiska Centralbyrån.

Svensson, A. (1971) *Relative achievement. School performance in relation to intelligence, sex and the home environment.* Stockholm: Almqvist & Wiksell.

The Swedish Institute (1987) *Equality Between Men and Women in Sweden.* Stockholm: The Swedish Institute.

Wernersson, I. (1977) *Könsdifferentiering i grundskolan.* (Sex differences in the compulsory school.) Göteborg: Acta Universitatis Gothoburgensis.

Wernersson, I. and Lander, R. (1980) *Pojkar och flickor i Furuhällskolan.* (Boys and girls in "Furuhällskolan".) University of Göteborg, Institute of Education (mimeo).

Wernersson, I. (1982) Sex differentiation and teacher-pupil interaction in the Swedish compulsory school. In *Sex stereotyping in schools. A report of the educational research workshop held in Honefoss, 5–8 May 1981.* Council of Europe. Lisse: Swets & Zeitlinger.

Wernersson, I., Lander, R. and Öhrn, E. (1984) Hur blev det med jämställdheten? Utvärdering av försöket "Jamstalld skola" (What became of gender equality? An evaluation of the programme 'Equal Schools'.) Stockholm: Arbetsmarknadsdepartementet, Jämställdhetssekretariatet.

CHAPTER 10

West Germany

ASTRID KAISER

Historical Background

THE HISTORY of education for girls in the German Federal Republic has been one of a hundred years' struggle for access to education (Brehmer, 1985).[1] The establishment of girls' secondary schools, the authorization of training colleges for women teachers at the beginning of the nineteenth century and an increasing convergence in the curriculum offered to boys and girls during the course of the twentieth century, all mark some of the clearly defined stages of this development (Kleinau, 1986). The early years of the twentieth century witnessed the first political campaigns led by feminist groups for the access of women to higher education (Clephas-Möcker and Krallmann, 1986). These campaigns also included the aim of integrating girls into all aspects of educational life, an aim which came more and more to the forefront of public attention over the ensuing years (Pfister, 1988). Full integration of pupils into co-educational secondary schools was initiated in the 1960s and completed within a few years and it seemed as if the goal of the early feminists had actually been achieved, despite some regional variations. Traditional single-sex schools and some sex differentiation in practical subjects, such as Needlework and Domestic Science, continued in the south of Germany, although to a lesser degree. On the whole, however, a universal school system developed, with entrance qualifications, curricula and option schemes open equally to both sexes.

Since the beginning of the 1970s, although girls have been quantitatively disadvantaged in the higher levels of the education system, nevertheless their overall position in the education system has steadily improved (Pross, 1972). Indeed, at the primary level girls achieve much higher grades than boys on the whole (Schümer, 1985). However, it is important to note that the increasing advance of girls up the "ladder of success" is often thwarted at the point of entry into "real life", where they have fewer prospects of teaching posts, are often advised to take lower paid and less highly regarded jobs and often remain without any career prospects. Explanations as to why this situation should come about have traditionally concerned differing attitudes and values on the part of girls and women.

187

It is only recently that the content of education has been the subject of feminist debate, reinforced by a nationwide conference on women and schooling held annually since 1983 and by research which has critically appraised the unquestioning optimistic consensus over co-education from the long-term perspective of girls. Since 1985 research has concentrated on discrimination against girls in classroom interaction, sex-stereotyping in textbooks and on sexist language (Block *et al.*, 1985). This kind of research tends to be dominated by indictment and negative criticism, with few concrete examples given and then mainly at a very general level. Collected volumes of research have such optimistic titles as "Women are Changing the School" and "Women are Changing Learning". In a typical recent article entitled "The Advancement of Women and the School" one can discern the emergence of a more defensive position (Kindermann *et al.*, 1987) in which the authors state their commitment to "combating all forms of direct and indirect discrimination against female pupils, teachers, academics and mothers of school-children" and their demand "that the achievements of women in the past and present are recognized at school and in lessons". Further, they demand that "vigorous improvements are made in the conditions of learning so that mothers can be relieved of the task of helping their children with homework and that girls and women enjoy equal rights in every aspect of school life" (Kindermann *et al.*, 1987, p. 196). It should be noted that the German school day starts earlier than in the United Kingdom and ends at lunchtime, which places a great onus on German mothers to care for children and to help with homework in the afternoons.

This chapter will briefly outline the structure of the education system in the Federal Republic. It will then summarize available information on girls' educational achievement and study patterns in compulsory, vocational and higher education, together with the position of women in teaching. In order to shed some light on quantitative differences in study patterns, qualitative research on classroom interaction, learning materials and girls' and boys' responses to teaching content will be examined.

The Education System of the German Federal Republic

Under the German Constitution, the entire school system, including the small private school sector, is under state control, mainly through the German Länder or federal states. A Standing Conference of Ministers of Education deals with matters of joint federal concern. Attendance at school is compulsory from the age of six to eighteen years, on a full-time basis for nine years (or ten in some Länder) and then with the possibility of part-time attendance for three years. Education is free and some state support grants are available to upper secondary school pupils.

The system consists of:

Kindergarten for three to six-year-olds. This is voluntary, mostly part-time and payment depends on parental income.

Grundschulen (primary schools) for six to ten-year-olds (or twelve in Berlin and Nordrheinwestfalen). These offer a basic curriculum in German Language, Social Studies, History, Geography, Physics, Biology, Mathematics, Chemistry, Religious Education, Music, Arts, Crafts and Needlework – all compulsory by law. Special schools for children with learning or behavioural problems also exist at primary and secondary level.

The secondary level consists of a tripartite system of Hauptschulen, Realschulen and Gymnasien, which corresponds roughly to the secondary modern, technical and grammar schools established in England and Wales under the 1944 Education Act. All now feature a two year "orientation stage", which enables transfer between the different types of schools. Transfer to the Gymnasien is also possible at a later stage after attendance at special classes. Hauptschulen offer a compulsory curriculum of German, Mathematics, Physics/Chemistry, Biology, Geography, History, Religious Education, Music, Arts, Civics, Social Studies, Physical Education and a foreign language. Classes are often streamed and pupils can enter vocational education on completion.

Realschulen prepare pupils for intermediate, non-professional work. They offer the same curriculum as Hauptschulen but on a more demanding level and also offer the possibility of taking two foreign languages. Pupils leave after six years with a certificate which enables them to enter employment or to attend a technical high school (Fachschule).

Gymnasien offer a nine year academic course, which prepares pupils for higher education or professional training. There have traditionally been three main types of Gymnasien specializing in Modern Languages, Classics or Mathematics and Science, plus some which specialize in other technological, arts and social science subjects. These are now largely being replaced by general Gymnasien. The compulsory curriculum of general schools includes German, Mathematics, Biology, Physics, Technology, Chemistry, History, Civics, Geography, Music, Art, Physical Education, Social Studies and at least two foreign languages. After the eleventh year of schooling, an extended range of options is available. Courses are divided into basic and intensive courses according to level of complexity and abstraction, number of hours taught per week and possibility of independent study. Most students elect to take two intensive courses, in anticipation of their university specialism, in addition to the compulsory curriculum. Most students take the Abitur at the age of eighteen or nineteen.

Gesamthochschulen or comprehensive schools also exist alongside the tripartite system in some of the northern Länder, such as Hessen and Nordrheinwestfalen.

Vocational education consists of a dual system of on-the-job learning and attendance at a Berufschule (non-advanced technical school) and is funded jointly by the state and by private enterprise. This lasts for two to three years and is mandatory for all those not in other forms of education.

Higher education consists of academic universities, colleges of education, tertiary technical colleges and other specialist colleges. The system has been greatly expanded since the 1950s when only 6 per cent of the age-group attended higher education. Entry depends mainly on grades gained in the Abitur and availability of places.

Although women and girls constitute about half the population, sex differences are seldom recorded in official statistics, with the exception of data on the age of marriage, patterns of inheritance and composition of the population. The only readily available official statistics which give sex differences in education are concerned with uptake of vocational education programmes. Patient research can unearth data on the representation of boys and girls in the various forms of education from school attendance registers, but more intensive work is required in order to assess patterns of achievement in state schools (Warm, 1985). This state of affairs is all the more striking when one considers that from the state's perspective, sex differences are far more readily definable characteristics than those of nationality and social class origin, which are more frequently used in official statistics. Even relatively new data collections on the education system give no information at all on sex differences in education.

Girls and Educational Achievement at School and in Further and Higher Education

The Compulsory School Years

On the whole, girls and boys are disproportionately represented in different types of education. Only in the first four years of primary school, the only universal form of comprehensive education in the Federal Republic, are the sexes present according to their proportional representation in the age range concerned. It was not until the publication of new data in the 1988 Statistisches Jahrbuch (Yearbook of Statistics) that it has been possible to establish the proportion of boys and girls in the population of primary school age through an examination of the birthrate. Even when figures are controlled for the slightly different birthrate of boys and girls, it now appears that boys are slightly over-represented in certain types of secondary school. In 1986 they constituted, for example, 52 per cent of pupils in the Hauptschulen, which are being increasingly labelled and devalued as "second-class" schools (Statistisches Jahrbuch der BRD, 1988). In addition, it is now possible to establish that, on the whole, the proportion of girls has for some years slightly exceeded the proportion of boys in the more prestigious Realschulen, as illustrated by Table 10.1 below and now matches the proportion of boys at the Gymnasien.

TABLE 10.1

Distribution of Pupils in Primary and Secondary Education

	1960		1970		1986	
	% Boys	% Girls	% Boys	% Girls	% Boys	% Girls
Grundschulen (primary) and Hauptschulen (intermediate schools)	51	49	51	49	52	48
Special Schools	60	40	60	40	61	39
Realschulen (Secondary Modern Schools)	48	52	47	53	47	53
Gymnasien (Grammar Schools)	60	40	56	44	50	50

Source: Author's own calculations from the Statistisches Bundesamt (1987).

These figures clearly show that on the one hand the representation of girls in special schools has been remarkably low, and on the other that their representation in the Gymnasien has been conspicuously on the increase in recent years. Although boys often attended more prestigious schools than their sisters up until the 1960s, this social advantage now seems to have disappeared in favour of more egalitarian or meritocratic principles.

When official statistics for the highest qualifications obtained at school are examined, girls appear to be performing well in relation to boys (Statistisches Jahrbuch der BRD, 1988). Of pupils who successfully completed the Schulabschluss (School-leavers Certificate) at Realschule 54 per cent were girls, while 47 per cent of students who successfully obtained vocational qualifications (including at night school and in comprehensive schools) were girls. Indeed, levels of attainment at the highest level of educational qualifications of the present generation of female school and college-leavers compare very favourably with those of the population as a whole, outstripping those of previous generations of women and the present generation of boys in all areas, except in vocational qualifications. Even more clear is the tendency of girls to outperform boys in yearly examinations and tests at school throughout their school careers. Girls have to repeat the year less often in primary schools (1.9 per cent of girls as opposed to 2.7 per cent of boys) and achieve better end-of-year results (Schümer, 1985). At the level of secondary education it seems that girls are gaining a clear edge in educational achievement, despite profound and continuing expectations of the greater success of boys on the part of teachers (Frasch and Wagner, 1982). However, according to recent research, sex differences in aspirations and in career and study goals emerge clearly at this level. A large-scale questionnaire-based survey of upper secondary pupils revealed that 20.6 per cent of female pupils and 8.8 per cent of male pupils did not intend to continue their studies at university. Of those who did, choices followed predictable and sex-specific lines, boys opting to a far greater extent for subjects in the spheres of business, technology and science with the greatest prospects (Küllchen and Sommer, 1989).

Vocational Education and the Labour Market

There are only a few areas in the labour market, as in the rest of society, which are not clearly differentiated according to sex (BMBW, 1980; Statistisches Jahrbuch der BRD, 1972). Despite a marked increase in the participation of women in the labour market since the 1970s, especially among mothers, women have in general taken up employment in the worst paid and most low status areas. In 1987, for example, women in manufacturing industries earned on average 69 per cent of the male rate, and women white-collar workers on average 64.5 per cent of their male colleagues' pay. When compared with the figures for the 1950s, when women industrial workers earned 54.3 per cent and women white-collar workers 56.4 per cent of the male rate of pay, it is apparent that the situation has improved to some extent, although not to anything like an equal degree (BMBW, 1980). In addition, from 1970 to 1979 the female rate of unemployment rose from 0.8 per cent to 5.2 per cent, compared with the rise in the male rate from 0.7 per cent to 2.9 per cent (BMBW, 1980). This higher rate of unemployment for women is partly a result of their increased rate of participation in the labour market, but it also clearly reflects a level of discrimination against women.

In the 1970s this lack of quantitative and qualitative progress in the labour market could be traced back to the under-representation of girls in vocational education and in the Gynmasien (grammar schools) (Linhoff and Sauer, 1976). However, since the beginning of the 1980s this supposed connection has not been able to stand up to the evidence, not only in academic studies but also in terms of vocational qualifications. Young women have increasingly used vocational education since the 1960s to enhance their skills (Kaiser, 1985). However, inequality of opportunity for girls is becoming increasingly evident in the options which girls take up in vocational education.

During the late 1970s and early 1980s, the Federal Ministry, working with the Länder and employers, set up a major series of projects to encourage the entry of girls and women into male-dominated areas of training (Byrne, 1987). These "model projects" were supported by payments of a substantial premium to employers who took part on the condition that projects would be monitored to provide a basis for future policies. Projects were established in rural and urban areas and across all spheres of employment. They were most successful where women constituted 15–20 per cent of trainees. Despite these efforts, women's occupational choices have remained in traditional areas (Braun and Gravalas, 1980). The labour market is still characterized by a high degree of vertical and horizontal job segregation by gender, which is reflected in the very different patterns of vocational education courses taken by young men and young women. These are illustrated in Tables 10.2 and 10.3 below.

In contrast, girls continue to enter predictable areas of training in vocational education where they are concentrated in a much narrow range of courses.

The clear divergence of choice between the sexes is striking, with no overlap between the sexes of the ten most popular courses for each sex. Only in the less popular courses does some measure of parity emerge, mainly in the areas of retail trade purchasing and purchasing for the wholesale trade.

Thus it can be seen that achievement in the education system does not open up equal opportunities in the world of work. Female trainees opt for careers with modest prospects, despite better achievements in vocational educational qualifications, for example in the area of Craft and Design, where girls achieved an 88.6 per cent success rate in the qualifying examinations to the boys' rate of 84.7 per cent in 1988 (BMBW, 1988). Even in the traditionally "male" areas of carpentry and heavy vehicle mechanics, girls achieved a higher

TABLE 10.2

Distribution of Male Students in Vocational Education, 1986

	(Ten most popular areas) in rank order
1. Heavy vehicle mechanics	7.5%
2. Electrics	4.8%
3. Machine fitting	4.5%
4. Painting and decorating	4.5%
5. Carpentry	3.3%
6. Plumbing and gas-fitting	2.9%
7. Business – import and export trade	2.8%
8. Banking	2.6%
9. Baking	2.6%
10. Industrial sales	2.4%
11. Total: Other courses – at less than 2% per course	62.1%

Source: Author's own calculations from the Statistisches Jahrbuch (1986).

TABLE 10.3

Distribution of Female Students in Vocational Education, 1986

	(Ten most popular areas in rank order)
1. Hairdressing	8.8%
2. Sales	7.9%
3. Secretarial work	6.9%
4. Technical sales	6.6%
5. Industrial purchasing	5.7%
6. Medical reception work	5.1%
7. Dental reception work	3.9%
8. Banking	3.9%
9. Shop assistants Retail	3.8%
10. Clerical work	3.2%
11. Total other courses at less than 2% per course	44.3%

Source: Statistisches Bundesamt (1986).

success rate, despite their low representation. Yet it appears that even today, girls of a "marriageable age" are prepared for a narrow range of possibilities for career development, while boys are able to utilize opportunities to the full at this critical phase in their life cycle.

Higher Education

Turning to the last and highest rung in the education system, one can see that the proportion of girls and young women in tertiary or higher education has increased in recent years, although not in proportion to their results in the qualifying examination, the Arbitur. Nevertheless, the proportion of women students at university has increased from 28 per cent in 1960–1961 to 31 per cent in 1970–1971 to 42 per cent in 1986–1987, a proportion still well below that of male students. Despite gains made in access to further and higher education and in formal qualifications, these have in general not been in the areas of study which lead to prestigious vocational and professional qualifications. In the less prestigious Gesamthochschulen (tertiary colleges), where a greater number of engineering-based courses are taught, in the church colleges, in art schools and in management colleges, the representation of women students appears to be no more equal than in the universities. Although the proportion of women students in non-university tertiary education has increased from 28 per cent of students in 1960–1961, women still only comprised 38 per cent of students in 1987–1988 in this sector (Statistisches Jahrbuch der BRD, 1988). Just as clear patterns of study are differentiated by gender in vocational education, a similar division can be discerned in higher education, setting the scene for entry into the labour market (Beck-Gernsheim, 1976). The most popular areas of study at university in 1987–1988 were sharply divided in rank order of importance and uptake by sex, as illustrated by Table 10.4 below.

TABLE 10.4

Distribution of Students in University Education by Sex and Study Area,
1987–1988

Male choice of subject in rank order	Female choice of subject in rank order
1. Electrical Engineering	Medicine
2. Mechanical Engineering	Law
3. Business Studies	German Language
4. Law	Teacher Education
5. Hotel Management	Biology
6. Information Technology	Hotel Management
7. Physics	English Language
8. Civil Engineering	Psychology
9. Chemistry	Architecture
10. Architecture	Chemistry
11. Biology	Sociology
12. Mathematics	History of Art
13. German Language	History
14. Economics	Mathematics
15. Political Economics	Social Education
16. History	Social Work
17. Teacher Education	Pharmacy
18. Journalism	Sports and Physical Education
19. Sports and Physical Education	Domestic Science and Nutrition

Source: Statistisches Jahrbuch der BRD (1988).

The Position of Women in Teaching

A similar sexual division of labour can be observed within the profession most favoured by women, namely teaching. Teachers in the Federal Republic earn on average a higher salary and enjoy more favourable conditions than their counterparts in many European countries, but women are still concentrated in those areas of the profession which command the lowest rates of pay, lowest status and worst conditions of work, in this case determined by the number of hours of class contact time per week. In virtually the whole of the Federal Republic the norm is of a twenty-three hour teaching week in the Gymnasien to a twenty-eight hour week in the primary schools, where women are largely concentrated. Rates of pay also increase with the level of school and show the same relative disparity as in the wider "dual labour market", even when the figures are controlled for part-time work, where women predominate. Table 10.5 below illustrates the sexual division of labour in teaching.

TABLE 10.5

Distribution of Teachers by Sex and by Type of School, 1986

	Female teachers	Male teachers	Total
Primary and Hauptschulen	65%	35%	100%
Special Schools	63%	37%	100%
Realschulen	51%	49%	100%
Gymnasien	36%	64%	100%

Source: Statistiches Jahrbuch der BRD (1989).

At the lower levels of primary education there are hardly any men to be found, whereas in the upper echelons of the secondary system, this situation is virtually reversed, with few women enjoying the status and privileges which this level of teaching confers. One reason for this is the length of time it takes to complete training and the probationary period. Many Gymnasien teachers are nearly thirty by the time they are fully qualified.

Organizational Features of the School and Classroom

Classroom Interaction

Complaints and criticisms about education today are often concerned with the dominance of verbal, and often didactic, teaching methods, which have changed little since the last century. Despite all the calls by educational reformers from the time of Pestalozzi onwards for a more practical form of education, and despite a continuing debate among educationalists about the value of teaching through the technique of questions and answers, this is still the most frequently used teaching strategy in classrooms today. If only because of the predominance of this method of teaching, it is particularly important to examine what actually goes on in classroom interaction. When female teachers are questioned about the extent of implicit sex discrimination in education, they flatly reject the idea that anything like this could go on in their classes, as so many researchers have found in Germany and in other countries (cf., Frasch and Wagner, 1982; Enders-Dragässer and Fuchs, 1987; Kaiser, 1985; Kaiser, 1988; Spender, 1985).

According to this research, it is quite clear that boys of all ages are in receipt of more praise and more censure from both male and female teachers, and are more accepted by them, even though male teachers tend to be adamant that they do not give more attention to boys than to girls. Boys' contributions in class are rated as more valuable and boys are defined as more worthy of help. This discrepancy is particularly paradoxical, given the higher scholastic achievements of girls and lends doubt to the idea that boys receive more praise, because they make more "praiseworthy"contributions in class. This subtle form of discrimination against girls, which goes against the meritocratic principle of equal opportunities, is particularly marked in school subjects in the traditionally "masculine" areas of Mathematics and the theoretical sciences, in which it is critical that girls think of themselves as on equal terms to boys. From the research cited above, it can be concluded that more than two-thirds of teacher-pupil interaction in primary and secondary schools is oriented towards boys and that the greater part of this is taken up by admonishments. Even when teachers are made aware of the problem and attempt to make classroom relationships more egalitarian, there is often little positive change. In a study conducted in 1985, for example, teachers were persuaded to make a conscious effort to devote more time to girls in their classes. Despite this, girls took up 42 per cent of classroom attention at the most, while boys in the class objected to the impression that girls were being unusually favoured (Barz, 1985). The author also noted that it was precisely the relatively modest educational achievements of boys which encouraged them to make concerted efforts to gain more teacher attention and the upper hand in class, resulting in a confirmation of conventional clichés about "strengths" and "weaknesses" in children's behaviour.

Qualitative differences in classroom interaction are even more striking than these quantitative differences. Boys dominate verbal interaction between pupils and teachers by trying to query or alter class exercises to suit their own learning skills and by ganging up on girls to discourage and interrupt their contributions (Skinnungsrud, 1985). A large-scale study of classroom interaction in primary and secondary schools conducted in Hessen in 1987 by Fuchs and Schmidt, for example, clearly showed that boys and girls employ different patterns of speech in class and concluded that boys frequently interrupt girls' contributions specifically in order to gain a monopoly of speech. Despite their scholastic competence, this creates a paradoxical burden for girls in co-educational classes, "who thus have the choice between two evils: to be sanctioned for their competitive male behaviour or to be disparaged as feminine and second class. (Their social and technical skills) are used but not recognized . . . Girls are the quiet losers in schools and boys the boisterous winners" (Fuchs and Schmidt, 1987, p. 87).

It is not only the differential amount of teacher attention and encouragement given to boys and girls but it is also often the actual content of the lesson which determines whether girls will seize the initiative to make a contribution in class, irrespective of their grasp of the subject matter at hand. A study of primary schools conducted by the author in 1987 found that, although in general boys made two-thirds of the verbal contributions in class, girls could make up to 60 or even 65 per cent of pupils' verbal contributions, when lessons were more concerned with issues about which girls felt strongly, such as exercises in conflict-resolution (Kaiser, 1988). This could indicate that it is the less "girl-oriented" content of lessons which reduces girls' share of interaction in class, and this has considerable implications for teachers.

So far discussion has been confined to a consideration of the process of gender differentiation at the level of formal instruction. However, wider issues impinge on classroom interaction and this is nowhere more evident than in the area of children's learning materials.

Reading Schemes and Textbooks

According to official school guidelines, educational content should be free of any sex bias. After all, what have letters, numbers or maps to do with sex discrimination? However, appearances can be deceptive. The example of textbooks shows that these are in no way as gender-neutral as their authors claim. To some extent early criticisms of the content of gender bias in textbooks, which centred on the limited representation of women and girls in children's readers in the early 1970s, are already "old hat" (Sollwedel, 1970). However, every year fresh analyses of the new material which is appearing on the market clearly point to the subordinate position in which girls and women are still portrayed in German, French, English, Mathematics, History, Geography, or Religious Education textbooks. Here, a short account of primary school books must suffice as an example of this widespread and substantial discrimination.

A comprehensive piece of research into children's reading schemes carried out by Schweitzer in 1985 showed that the early critiques of reading schemes did result in a more realistic depiction of women in some individual publications (Schweitzer, 1985). However, many of these were not reprinted "for economic reasons" and simply disappeared from the market or were not reprinted in the same format, with the result that by the late 1980s there had been something of a retrenchment in this area, with a return to the old clichés. In particular, the following characteristics can be singled out for criticism:

— mothers are portrayed in a stereotypical and anachronistic way, as solely confined to and primarily responsible for the home;
— social relations within the family are depicted in a hierarchical manner;

— the workplace is depicted as being dominated by men, who are always in superior positions;
— girls are depicted as unadventurous, passive and non-assertive (Schreier, 1979).

According to Schweitzer this list of criteria can be applied in principle to textbooks in all school subjects, as a yardstick for gauging equality of opportunity. Even a cursory glance at this list shows how little progress there has been in developing an equal and accurate depiction of men and women in educational publishing.

Gender Differences in Learning Materials and Aptitude

Although textbook analysis is a fairly uncontroversial area, since bias in children's books is relatively easy to substantiate, it may nonetheless provide useful guidance for parents helping children to read at home. However, it is also essential that more detailed research into the actual content of lessons is undertaken, since learning materials are indicative but not representative of all that is taught in schools.

Up until the late 1980s research into children's development has mostly concentrated on the early years of education, and either tends to take rather crude indicators such as entries in teachers' reports as measures of actual instruction, with little to say about the sex-specific significance of such entries, or it has concentrated on extrapolating general developmental capabilities of children from the actual content taught, treating sex differences in aptitude as a marginal issue (Baake, 1984; Kaiser, 1986). In a further research project into thematic approaches to learning, I made a first attempt at establishing which cognitive processes are developed in boys and girls at primary school (Kaiser, 1986). The research was restricted to a representative sample of five different teaching themes: environmental issues (for example, recycling paper), pocket money, "school breakfasts" (as the German school day starts much earlier than in the United Kingdom young children are often given breakfast at school), advertisements for sweets and factory work. The latter theme was chosen as a particular test-case, to highlight how boys and girls can be subject to contradictory pressures from the hidden curriculum, as it has been amply documented as being treated as a sex-specific area in schools.

In the context of the sub-theme of the "ideal factory", children were asked a set of standard open-ended questions, which included the following:

— What kind of factories are there?
— What kind of factories would you design or build?

Children were then divided into groups and asked to draw their own factories, prompted by examples in photographs. In most classes groups were divided, in accordance with the children's wishes, into single-sex groups, as is usual in primary schools. A spokesperson for each group then shared the groups' designs with the class.

The results of the project can only be sketched in outline at this point. In their verbal descriptions and pictures of factories, girls tended to present more human life, with a variety of male and female workers depicted at their jobs. In contrast the boys' group hardly featured any human beings in their designs at all. Complex, technical constructions in which units were connected through cables, pipes and electrical wires, were the general rule here, while such technical elements hardly entered into the girls' presentations (Kaiser, 1986).

What these findings could indicate is that the approach of boys and girls to supposedly gender-neutral themes is already clearly very different, even before they are presented with material which may be more related to the perceived interests of either group. This conclusion would imply that gender differentiation in the classroom cannot be reduced by simply introducing more equal learning materials and curricula. Traditional social patterns, expectations and life experience result in differentiation between the sexes and the continuing devaluation of women's achievement. Measures adopted to promote the structural equality of girls in the education system will therefore only be partially successful, even if they have some effect on increasing gains in skills and competence or in general social influence. However, as long as relationships in society remain deeply sexist, educational change on its own will always stumble up against structural barriers.

References

Baake, D. (1984) *Die 6 bis 12 jährigen* (Six to twelve-year-olds). Weinheim: Beltz.

Barz, M. (1985) Jungengewalt gegen Mädchen (Boys domination of girls). In R. Valtin and U. Warm (Eds.) *Frauen machen Schule* (Women make school). Frankfurt: Arbeitskreis Grundschule e.v.

Beck-Gernsheim, E. (1976) *Der geschlechtsspezifische Arbeitsmarkt* (The sexual division of labour). Frankfurt: Fischer.

Block, J. Pfister, G., Rieger, U. and Schmeling, C. (Eds.) (1985) *Feminismus in der schule* (Feminism in School). Berlin: Frauen und Schule Verlag.

Brehmer, I. (1985) Zur Geschichte weiblicher Bildung (A history of women's education). In R. Valtin and U. Warm (Eds.) *Frauen machen Schule* (Women make school). Frankfurt: Arbeitskreis Grundschule E. V.

Braun, F. and Gravalas, B. (1980) *Die Benachteiligung junger Frauen in Ausbildung aund Erwerbsstätigkeit* (Discrimination against young women in wages and training). München: Juventa.

Bundesministerium für Bildung und Wissenschaft (Ed.) (1980) *Zur Situation der Frauen in der beruflichen Bildung* (The situation of women in vocational education). Bonn: Press-und Informationsamt.

Bundesministerium für Bildung und Wissenschaft (Ed.) (1988) *Berufsbildungsbericht*, (Report on vocational education). Bonn: Press-und Informationsamt.

Byrne, E. (1987) Gender in education: educational policy in Australia and Europe, 1975–1985. *Comparative Education*, 27 (1).

Clephas-Möcker, P. and Krallmann, K. (1986) Frauenstudium in der Weimarer Republik und im Dritten Reich (Women's Studies in the Weimer Republic and the Third Reich). In Interdisciplinäre Forschungsgruppe Frauenforschung (Eds.) *Ringvorlesung Neuere Arbeitsergebnisse aus der Frauenforschung* (Preface to new work in the area of research into women's studies). Bielefeld: Universitätsdruck.

Enders-Dragässer, U. and Fuchs, C. (1987) Der heimliche Lehrplan der Geschlechterziehung in der Schule am Beispiel der Interaktionen (The hidden curriculum in sex education at school as an example of interaction). In A. Prengel *et al.* (Eds.) *Schulbildung und Gleichberechtigung* (Education and equality). Frankfurt: Nexus-Verlag.

Frasch, H. and Wagner, A. C. (1982) Auf Jungen achtet man einfach mehr . . . (One simply notices boys more . . .). In I. Brehmer *Sexismus in der Schule* (Sexism in school). Weinheim: Beltz.

Fuchs, C. and Schmidt, P. (1987) Weiblichkeit und Männlichkeit in den Interaktionen des Unterrichts (Femininity and masculinity in classroom interaction). In G. Kindermann *et al.* (Eds.) *Frauen ändern Schule* (Women are changing the school). Berlin: Frauen und Schule Verlag.

Kaiser, A. (1985) *Schulfrühstuck-oder was haben die Mädchen im Sachunterricht zu sagen?* (Breakfast at school – or what have girls to say in class?). Frauen und Schule, **8**, 4.

Kaiser, A. (1986) *Schulervoraussetzungen für sozio-ökonomischen Sachunterricht* (Pupils' expectations in social studies). Bielefeld: Universitätsdruck.

Kaiser, A. (1988) Didaktische Differenzierung statt Konstruktion (Differentation rather than Co-education in teaching). In G. Pfister (Ed.) *Zurück zur Mädchenschule?* (Back to girls' schools?). Pfaffenweiler: Centaurus.

Kindermann, G., Mauersberger, B. and Pilwousek, I. (Eds.) (1987) *Frauen ändern Schule* (Women are changing the school). Berlin: Frauen und Schule Verlag.

Kindermann, G. (1987) Förderung der AG Frauen und der Schule (The advancement of women and the school). In G. Kindermann *et al.* (Eds.) *Frauen ändern Schule* (Women are changing the school). Berlin: Frauen under Schule Verlag.

Kleinau, E. (1986) Zur Geschichte des höheren Mädchenschulwesens im 19 Jahrhundert (A history of girls' secondary education in the nineteenth century). In Interdisziplinäre Forschungsgruppe Frauenforschung (Eds.) *La Mamma: Beiträge zur sozialen Institution Mutterschaft* (Contributions on the social institution of motherhood). Köln: Volksblatt – Verlag.

Küllchen, H. and Sommer, L. (1989) Beruf- und Lebensvorstellungen von Schulerinnen and Schulern. (Career and life aspirations of male and female pupils). In Interdisziplinäre Forschungsgruppe Frauenforschung (Eds.) *La Mamma: Beiträge zur sozialen Institution Mutterschaft* (Contributions on the social institution of motherhood). Köln: Volksblatt-– Verlag.

Linhoff, U. and Sauer, B. (1976) *Berufliche Bildungschancen von Frauen* (Equal opportunities for women in vocational education). Gottingen: Sofi.

Nave-Herz, R. (1972) *Das Dilemma der Frau in unserer Gesellschaft: Der Anachronismus der Rollenerwartungen* (The dilemma of women in society: the anachronism of role expectations). Neuwied: Luchterhand.

Pfister, G. (1988) Die Geschichte der Koedukation – eine Gesichte des Kampfes um Wissen und Macht (The history of co-education: a story of struggle for knowledge and power). In G. Pfister (Ed.) *Zurück zur Mädchenschule?* (Back to girls' schools?). Pfaffenweiler: Centaurus.

Pross, H. (1972) *Über der Bildungschanchen für Mädchen in der BRD* (Concerning equal educational opportunities for girls in the German Federal Republic). Frankfurt: Suhrkamp.

Schreier, H. (1979) *Sachunterricht – Themen und Tendenzen* (Teaching content – themes and tendencies). Paderborn: Schoning.

Schümer, G. (1985) *Geschlechtsunterschiede im Schulerfolg* (Sex differences in educational achievement). In R. Valtin and U. Warm (Eds.) *Frauen machen Schule* (Women make school). Frankfurt: (Arbeitskreis Grundeschule ev).

Schweitzer, I. (1985) Auch heute noch: Sexismus in Fibeln? – Eine Analyse (Sexism in children's books? The debate continues). In R. Valtin and U. Warm (Eds.) *Frauen machen Schule* (Women make school). Frankfurt: (Arbeitskreis Grundeschule ev).

Sollwedel, I. (1970) Des neue Frauenbild in den Lesebüchern (The new image of women in children's readers) *Informationen für die Frau 6*, **19**.

Skinnungsrud, T. (1985) Mädchen im Klassenzimmer: warum sie nicht sprechen (Why girls don't speak in class) *Frauen und Schule*, **3** Aug.

Spender, D. (1985) *Frauen kommen nicht vor* (Why girls are not getting ahead). Frankfurt: Fischer.

Statistiches Bundesamt Wiesbaden, 1987 Bildung im Zahlenspiegel. Stuttgart: Mainz.

Statistisches Jahrbuch der BRD (Statistical Yearbook of the German Federal Republic) (1972) Wiesbaden: Statistisches Bundesamt.

Statistisches Jahrbuch der BRD (Statistical Yearbook of the German Federal Republic) (1986) Wiesbaden: Statistisches Bundesamt.

Statistisches Jahrbuch der BRD (Statistical Yearbook of the German Federal Republic) (1988)
　　Wiesbaden: Statistisches Bundesamt.
Statistisches Jahrbuch der BRD (Statistical Yearbook of the German Federal Republic) (1989)
　　Wiesbaden: Statistisches Bundesamt.
Warm, U. (1985) *Aktuelle Grundschulstatistik* (Current primary school statistics). Grundschule
　　17, 2.

Note

1. This chapter was written before the events of Autumn, 1989, which began the process of the reunification of Germany. The effects of the accession of the German Democratic Republic to the Federal Republic will be very complex, not least in the field of social and educational policy in relation to gender, a matter of concern to women's representatives in both Germanys [Ed., August 1990].

CHAPTER 11

Europe: An Overview

MAGGIE WILSON

State Policy

Co-education has been considered by national educational authorities as something of a universal panacea to the great disparity in the educational opportunities offered to boys and girls which existed in most countries until the end of the 1970s. By the late 1970s, this policy had been introduced in the state sectors of all but two of the countries under review. Single-sex schools continue to exist in the independent and state sectors in Ireland and, to a lesser degree, in England and Wales. Some subjects, such as Physical Education and Crafts, are still taught in single-sex classes in Poland, Belgium, Spain, Greece, West Germany and England and Wales. Partly through the impact of such international legislation as the European Community Directive on the Equal Treatment of Men and Women Workers, governments have introduced equal opportunities legislation with varying degrees of political will and commitment and with a varying degree of reference to educational matters.

The Swedish state has, for example, maintained a strong stance in the area of equality of educational opportunity since the late 1960s, supporting both research and action programmes, as well as attempting to secure equal participation through the formal mechanism of the curriculum. Equal opportunities have been a major foundation-stone of state educational policy in Poland since 1965 and an explicit feature of Greek policies since the mid-1970s, while the Spanish government has lent some weight to equality issues since the 1980s. In Greece and Spain, equal opportunities issues have been given particular prominence through specialist semi-independent agencies within ministries and in Sweden through a specialist government division and representative council. In Ireland the Council on the Status of Women, established in 1973, has been greatly strengthened by the appointment of a minister responsible for women's affairs in 1982. Although there has generally been a lack of central government support in England and Wales, some local educational authorities have responded to pressure from local schools, teachers and women's groups to establish equal opportunities policies in the areas under their jurisdiction. In West Germany, a similar picture of a lack of central government support and some initiatives in individual Länder prevails, while in France and Belgium the Ministries of Education have responded to equal opportunities in a rather tardy and lukewarm way. The role of the European Community in giving impetus to equality issues is specifically acknowledged in the cases of Ireland, Spain, Greece and Belgium.

State support for equal opportunities issues in education has had some demonstrable results, as the summary below illustrates. Where state policy has been most successful has been in outlawing direct discrimination in terms of formal access to institutions or courses of study; in establishing common curricular goals; in setting principles and targets; in highlighting and monitoring areas of practice on a national scale and in funding start-up costs for specific programmes. However, as Kirp asserts, states cannot be expected to decree gender justice. The Big Sister state, which could enforce sufficiently stringent measures while over-riding popular opinion, would be deemed undesirable in democratic societies (Kirp *et al.*, 1987). This is not to say that sex discrimination in education can be removed by rational discussion and knowledge of the issues alone, but merely to acknowledge the political contribution, both past and potential, of concerned groups among teachers, parents, administrators and women's groups at all levels of the education system, a contribution which has often been underestimated (Weiner and Arnot, 1987; Lovenduski, 1988).

Despite an explosion of activity in informal groups since the 1970s, women have been less successful in gaining ground within mainstream political parties. Table 11.1 below illustrates the level of women's participation in the lower Parliamentary houses of the countries under review. The representation of women in the European Parliament and at local authority level has been slightly higher, but representation at national cabinet level is particularly low. Apart from Sweden and Norway, which have a greater proportion of women ministers, nearly all European women ministers hold portfolios in education, social welfare, the family and sports and recreation rather than in finance, defence, justice or industry (EOC, 1987).

While participation in mainstream politics may be rejected as a valid goal by some feminists, it nevertheless remains one of the major ways of gaining

TABLE 11.1

Percentage of Women Elected to the Lower Houses of Parliament in Selected European Countries as at 1988

Belgium	7.5
France	5.9
Greece	4.0
Ireland	8.4
Spain	6.0
Sweden	33.0
United Kingdom	6.3
West Germany	15.4

Source: *Women of Europe Ten Years On*, Women's Information, CEC (1988).

some measure of control over the levers of power and of influencing state policy in the area of equal opportunities for women and men. Although women in powerful positions may not necessarily support such policy, as has been the case in Britain and the United States, political participation provides the starting point for effecting change at the heart of the system.

Girls and Equal Educational Opportunities

Attainment

The evidence presented from the nine countries under review suggests that the introduction of co-education and of a number of measures to promote equality of educational opportunity has had some success in improving the educational life-chances of girls, particularly in terms of access to upper secondary and higher education. In the nine countries under review, the proportion of female university students nearly matches that of male students and is greater in Sweden, Poland and France, as Table 11.2 below shows, although women students are still under-represented at postgraduate level.

At the primary school level, interesting national differences in test data on levels of attainment emerge. Although data from Spain support the view that there are distinct sex differences in cognitive skills, such as verbal skills or abstract reasoning, this pattern is not supported by data from Sweden, Greece and West Germany, while research in this area in England and Wales presents mixed and inconclusive evidence. More boys than girls are required to repeat the school year in Belgium, Greece, France, Spain and West Germany after failure at the lower levels of the education system. Results at the upper secondary level also point to the superior mean academic performance of girls in relation to boys in academic studies in Sweden, Spain, Greece, West Germany, France and Belgium, although clearly significant differences in performance exist within each group. A more complicated picture emerges in data from Ireland and England and Wales while Polish data indicates that boys have a slight edge in school performance on average. Where girls and

TABLE 11.2

Representation of Female Students as a Percentage of Full-Time University Students, 1986–1987, Selected European Countries

Belgium	48	Ireland	48
England and Wales	46	Poland	52
France[a]	53	Spain	49
Greece	48	Sweden	56
		West Germany	42

[a] Figure excludes the grandes écoles.
Source: Author's compilation from individual chapters and UNESCO *Statistical Yearbook* (1988).

young women have entered "non-traditional" areas of study, such as in vocational education in West Germany or in higher education in Greece, there is some evidence to suggest that this form of "self-selection" results in their slightly superior performance on average in relation to their male peers (Kontogiannopoulou-Polydorides, 1989; BMBW, 1988). Research conducted in Poland, however, suggests that male students have a very slight edge in performance in Physics at the university level (Szydlowski and Dudziak, 1985).

Little of the data presented includes analysis of other factors, such as social class or rural-urban differences. Exceptions to this general rule, such as in the 1985 Polish study by Zaborowski and Karpinczyk, lend support to the view that social differences can compound gender differences in attainment, and indicate that there is a need for more sustained research which fully explores the complexity of patterns of pupil and student performance.

Patterns of Study in Secondary and Further Education

National education systems vary considerably in their organizational arrangements for secondary education, particularly in the degree to which pupils are channelled into different types of programmes, the extent to which they can specialize between options and at what age this occurs. Where secondary education is divided between academic and vocational programmes or institutions, there is a strong pattern of female "under-representation" in vocational education and "over-representation" in academic education. For example 53 per cent of students on Swedish academic programmes in 1987 and 57 per cent of students on Greek general education programmes in 1985 were female, compared with 36 per cent of students on Swedish and 20 per cent of students on Greek vocational education programmes in those years. In education systems where upper secondary education is divided into academic, vocational and technical programmes or institutions, girls are even less likely to be found in the technical sector. For example, in Belgium in 1984–1985 15.82 per cent of students in technical education and 24.51 per cent in vocational education were female. An exception to this pattern is the example of Poland where 55 per cent of students in technical high schools were female in 1985–1986. Such data needs to be treated with caution, as the content and also the status of programmes varies considerably under these general headings. However, there is a strong possibility, asserted in both the Belgian and Greek contexts, that girls' increasing participation in academic upper secondary programmes may actually do them a disservice if they do not go on into higher education and thus leave school poorly equipped for the job market.

Within upper secondary education, the trends in curricular differentiation outlined in the 1986 OECD report remain. Although direct comparisons between national patterns are problematic at this level and at the level of higher education, because of variations in subject classification, nevertheless the strong pattern which emerges is that girls still opt for the Arts and Humanities in great numbers as soon as the education system permits them to specialize. For example, 82 per cent of candidates for the French Baccalauréat in Literature and Philosophy in 1988, 87 per cent of students on the Humanities programme in Sweden in 1987 and 88 per cent of pupils on the Polish Humanities programme in 1984–1985 were female. Girls comprised only 34 per cent of candidates for the French Baccalauréat in Mathematics and Science in 1988, 45 per cent of students on the Science options in Spain in 1984–1985 and a third of the candidates for A-Level Physics in England and Wales in 1985–1986. In the Republic of Ireland in 1985–1986 only 9.4 per cent of female candidates for the School Leaving Certificate took Physics, 16 per cent took Chemistry and 0.5 per cent Technical Drawing. However, where available data covers the time period in which there has been a greater degree of official support for equal opportunities policies in education, a distinct shift in patterns of study is discernible. In Sweden, for example, there has been a 10 per cent increase in the number of girls studying Science in upper secondary schools between 1976 and 1987, so that girls now comprise 50 per cent of Science students at this level. In England and Wales the number of girls studying Chemistry to A-Level increased by 42 per cent and Mathematics by 80 per cent between 1975–1976 and 1985–1986. The Belgian case study also illustrates the increasing uptake of Mathematics options by girls, while Irish data on single-sex schools illustrate dramatic changes in the proportion of boys and girls taking Accountancy and Business Studies as well as Physics and Chemistry between 1972–1977 and 1985–1986.

Within the Sciences, marked patterns of female preference are still to be found. In Poland, for example, where girls comprise 72 per cent of students in academic high schools, 76 per cent of pupils taking options in Biology and Chemistry were female in 1985–1986 as compared with 53 per cent taking options in Mathematics and Physics. The newer school subject area of the Social Sciences also seems to be emerging as something of a feminine enclave, although to a lesser degree than the Arts. Thus, for example, 62 per cent of students on the Economics programme in Sweden in 1987 and 61 per cent of candidates for the French Baccalauréat Series B (largely in Social Sciencies) in 1988 were female.

Within vocational education, an even more entrenched concentration of girls into a restricted range of programmes may be observed. There is a strong congruence between the five most popular areas of vocational education among female students in the nine countries studied, also influenced to a certain extent by national economic circumstances. The areas in which 80 per cent of female vocational education students in Belgium were concentrated in 1984–1985 are typical, namely textiles, sales, domestic science, art and welfare work. To these could be added: hairdressing (Spain, West Germany), administration and clerical work (Spain, England and Wales, West Germany,

Sweden and France), nursing and paramedical courses (France, Sweden, Spain), catering and food technology (Sweden, England and Wales). This pattern is continued in technical tertiary education, where the three most popular areas of study among French female students, namely paramedical studies, visual arts and administration, are typical. This contrasts with the low proportion of female students on technical vocational programmes. For example, only 10 per cent of candidates for the French Baccalauréat in industrial training and 15 per cent of candidates for the French CAP and BEP diplomas in the manufacturing and extractive sectors were female in 1988, while in Sweden only 3 per cent of students of Motor Mechanics were female in 1987. In Poland a greater proportion of girls and young women study Technology at the level of secondary and higher education, but are still in a minority at roughly 20 per cent of students in 1985–1986. From the limited evidence available, it appears that girls are entering the area of information technology in significant, but not equal, numbers to boys. For example, 32 per cent of candidates for the French Baccalauréat in this area in 1988 and 16 per cent of A-Level candidates in England and Wales in 1985–1986 were female.

Three main points for consideration arise from this data. The first concerns the relationship between state policy and patterns of curricular choice. There is a considerable variation in the commitment of governments to effecting change in this area, even in the extent to which state departments monitor patterns of curricular choice. The production of up-to-date official statistics must be a starting point here. Where conscious efforts have been made to delay specialization between options or branches of education, as in Sweden, there is less opportunity for a predictable polarization between the sexes in terms of choice of studies to emerge. In order to recruit more girls into the area of Science and Technology, strenuous efforts have to be made to change the image of these subject areas, particularly in the case of technical subjects. This may partly be a question of finding ways in which to relate content to the scientific and technical equipment which surround girls in their everyday lives, as well as of recruiting more female teachers into these subject areas. Single-sex groups within laboratory-based classes may also give girls the confidence to exercise their skills and to discover the excitement of scientific research, without the need to use science lessons as a testing ground for gender identities (Measor, 1984; Whyte, 1985). Constructional activities for boys and girls in pre-school education and Science education at primary school level are crucial here, as well as the opportunity for boys and girls to experience the full range of technical and scientific subjects. "Second-chance" courses in "non-traditional" areas may also help to widen the vocational choices of boys and girls at a later stage.

Secondly, concentration on the under-representation of girls in Science and Technology is often at the expense of the question of the under-representation of boys in the Arts, Humanities and Foreign Languages. With increasing European integration, linguistic competence will be an invaluable asset to many school leavers and graduates in skilled manual work, as well as in professional work. While this is already recognized in the education programmes of such countries as Sweden or West Germany, boys may be ill-served by their lack of skills in this area in countries such as England and Wales, which lag behind in this respect. Similarly, advanced communications and design skills, largely developed in female-dominated areas of study in upper secondary and higher education, should also be considered an advantage in preparation for working life. In the United Kingdom there is also evidence to suggest that some employers use formal qualifications as a screening device for other attributes and regard subjects studied or degree discipline as one element among many (Moore, 1983; Roizen and Jepson, 1985). Beyond the narrow conception of education in purely vocational terms, girls and boys can be impoverished by the lack of a deep understanding of, for example, historical change, and of a vocabulary in which to express their responses to such change, as much as by a lack of understanding of the world of science.

Finally, patterns of subject choice may be rooted in factors which are beyond the influence of the state, the education authorities or the school. The arguments developed in the Belgian, French and Greek contexts suggest that the labour market itself may provide the strongest determinent of occupational choice. While formal and organizational barriers to subject choice have largely been removed, freedom of educational choice may be a somewhat illusory concept in societies where equality of opportunity in employment and in the home lags so patently behind equality of opportunity in education. Rather than acting as "stubborn traditionalists" in terms of study choices, girls may in fact be acting on an accurate appraisal of their best chances of employment and of combining their activity in the public sphere with their responsibilities in the private sphere of the home.

Patterns of Study in Higher Education

In higher education divergent patterns of study choice similar to those outlined in the 1986 OECD report are again apparent. Although the differing status of types of institution and differing classification of subjects makes direct national comparisons in this area somewhat unreliable, Table 11.3 below gives an indication of the patterns of study choice of female students in higher education.

From this data it is clear that women students, apart from those in Poland, are still greatly under-represented in the Natural Sciences, Mathematics and Computer Studies, and particularly in Engineering and Technology. Male students are correspondingly under-represented in Educational Studies, the Humanities and the Fine Arts. A more even gender balance is apparent in general in the Social and Behavioural Sciences, in Law, Administrative and Business Studies. Other subject areas, such as Architecture and Town

TABLE 11.3

Percentage of Female Students in Tertiary Education in Selected Subject Areas and by Selected Country[a]

	Belgium 1986	France[c] 1988	Greece 1985	Ireland 1985	Poland 1986	Spain 1985	Sweden[b] 1986	United Kingdom[b] 1985	West Germany 1985
Natural Sciences	37	33	37	51[d]	63	45	38	32[d]	31
Mathematics and Computer Studies	30	—[d]	35		65	37	26		23
Medical and Health Sciences	63	45	54	45	73	59	72	78	65
Engineering	15	37	17	11	15	10	20	6	6
Law	46	54	56	46	76	46	47	—[d]	39
Social and Behavioural Sciences	50	46[e]	51	54	55	47	55	42	39
Educational Studies and Teacher Training	70	—[d]	77	71	78	68	77	63	73
Humanities and Theology	56	69[f]	66	58	66	65	63	62	60
Fine and Applied Arts	50	—[d]	61	64	53	53	58	58	51
Architecture and Town Planning	33	—[d]	48	23	46	21	54	—[d]	37
Administrative and Business Studies	50	—[d]	50	45	62	44	47	—[d]	41

[a] Includes non-university tertiary education.
[b] Includes multiple counting of students enrolled in more than one field.
[c] Derived from chapter in this collection – other information not available.
[d] Figures not given separately.
[e] Economics only.
[f] Arts only.
Source: UNESCO *Statistical Yearbook* (1988), Paris: UNESCO.

Planning, vary quite widely in their patterns of recruitment between countries, although show an increase in female participation rates. It is interesting to note the increasing gender balance in the Medical Sciences, although figures, which include those for Nursing Studies in Sweden and the United Kingdom, have to be treated with caution. In the United Kingdom, for example, the proportion of female students training to be doctors or dentists was 53 per cent in 1986–1987.

Within the Sciences at this level, Physics is again the discipline least favoured by female students, even in Poland where there is overall a greater proportion of female Science students than in Western European countries. Despite the relatively high recruitment of women students into the Sciences in Poland, it is interesting to note that the proportion of female Engineering students lags behind the proportion in Greece, Sweden and France. From limited data available, it appears that women students within this field favour Civil Engineering and are least attracted to Mechanical Engineering, which again raises questions about the image of these disciplines and about prior childhood and scholastic experience.

Within other subject clusters, such as the Social and Behavioural Sciences, an area of increasing "feminization", gender differences between branches, such as Politics or Social Welfare exist. In Business and Administrative Studies, gender differences in recruitment to, for example, Marketing and Personnel Management courses, can be quite marked.

The same questions about the relative status of subject areas posed in the context of upper secondary education also apply at this level. In several countries there have been concerted campaigns to encourage more women students into Science and Technology courses, with varying degrees of success. To what extent such campaigns reflect a genuine governmental commitment to equal educational opportunities and to what extent they are motivated by short-term manpower planning considerations, is a debatable point. At any rate, the current canon of faith, which decrees that qualifications in Science and Technology are always superior to those in other subject areas, needs to be more fully explored. Whether more women students are now applying for such areas as Law and Medicine because of their humanistic orientation or because of the relatively high market value of such qualifications is also an open question. What remains to be seen is whether the social cachet of professional qualifications is eroded by increasing "feminization" *per se*, or whether male students have simply deserted areas of work, such as teaching, where prospects have declined, leaving them more open to female entry.

A further problem in any discussion of gender inequality at this level lies in the fact that students in tertiary education represent a small minority of the population as Table 11.4 below shows. They are also drawn disproportionately from certain social backgrounds, despite the dramatic growth in the number of places in higher education from the mid-1960s onwards. In 1986–1987, for example, 31 per cent of university students in France and

TABLE 11.4

*Enrolment of Students in Tertiary Education as
% of 19–24-Year-Olds, Selected Countries*

Country	Year	% 19–24-year-olds
Belgium	1986	30.6
France	1986	30.2
Greece	1984	23.4
Ireland	1984	21.6
Poland	1984	16.9
Spain	1986	31.8
Sweden	1986	37.4
United Kingdom	1985	22.4
West Germany	1985	29.8

Source: UNESCO *Statistical Yearbook* (1988) Paris: UNESCO.

45 per cent of students in higher education in England and Wales were from a professional-managerial background, despite the fact that those groups represented a much lower proportion of the population as a whole. In the most prestigious institutions, such as the French grandes écoles, the proportion of students from a professional-managerial background is significantly higher (Bourdieu, 1989). Whether bright middle-class girls have been able to take advantage of the expansion of opportunities at the expense of working-class boys is a question which needs further research and exploration. There is also some evidence to suggest that as higher education has expanded to meet demand, systems are becoming more differentiated in terms of the status of institutions and courses. Some prestige areas, such as the grandes écoles in France, remain relatively exclusive in terms of both social class and gender: another form of "shifting the goal posts" to the advantage of those who are already privileged.

Qualitative Research

In terms of teacher attitudes, teaching materials and classroom interaction, a number of strong patterns emerge from the research evidence presented. Most early research in this area concentrated on images of girls and women in school textbooks and children's reading schemes, and it is interesting to note national variations here in the prominence given to this kind of activity. Where official support for equality issues has been relatively recent, such as in Spain, or weak, as in West Germany, such issues seem to provide a concrete starting-point for research and campaigns. It is also of interest to note the apparent absence of such research in Poland, where state support for formal educational equality has been strong. Research in this area in Spain, West Germany, England and Wales, Belgium and Greece confirms that school books present a skewed and restricted range of images of girls and women, as marginal to society and largely confined to the home. There is a general, although unproven, assumption that this negative and distorted view of reality has a strong influence on the self-image of girls and boys, a hypothesis which needs to be explored in greater depth. The West German experience offers an insight into the mismatch between the publishing market and official school guidelines, which raises questions about the degree to which official sponsorship of educational publishing could or should be used to bring about change in this area.

Again, there is a marked similarity in accounts of teachers' attitudes towards gender issues, which contrast teachers' expressed commitment to the principle of equal educational opportunities or "gender-neutral" teaching strategies with the level of practice. Although teachers often deny that differential treatment of boys and girls exists in classrooms, case studies from Belgium, Spain, Sweden, Greece, West Germany and England and Wales chart the great amount of attention which teachers give young boys, albeit in the form of both praise and censure, and their overtly expressed preference for teaching boys, especially at the upper levels of school and in certain subject areas, such as in Science and Mathematics. According to such studies, boys are quick to exploit this advantage in class in order to divert what goes on in the classroom towards their own interests. Case-study material of young children in Sweden and older pupils in Belgium, West Germany and England and Wales show how strong voluntary divisions between the sexes can be in nominally co-educational classes. Conflicting conclusions are presented in one French case study (Sirota, 1988), which suggests that girls are advantaged in the short term by their apparent adherence to the "good pupil" image in class, while research into the ethos of single-sex schools in Ireland suggests that girls' schools present girls with the contradictory goals of academic success and conformity to a feminine ideal (Lynch, 1989a). Only one study cited explored teachers' attitudes towards the future social roles of male pupils (Subirats and Brullet, 1984). This kind of research tends to lead to the conclusion that "girls are the quiet losers while boys are the boisterous winners", in terms of self-esteem rather than school performance. This has implications for in-service work with teachers, experiments in single-sex groups, such as those reported in some English schools, and for a wider definition of careers guidance which encompasses consciousness-raising as well as information and counselling. The apparent lack of research into teachers' attitudes towards the development of boys' self-images and range of possible masculine role models is also an issue which needs to be further explored.

Data from Belgium and England and Wales illustrate similar sex differences in children's out-of-school play activities and reading habits, which may exert a strong influence on future study options. It is interesting to note here that sex differences in teenagers' attitudes towards technology presented in a Polish case study (Szydlowski and Dudziak, 1987) were not as strong as sex differences in the "scientific" out-of-school activities of eleven-year-olds in an English case study (Johnson and Murphy, 1986), given the marked difference in the level of girls' uptake of the Sciences in those two countries. The

conclusion of the German case study by Kaiser (1986), which suggested that
children's responses to learning content and materials may be shaped by
gender differences fostered in the family, makes for interesting reading
alongside data from Ireland (Lynch, 1989b), France (Sirota, 1988), Belgium
(Peemans-Poulet, 1984) and the European Commission (Women of Europe,
1987) on attitudes to domestic role-sharing. The implications of this research
are that changes in the sexual division of labour at home are fundamental to
children's development, as well as to equality between the sexes in the paid
labour market. The extent to which overt parental attitudes and the "hidden
curriculum" of schools, in classroom interaction or learning materials, do in
fact influence girls is a debatable point. Girls have, after all, proved to be
increasingly successful in the education system in quantitative terms. Research
into questions of self-esteem and self-identity may in fact underestimate the
degree to which girls are capable of contesting their inferior status in co-
educational classrooms, even if they do so in a more subtle way than boys.
Such research can also lead to a "deficit model" of girls, as being responsible
for their own lack of assertiveness and for the restricted scope of their
ambitions and occupational aspirations in a context divorced from the impact
of the wider labour market. Occupational aspirations are also likely to vary
between different social groups with different cultural experiences. However,
such research can be of great value in giving insight into the full range of
experiences of girls in school, rather than simply measuring success in crude
quantitative terms.

Women in Teaching

Teaching represents one of the first areas of the labour market with which
young children will have contact and here there are remarkably consistent
patterns of employment between countries. Over 90 per cent of pre-school
teachers in France, Greece, Sweden, Spain, and England and Wales are
female, and the proportion of primary teachers who are female ranges from
61 per cent in Spain in 1985–1986 to 79 per cent in England and Wales and
Ireland in 1988–1989. Secondary education is less of a female enclave, with the
proportion of female teachers ranging from 44 per cent in Sweden in
1986–1987 to 55 per cent in France in 1985–1986. Figures for the number of
women in school leadership roles, presented in the chapters on France,
Sweden, Ireland and England and Wales, suggest that women are greatly
under-represented in senior posts, in both absolute and relative terms. The
proportion of female students of teacher education ranges from 67 per cent in
Poland in 1985–1986 to 78 per cent in England and Wales in 1986–1987,
although such figures have to be treated with caution as universities are not
always the sole providers of teacher education. These figures do, however,
suggest that teaching is becoming an increasingly "feminine profession" except
in some academic subject areas in upper secondary education, in vocational

education or where particular types of school are considered to be of higher status, such as the West German Gymnasien. It is significant that few accounts of the sexual division of labour in schools include the predominantly female support services of cleaners, secretaries, canteen assistants and technicians, who are often paid at a lower rate in the public sector than in equivalent private sector employment. Were such jobs to be included in data on employment in schools, the way in which schools mirror vertical job segregation (i.e., by rank) as well as horizontal job segregation (i.e., by employment sector) in the wider labour market would be even more apparent.

Data on the representation of women on university staff in France, Greece, Ireland, Spain, Poland and England and Wales supports a similar picture. Although there is some variation in the degree to which women have succeeded in entering academia, the proportion of women on academic staff at this level of education rarely exceeds 25 per cent, with the exception of Poland and some Eastern European countries (Moore, 1987). Women are again concentrated at the lower levels and the proportion of women professors ranges from 0.7 per cent of professors at the Technical University at Poznàn in Poland in 1985 to 9 per cent of university professors in France in 1985–1986. Where data is given on the distribution of women university staff by subject area, such as in the Polish and Greek contexts, it is apparent that the degree of concentration among women university staff in certain subject areas is greater than among women students and that female academics are under-represented even in those areas where women students are in the majority. So, for example, in 1986, 34.6 per cent of Veterinary Science students in Greece were female as compared with 1.68 per cent of senior and 19.44 per cent of middle-grade academics in that area and 44 per cent of Economics students were female as compared with 7.01 per cent of senior and 14.14 per cent of middle-grade academics. Only at the lower academic grades did a rough level of parity exist. The case studies of the two universities in Poland presents a particularly complex and interesting variation. Given the high number of women students of the Sciences in Poland, the disparity between the proportion of women staff and students at the A. Mieckiewicz University in 1985 is particularly marked. The relatively high proportion of women members of staff in certain Engineering disciplines at the Technical University of Poznàn raises questions about both the status of the two types of institution in Poland and the commitment and determination of women in "non-traditional areas", despite some evidence of ambivalent attitudes among female Polish scientific research workers (Szydlowski and Dudziak, 1987).

Data on the use of part-time and temporary labour in Irish schools suggests that analysis of employment contracts in schools and higher education might reveal an even stronger pattern of gender inequality. Little scholarly attention has been paid to academic or bureaucratic leadership roles within academic institutions or on national or regional boards of education (Moore, 1987). The significance of this kind of research lies not only in its demonstration of inequality in one of the major sectors of female employment. It also points to the consequences of this inequality in terms of the development of the role expectations of boys and girls, since the teaching profession itself arguably provides one of the major "feedback loops" from the labour market. The division of labour within teaching perpetuates the assumption that men have little to contribute to the care and upbringing of young children and that women have little to contribute to management and decision making. This will continue in turn to generate unequal practices until a greater diversification of roles exists, through such measures as the recruitment of more men into the lower levels of the education system as well as the recruitment of more women into subject areas and positions of seniority in which they are under-represented at the levels of secondary and higher education. The vigorous applications of equal opportunities policies in terms of appointments, in-service training and promotion within educational institutions and authorities are also clearly of paramount importance.

Women and the Labour Market

Data from the countries under review confirms the general trends outlined in the 1985 OECD report on women and employment (OECD, 1985). The proportion of women at work ranged from 21 per cent in Spain to 82 per cent in Sweden in 1985, with the West German rate of participation, at 34 per cent, about average. Women are thus numerically an important part of the labour force, and have taken advantage in particular of the expansion of opportunities for employment in the service industries and in the public sector. In Greece, for example, in 1978, a peak period for expansion in the public sector, 40 per cent of all new appointments were women, compared with 31 per cent of existing appointments. In France in 1984 women occupied 52 per cent of all service sector jobs and this sector represented 78 per cent of jobs occupied by women employees as a whole. As several of the contributors to this book attest, the public sector of employment has attracted women for positive reasons – appointments, working conditions and opportunities for promotion are perceived to be fairer, more explicit and subject to state regulation. However, this has not undermined the overall pattern of the restricted range of occupations in which women employees are to be found. Even in Sweden, where there has been a positive state policy of encouraging women to enter non-traditional areas of work, women were still to be found in only 56 out of 161 occupations in 1987, and are still largely concentrated in the typical areas of nursing and welfare work, teaching, secretarial, clerical and retail work.

This kind of data also masks inequalities within the female workforce itself, where the very low paid and dirty jobs, such as industrial cleaning or jobs with extremely poor conditions of employment, such as piecework assembly jobs in the home, have increasingly been taken up by migrant workers. Profiles of national patterns of employment also tend to ignore the repetitive and low-paid jobs occupied by young women in agriculture, assembly-line plants or the "rag trade" in branches of Western companies located in the Caribbean, Central America and Southeast Asia, which are arguably just as much a part of the same system (Leacock and Safa, 1986).

Although the same general patterns are to be found in the employment situation of women in Poland, the diversification of study choices in secondary and higher education has contributed to expanding the range of occupational opportunities for women. As data on the employment patterns of graduates shows, women comprise a far greater proportion of the workforce in Poland in such occupations as the law, architecture, dentistry and chemistry than in Western European countries. In 1985–1986, for example, 45 per cent of Polish lawyers were women as compared with 15 per cent of lawyers in the United Kingdom in 1987, and 39 per cent of Polish architects were women, as compared with 5 per cent in the United Kingdom. Although Polish women are in the minority in most of the branches of engineering, they have still penetrated these areas to a greater extent than in Western Europe. For example, 59 per cent of Polish food industry engineers, 38 per cent of civil engineers and 16 per cent of electrical engineers in 1985–1986 were women. In 1985 in France women comprised only 6 per cent of all engineers at the higher professional level. Changes in Polish economic life underway in 1990, in particular the privatization programme, may significantly alter this picture since, as outlined above, women have made more advance in general in the public sector of employment.

In addition to the generally low representation of women in the full range of professional and managerial work, it appears that the "pay-off" for graduate qualifications, as well as for lower level qualifications, has not been the same for women as for men. Although other factors, such as seniority and length of service, may come into account, these do not appear to offer a full explanation of differences in levels of pay between men and women in non-graduate work. Calculations in the Greek context that 90 per cent of pay differentials can be attributed to a measure of sex discrimination are instructive here (Psacharopoulos, 1980). In Belgium, in common with many other countries, the unemployment rate for women has been shown to be greater than for men with the same level of formal qualifications, while in Sweden, in 1986, the unemployment rate for women who had trained for non-traditional areas was higher than that of men. This suggests that sex discrimination in the labour market has persisted, despite European legislation on equal pay and treatment of employees and similar national legislation in the countries under review.

As Kontogiannopoulou-Polydorides rightly asserts, there is always a danger in underestimating the impact which enhanced educational opportunities for girls will have on employment patterns over time. Although the medical profession is, for example, male-dominated in most Western European countries, the gender balance within the intake of medical students is now more or less equal in most countries and so we can expect to see the profession balanced in numerical terms within the next twenty or thirty years. However, if present trends persist, women may still be concentrated in the less favoured areas of community and psychiatric medicine, paediatrics, general practice and radiology, and may not rise to the levels of the top consultants or medical researchers (Lawrence, 1987; Alterkruse and McDermott, 1988, for an account of medicine in the United States). Moreover, confining research to women "at the top" disregards the areas of nursing, hospital cleaning, catering, and other services, which have remained deeply entrenched and often poorly paid female areas of employment.

A further example of deep-rooted patterns of inequality in employment is the sphere of television, an area which has been generally bypassed in educational research, despite its enormous impact on the lives of young people in Europe. Important as an employment sector in its own right, television also presents a range of possible role models for children. It has been estimated that the average European citizen will spend twice as much time in front of a television screen as in the classroom. Yet, according to European survey data, women are still depicted on television in a remarkably narrow range of roles, especially in advertising and serials. Here women are seen to be dependent on their appearance and charm in the few work situations in which they appear and are otherwise largely confined to the private sphere. Although women have become far more visible in news programmes, most on screen journalists are younger than their male counterparts, are often conventionally glamorous and do not wear glasses (Women of Europe, 1988). Behind the scenes, women are still greatly under-represented among technical staff and at the middle and senior management levels. Sixty per cent of women employed in television in 1986 were in secretarial and clerical jobs and women comprised 4 per cent of technicians, 26 per cent of middle-level and 8 per cent of senior production staff, and 7 per cent of boards of directors (Gallagher, 1986). Despite a commitment to equal opportunities issues in employment in companies in England, West Germany and the Netherlands, there had been overall little change in employment patterns by sector or by level over the previous ten years.

This supports the view that changes in employment patterns, even in "modern" sectors of the economy, will not automatically follow from improvements in girls' educational qualifications. The European Commission and individual television companies have launched action programmes in the critical area of television since the early 1980s, which have underlined the importance of undertaking concerted reviews of employment practices as well as initiating measures to redress imbalances. While these have met with varying degrees of success in this particular sphere, without such measures girls and women will continue to confront restricted opportunities in the labour market, whatever progress they may have made in educational terms. As the experiences of the nine countries reviewed have shown, the question of equal opportunities in education cannot be viewed in isolation from the question of equality of opportunity in the labour market and the wider social world.

In the 1990s most Western European countries will face a severe shortage in skills, fewer school-leavers and increased international competition. Between 1990 and 2010 there is predicted to be a rapid change in the age-structure of the population, before it again reaches a period of stability. Countries will be affected by the shortfall of young workers to differing degrees, as Table 11.5 below shows, although it should be noted that this data does not take into

TABLE 11.5

Projected Decline in the Number of Young Workers Aged 15–34 in Selected European Countries

	Base = 100% at 1980	
	1990	2010
Belgium	96.4	79.1
France	99.1	87.9
Greece	105.8	95.8
Ireland	110.5	114.8
Spain	113.0	99.2
Sweden	97.0	84.3
United Kingdom	101.5	86.3
West Germany	101.0	67.4

Source: Adapted from: R. Hazeman and G. Nicoletti: *Ageing populations: economic effects and implications on public finance*, OECD Working Paper No. 61 (1989), Table 2.

account the possible effects of immigration and emigration. Trends towards earlier retirement may also differ between countries. Nevertheless, the implications of these demographic factors are that women will be in increasing demand in the labour market. The British Equal Opportunities Commission has described this as "a once-in-a-lifetime chance to bring equal opportunities firmly into the mainstream of British life" (EOC, 1988, p. 1). Those researchers who take a longer-term historical perspective of such issues may be inclined to less optimism, given the use of women as a reserve army of labour in two world wars. In the 1990s the critical point is to ensure that the emancipation of women is not used as a temporary convenience in a time of labour shortage.

References

Alterkruse, J. and McDermott, S. (1988) Contemporary concerns of women in medicine. In S. Rosser *Feminism within the sciences and health-care professions: overcoming resistance.* Oxford: Pergamon.

BMBW (Bundesministerium für Bildung und Wissenschaft) (1988) *Berufsbildungsbericht* (Report on vocational education). Bonn:

Bourdieu, P. (1989) *La noblesse d'état.* Paris: Editions de Minuit.

Equal Opportunities Commission (1987) *Men and women in Britain: a statistical profile.* London: HMSO.

Equal Opportunities Commission (1988) *From policy to practice: an equal opportunities strategy for the 1990s*. Manchester: EOC.

Gallagher, M. (1986) *Employment and positive action for women in television organisations of the EEC Member States*. Brussels: CEC.

Hazeman, R. and Nicoletti, G. (1989) *Ageing populations: economic effects and implications on public finance*. OECD Working Paper 61, Table 2, Paris: OECD.

Johnson, S. and Murphy, P. (1986) *Girls and Physics*. London: Assessment of Performance Unit, HMSO.

Kaiser, A. (1986) *Schülervoraussetzungen für sozio-ökonomischen Sachunterricht* (Pupils' expectations in Social Studies). Bielefeld: Universitätsdruck.

Kirp, D., Yudof, M. and Franks, M. S. (1987) Gender in the house of policy. In M. Arnot and G. Weiner (Eds.) *Gender and the politics of schooling*. London: Hutchinson/Open University.

Kontogiannopoulou-Polydorides, G. (1989) Achievement at university. Research in progress, partially published in "The main characteristics of the entrance examination". In Vervakian Alumur Association *The transition from secondary to tertiary education*. Athens:

Lawrence, B. (1987) The fifth dimension: gender and general practice. In A. Spencer and D. Podmore *In a man's world: essays on women in male dominated professions*. Oxford: Pergamon.

Leacock, E. and Safa, H. (Eds.) (1986) *Women's Work*. South Hadley, MA: Bergin and Garvey.

Lovenduski, J. (1988) The women's movement and public policy in Western Europe: theory, strategy, practice and politics. In M. Buckley and M. Anderson *Women, equality and Europe*. Basingstoke: Macmillan.

Lynch, K. (1989a) The ethos of girls' schools: an analysis of differences between male and female schools. *Social Studies*, 10 Nos. 1–2, pp. 11–81.

Lynch, K. (1989b) *The hidden curriculum: reproduction in education, a reappraisal*. London: Falmer Press.

Measor, L. (1984) Gender and the sciences pupils' gender-based conceptions of school subjects. In M. Hammersley and P. Woods (Eds.) *Life in school*. Milton Keynes: Open University.

Moore, K. (1987) Women's opportunities in higher education. *Comparative Education*, 23 (1).

Moore, R. (1983) Further education, pedagogy and production. In D. Gleason *Youth training and the search for work*. London: RKP.

OECD (1985) *The integration of women into the economy*. Paris: OECD.

OECD (1986) *Girls and women in education*. Paris: OECD.

Peemans-Poulet, M. (1984) *Partage des responsabilités professionelles, familiales et sociales* (The division of family, social and occupational responsibilities). Brussels: CEC.

Psacharopoulos, G. (1980) *Sex discrimination in the labour market*. Paper presented at the Modern Greek Studies Symposium, Philadelphia, Pennsylvania, 14–16 Nov.

Roizen, J. and Jepson, M. (1985) *Degrees for jobs – employers expectations of higher education*. Guildford: SRHE and NFER-Nelson.

Sirota, R. (1988) *L'école primaire au quotidien* (Daily life in the primary school). Paris: Puf.

Subirats, M. and Brullet, C. (1984) *Rosa y azul. La transmision de los generos en la escuela mixta* (Pink and blue. The transmission of sex-roles in the co-educational school). Madrid: Instituto de la Mujer.

Szydlowski, H. and Dudziak, G. (1985) Women in the natural sciences at A.Mieckiewicz University and the Technical University at Poznàn. In *GASAT 3 Congressbook*. London:

Szydlowski, H. and Dudziak, G. (1987) Research work of men and women in Science and Technology. In *GASAT 4 Congressbook*. Ann Arbor:

UNESCO (1988) *Statistical Yearbook*. Paris: UNESCO.

Weiner, G. and Arnot, M. (1987), Teachers and gender politics. In M. Arnot and G. Weiner (Eds.) *Gender and the politics of schooling*. London: Hutchinson/Open University.

Whyte, J. (1985) Girl friendly science and the girl friendly school. In J. Whyte et al. *Girl-friendly schooling*. London: Methuen.

Women of Europe (1987) *Men and Women of Europe*. Supplement 26. Brussels: CEC.

Women of Europe (1988) *Women and television in Europe*. Supplement 28. Brussels: CEC.

Women's Information Bureau (1988) *Women of Europe Ten Years On*. Brussels: CEC.

Zaborowski, I. and Karpinczyk, P. (1985) *Students' achievements in physics: results of an all-Polish inquiry 1981–1988*. Warsaw: IKN.

CHAPTER 12

Conclusion

MAGGIE WILSON

ANALYSES of approaches to gender issues at the level of research or political activity usually emphasize common strands within the women's movement, such as its understanding of politics as rooted in personal issues, a common stance against sex discrimination and its commitment to group solidarity. However, within this broad framework of agreement, differences in perspective are marked and can have strong repercussions on approaches to educational issues. Distinctions have been drawn, for example, between an "equal opportunities" and an "anti-sexist" perspective on educational policy (Weiner, 1985), between liberal, socialist and radical ideologies in the political sphere (Lovenduski, 1988) and between "fundamental" and "implementary" perspectives within educational research (Acker, 1984).

At the governmental level the most successful approaches have undoubtedly been underpinned by egalitarian or liberal arguments, which stress attainable change within the education system. The assumption is that women are prevented from the full realization of their potential by the intended or unintended consequences of social practices in school through direct or indirect sex discrimination, and through socialization into traditional sex roles and ways of thinking. Within a competitive society, individuals should be able to start from the same touch-line, unhindered by any disadvantages which might accrue from their birth, degree of ability or disability, sexual orientation, nationality, gender, enthnicity or social origin. Where such arguments have coincided with concerns, derived from human capital theory, about the underutilized reservoir of female labour, and consequent wastage of talent, they have found the warmest reception by governments, as the campaign to recruit more women into science and technology illustrates. Stress is placed within this approach on changing attitudes, and public opinion, on legal action and campaigns within the existing framework. In the educational sphere, questions are raised about choice within the curriculum, school organization, in-service education, opportunities for female staff as well as pupils and students, and about the often anachronistic images of girls and women in educational literature.

Critics of this approach stress its limitations. Radical feminists argue that sex inequality in society does not stem from a lack of opportunity, but from age-old social arrangements based on patriarchal power relations, institution-alized primarily in the family, which impede women's full development irrespective of the political structures in which they live. This, it is maintained, is both mirrored in and reinforced by the school, for example in the way in which the organization of the whole school day depends on the availability of mothers to fetch and carry children and where "parental" involvement in school life usually means maternal involvement. In addition, there is little recognition of women's experiences or contribution to knowledge. Lessons which marginalize the part which women have played in the process of historical change hardly enhance the self-esteem of young girls. In this approach, stress is thus placed in the educational sphere on changing the content of knowledge itself, on re-evaluating conventional subject hierarchies, on changing educational practice so that it is not assumed that pupils are passive recipients of knowledge and on creating, where appropriate, single-sex, girl-centred groups to counteract the pressures on girls in co-educational settings. This overall perspective has therefore profound educational and social repercussions and has gained most ground within networks of small groups, research cooperatives and women's studies circles. Here again there is considerable variation in attitudes towards separatism as a tactic or as a principle.

Among some writers there is also a growing recognition that there is another side to the coin of sex differentiation (Byrne, 1987). Boys who do not fully conform to conventional masculine role models may also suffer the acute emotional pressure of being seen as "failed men", which may haunt them throughout their lives.

A further set of criticisms of the liberal argument for equality of opportunity revolve around the degree to which, it is maintained, women experience a double oppression, in the labour market as well as the home. Socialist analyses argue that women are generally to be found in the "secondary" labour market, where there are few training or career opportunities, low levels of pay and where there is little occupational autonomy. Women thus constitute part of a "reserve army of labour", drawn on in times of labour shortage and disposable in periods of recession (Barron and Norris, 1976). Although improved educational opportunities may have some effect in enabling some girls and women to enter the primary labour market, for example in banking or administration, the great majority of girls will be left untouched by such gains, unless the sexual division of labour within the labour market is redressed. Within this approach, activity in the educational sphere is therefore supported, but greater emphasis is placed on activity within trade unions and political parties and movements.

In practice, it is considerably harder to make such distinctions. Alliances are forged at the personal, institutional and political levels to pursue overlapping goals. A women's research group, for example, which disseminates information among a network of groups and is active in lobbying the European Commission over community policy, or a mixed group of staff within a school, which is monitoring the employment of part-time and casual staff, may be hard to define in such terms. A variety of different emphases in approach have been apparent within the contributions of individual writers to this book. All have pointed out the need for vigorous change within the education system, and for change which is based on new principles of educational and social organization. Extrapolating from such views, an attainable agenda for change in the sphere of education is outlined below. In some chapters there is also a recognition that change within the education sphere alone is insufficient, if yet another generation of educated young women are not to come face to face with often insuperable barriers in the sphere of employment. An agenda for change in this sphere is therefore also included and both sets of strategies should be seen as complementary, if progress is to be made. However, both agendas are delimited, and do not encompass activity within trade unions and other interest groups, among parents or the mass media, so cannot on their own challenge deeply rooted assumptions about the roles which men and women play in society.

On a personal and very English note: I recently attended a reunion of the highly academic and competitive women's university college which I had attended as an undergraduate. A suggested future social event was a husbands' cricket match, to which the graduate wives would bring along sandwiches, tea and children – and at which they would presumably applaud their men's prowess. As the current college principal objected: "But this is all about being players and not spectators."

An Agenda for Change in the Sphere of Education

Governments should:
— declare a firm and vigorous commitment to equality of opportunity in education;
— establish a common core curriculum for girls and boys up to the age of sixteen;
— review the structure of upper secondary technical and vocational education to ensure that there is sufficient opportunity for transfer between programmes or institutions, as appropriate;
— gather comprehensive national statistics on equal opportunities issues in education, including uptake of subjects at all appropriate levels, pupil attainment and deployment of personnel;
— undertake major national investigations into equal opportunities issues in education, such as curricular differentiation;
— sponsor pilot projects of good practice at all levels of education;
— make available grant assistance for "second-chance education" through access courses or distance learning;

— institute a policy of positive discrimination, e.g. minimum quotas or special measures to attract girls on to vocational training programmes.

Local educational authorities or other employing bodies should:
— formulate equal opportunities policies and issue guidelines to good practice;
— ensure that there is a balanced distribution of men and women at all levels of education, including school boards and governing bodies;
— employ equal opportunities consultants at all levels of education;
— review and monitor employment procedures, including applications, appointments, training and promotion, paying particular attention to the use of part-time and temporary contracts;
— review the distribution of men and women teachers in subject-areas and take steps to redress imbalances;
— sponsor pilot projects of good practice at all levels of education;
— initiate in-service courses to raise awareness of equal opportunities and sex discrimination among teachers, educational administrators, advisers, librarians and other educational personnel;
— provide facilities, such as crèches, to enable women to undertake retraining or second-chance educational courses.

Nursery schools should:
— establish a working party of staff and parents to review practice;
— encourage all children to take part in mechanical and constructional activities, and in all types of play activity;
— establish teacher and parent working parties to evaluate children's reading schemes;
— stimulate all children's early language development;
— ensure that pictures, posters and wall displays depict boys engaged in quiet activities as well as girls in more adventurous roles;
— ensure that boys are able to give full expression to their emotions and that language used in addressing boys and girls is similar;
— examine expectations of behaviour among girls and boys to ensure parity of treatment.

Primary schools should:
— establish a programme of school-based self-evaluation through a working party led by a key member of staff to review practice;
— ensure that girls are not asked to undertake certain duties and boys others, for example, helping with technical equipment;
— review teachers' classroom strategies to try to counteract unequal treatment;
— ensure that boys and girls are not asked to undertake different types of thematic work;
— choose some adventure stories where girls or women are the central characters;

— choose teaching and display materials which depict girls in active roles and women in non-traditional jobs and which avoid those which are sexist by omission or distortion;
— invite men and women in non-traditional areas to talk to pupils;
— ensure that expectations of behaviour and achievement and sanctions against misbehaviour are not sex-stereotyped;
— ensure that boys and girls are not divided into separate groups for assembly, lining up or in the classroom and that boys do not monopolize playground space;
— offer boys and girls equal facilities and encouragement in sporting activities;
— avoid making sex-stereotyped assumptions about parental involvement and responsibilities.

Secondary schools should:
— establish a programme of school-based self-evaluation through working parties led by a senior responsible member of staff to review subject areas and whole-school issues;
— ensure that the timetabling of options does not steer pupils towards traditional clusters of choice;
— ensure that all pupils have the opportunity to take Crafts subjects as a matter of course;
— offer "second-chance" crash courses at the upper levels of secondary education in traditionally "masculine" or "feminine" subject areas, such as Crafts or Languages;
— review the image and content of Science and Technology courses and seek ways in which to make these more "girl-friendly", for example by stressing the achievements of women scientists, by including jewellery-making in metalwork, or by considering changes in the titles of courses;
— pay attention to the use of classroom and playground space by pupils, to expectations of behaviour and achievement, and to sanctions and tasks assigned, to ensure that double standards are not in operation;
— offer boys and girls equal facilities for sports and recreational activities;
— examine the reward structure of the school to ensure that similar rewards are given for similar achievements and that positions of responsibility among pupils are equally divided;
— monitor comments in pupils' records of achievement or reports to ensure that these are not sex-biased;
— ensure that the public face of the school, in terms of publicity materials, school brochures and special events, conveys a commitment to equality of opportunity;
— raise equal opportunities issues among governing bodies and parent-teacher associations;

— monitor profiles of school-leaver destinations as part of a thorough review of guidance procedures;
— establish properly planned courses of vocational guidance from the age of thirteen, linking academic with personal and vocational counselling and creating an awareness of careers options among all members of staff;
— review careers guidance materials with a view to eliminating sex-stereotyping;
— try to ensure that work-experience schemes do not channel pupils solely into traditional areas;
— invite visiting speakers in non-traditional areas of work and arrange discussions of sex equality issues in employment among pupils;
— review teachers' classroom strategies to try to counteract unequal treatment;
— review teaching materials in all subject areas to eliminate materials which are sexist by omission or by distortion;
— raise issues of sexuality (with parental permission) in single-sex groups.

Colleges and Institutes of Further and Higher Education should:
— include a written policy on equality of educational opportunity as a central part of stated institutional policy, covering staff, support staff and students;
— ensure that equal opportunities issues are fully explored in initial and in-service teacher education programmes, where provided;
— provide courses to enable mature students to enter higher education, such as access, returner and taster courses, and compensatory courses in non-traditional subject areas, and ensure that admissions requirements are sufficiently flexible;
— offer the option of combined courses which straddle the Arts-Sciences divide;
— review employment procedures, including applications, appointments, promotion and training opportunities, and the use of part-time and casual staff;
— monitor and review recruitment of students and admissions requirements, taking steps to encourage male and female students to apply for non-traditional areas;
— monitor and review student numbers on and performance in courses and subject options;
— establish interdepartmental women's research and study circles to find ways of introducing a feminist perspective in courses;
— provide subsidized nursery and crèche facilities and an after-school play scheme;
— provide a programme of staff development for support staff and academic staff, which includes an enhanced management programme for women;
— support job-share and career-break schemes;

— appoint a full-time equal opportunities officer to work with a senior member of management;
— maintain a gender balance on college committees;
— establish a women's consultative committee which would report regularly to the Academic Board of the college;
— examine teaching and publicity materials for sexism;
— design marketing and publicity strategies which are specifically aimed at attracting girls and women;
— examine careers guidance materials for sex bias;
— establish a "student-friendly" grievance procedure for cases of sexual harassment;
— examine any evidence of differential spending, e.g. on sports facilities.

An excellent comprehensive account of recommendations for school based policy and practice is provided in K. Myers (1987) *Genderwatch*, London: Equal Opportunities Commission/School Curriculum Development Committee, and a good list of the performance indicators of "Ideal College" is included in a project report of the Further Education Unit of the Department of Education and Science of England and Wales (1989), entitled *Equal Opportunities (Gender) Policy and Practice in Colleges of Further Education.*

An Agenda for Change in the Sphere of Employment

Governments should:
— provide a strong legislative framework for anti-discrimination legislation and should vigorously maintain equal opportunities policies in periods of recession;
— provide legislative protection for part-time workers and home workers including parity of rights to social security and pensions;
— ensure that women are fully represented at all levels of decision making;
— establish minimum wage legislation which covers small enterprises;
— address specifically female patterns of unemployment and provide training or retraining programmes aimed at expanding vocational opportunities, particularly in those areas in which women are present but in low numbers or in occupations without a strong history of sex-stereotyping;
— offer wage subsidies to employers to operate affirmative action training, especially in expanding economic areas. This should also extend to recruitment, placement and support within jobs;
— consider contract compliance policies or clauses in government employment contracts to encourage affirmative action programmes;
— ensure that the public sector sets an example of good practice in its own employment procedures. This should include the monitoring of applications, appointments, training and promotion and the establishment of a programme to redress imbalances, possibly through the employment of equal opportunities consultants;

— provide high quality child-care services to all, extend tax relief to include child-care expenses, and provide tax incentives to employers to invest in workplace nurseries and compensate for loss of earnings incurred by those who care for the sick or disabled at home;

— provide paid parental leave, possibly through a system of leave-credits, for at least eighteen months;

— provide legal protection against direct or indirect discrimination during parenthood;

— harmonize school hours with the working day or provide free holiday, after school day-care and activity centres;

— ensure that women employees enjoy parity of taxation, pension rights, and social security;

— introduce mechanisms for ensuring that policies are coordinated and fully integrated into ministerial structures, such as the employment of an independent "ombudsman" with direct access to decision making and a consultative body of representative groups.

Employers should:

— ensure that women are represented at all levels of decision making;

— systematically review and monitor recruitment procedures, promotion policies and appraisal procedures, ensuring that women are aware of training opportunities and are encouraged to take these up;

— encourage men and women to enter non-traditional areas of work;

— provide support for women in non-traditional occupations and provide priority places for women on training schemes, especially in growth areas such as new technology;

— introduce flexi-time schemes and job-sharing arrangements;

— provide company or organization based child-care facilities and after-school care;

— ease age-limits for entry and any unnecessary educational requirements for occupational entry;

— recognize the value of applicants' experiences outside the sphere of paid work;

— review mobility policies, giving special consideration to family responsibilities;

— ensure that part-time workers enjoy the same rights, protection and opportunities as full-time workers and receive equivalent remuneration;

— review job evaluation procedures to establish comparability of jobs;

— provide protection for seniority in periods of parental leave.

References

Acker, S. (1984) Sociology, gender and education. In S. Acker, J. Megarry, S. Nisbet and E. Hoyle *World yearbook of education 1986: women and education.* London: Kogan Page.

Barron, D. and Norris, G. M. (1976) Sexual divisions and the dual labour market. In D. L. Barker and S. Allen *Dependence and exploitation in work and marriage*. London: Longman.

Byrne, E. (1987) Gender in education: educational policy in Australia and Europe 1975–1985. *Comparative Education*, **23** (1).

Further Education Unit of the Department of Education and Science of England and Wales (1989) *Equal Opportunities (Gender) Policy and practice in colleges of further education*. London: HMSO.

Lovenduski, J. (1988) The women's movement and public policy in Western Europe: theory, strategy, practice and politics. In M. Buckley and M. Anderson *Women, equality and Europe*. Basingstoke: Macmillan.

Myers, K. (1987) *Genderwatch*. London: Equal Opportunities Commission/School Curriculum Development Committee.

Weiner, G. (1985) Equal opportunities, feminism and girls: and introduction. In G. Weiner *Just a bunch of girls*. Milton Keynes: Open University.

Index

Notes on the Contributors

Isabel Alberdi Alonso has been a Member of Parliament for the Madrid Constituency since 1989. She was Deputy Director of the Spanish Instituto de la Mujer from 1985 to 1988 and was appointed Director in 1988, in charge of organizing the newly-created Directorate General of Women's Affairs for the City of Madrid. She has a particular interest in equal opportunities in education and sexism in Spanish schools and has written several articles on these themes.

Ines Alberdi Alonso is a lecturer in Sociology at Complutense University, Madrid, with particular responsibility for the Sociology of Education. She has written several articles about girls and education and women in the family, and is the author of *La mujer, Cien Años de su Historia* and *El impacto de las Neuvas Tecnologicas en la Formación y el Trabajo de las Mujeres*. She has been a member of the United Nations Institute of International Research and Training for the Advancement of Women since 1986, and is the Advisor for Women and Development in the Interamerican Development Bank.

Frédéric Charles is currently a research associate in Sociology at Oxford University Department of Educational Studies. His main area of research interest is changing social patterns in the recruitment of student teachers in the past forty years in England and France, and "the parallel changes in the students' relationship with their training and their profession". He is the author of *Instituteurs: un coup au moral (genèse d'une crise de reproduction)*.

Grazyna Dudziak is an assistant lecturer and researcher in Physics at the A.Mieckiewicz University in Poznàn. She is particularly interested in pupils' attitudes to technology and has contributed papers on this area and on women in science to several European conferences. She is currently undertaking research for a Ph.D. in experiments in teaching methods in undergraduate laboratory work in Physics.

Astrid Kaiser is a primary school teacher, working with children from Russia and Poland. She has been a lecturer in primary education at Bielefeld University and has taught in schools in Marburg and Kassel. Her publications include *Die Sozialisation von Lehrerstudenten* (The Socialisation of Student-

Teachers) and *Deutsche Pädagoginnen der Gegenwart* (Women in German Education).

Kathleen Lynch is a lecturer in Sociology in the Education Department of University College, Dublin. She is the author of *The Hidden Curriculum: Reproduction in Education, A Reappraisal* and joint editor of *Ireland: a Sociological Profile*. Her current research interests include equality issues in education and concepts of work, and she has also worked with the homeless in Dublin.

Nadine Plateau is a teacher of Dutch and English and has over twenty years' teaching experience in Belgium and Africa. She is a member of the steering committee of the Université des Femmes, a women's studies centre in Brussels, where she also lectures regularly. She has written articles on co-education and gender differentiation in Belgian schools, is editor of *La Chronique Feministe* and has a particular interest in European and Belgian equal opportunities policies.

Georgia Kontogiannopoulou-Polydorides is a Professor in Educational and Social Policy in the Department of Education at the University of Patras. She has contributed articles to international and Greek journals, and has presented papers to international conferences. Her research interests include sociological analysis of student achievement (IEA studies), gender issues in education, education and development and the impact of new technologies on equality of educational opportunity.

Henryk Szydlowski is Head of Experimental Physics in the Department of Education at the A.Mieckiewicz University in Poznàn, where he has taught for over thirty years. He has published several Physics textbooks for university students and contributed research papers on student and pupil attitudes to science and technology to several international conferences.

Inga Wernersson is a lecturer in the Department of Education and Educational Research at the University of Gothenburg. Her main research interests are sex differences and sex differentiation in the classroom and ideologies of gender equality. Her dissertation (1977) was on sex role conceptions and teacher-pupil interaction in the compulsory school. She has published articles and reports on male preschool teachers, social class and sex roles, ideologies of gender equality, gender and power and sex differences in young children's "occupational choice". Her current research projects are (1) a review of research on sex differentiation in the classroom and (2) development of theoretical models of sex differences in social outlook.

Maggie Wilson is a Senior Lecturer in Education at Oxford Polytechnic and has taught in London and West Germany. She has a particular interest in gender issues in education, multicultural and development education and comparative education. She is the author of *Know Your Rights: Immigration and Race*.